The Field of Water Policy

Bringing together the analysis of a diverse team of social scientists, this book proposes a new approach to environmental problems. Cutting through the fragmented perspectives on water crises, it seeks to shift the analytic perspectives on water policy by looking at the social logics behind environmental issues. Most importantly, it analyzes the dynamic influences on water management, as well as the social and institutional forces that orient water and conservation policies. The first work of its kind, *The Field of Water Policy: Power and Scarcity in the American Southwest* brings the tools of Pierre Bourdieu's field sociology to bear on a moment of environmental crisis, with a study of the logics of water policy in the American Southwest, a region that allows us to see the contest over the management of scarce resources in a context of lasting drought. As such, it will appeal to scholars in the social and political sciences with interests in the environment and the management of natural resources.

Franck Poupeau is Director of Research at the French National Center for Scientific Research (CNRS) and he has been the co-director of the joint international unit for Interdisciplinary and Global Environmental Studies (UMI iGLOBES, CNRS/University of Arizona) from 2012 to 2017. He is the co-editor of several books on water policy: *Water Bankruptcy in the Land of Plenty* (2016), *Water Regimes: Beyond the Public and Private Sector Debate* (2016), *Water Conflicts and Hydrocracy in the Americas: Coalitions, Networks, Policies* (2018).

Brian F. O'Neill is a doctoral candidate in the Department of Sociology at the University of Illinois at Urbana-Champaign, USA, and at the Center for Research and Documentation on the Americas (CREDA, CNRS/Université Paris III La Sorbonne Nouvelle).

Joan Cortinas Muñoz is a postdoctoral researcher at the Centre de Sociologie des Organisations, Sciences Po Paris, France. Previously, he worked at the UMI iGLOBES, CNRS/University of Arizona.

Murielle Coeurdray is a postdoctoral researcher at the UMI iGLOBES, CNRS/ University of Arizona.

Eliza Benites-Gambirazio is a post-doctoral researcher at the CNRS (French National Center for Scientific Research). She is affiliated with the Centre Max Weber (University Lyon 2).

Routledge Advances in Sociology

21 Globalization, Uncertainty and Late Careers in Society
Edited by Hans-Peter Blossfeld, Sandra Buchholz, and Dirk Hofäcker

22 Bourdieu's Politics
Problems and Possibilities
Jeremy F. Lane

23 Media Bias in Reporting Social Research?
The Case of Reviewing Ethnic Inequalities in Education
Martyn Hammersley

24 A General Theory of Emotions and Social Life
Warren D. TenHouten

25 Sociology, Religion and Grace
Arpad Szakolczai

26 Youth Cultures
Scenes, Subcultures and Tribes
Edited by Paul Hodkinson and Wolfgang Deicke

27 The Obituary as Collective Memory
Bridget Fowler

28 Tocqueville's Virus
Utopia and Dystopia in Western Social and Political Thought
Mark Featherstone

29 Jewish Eating and Identity Through the Ages
David Kraemer

30 The Institutionalization of Social Welfare
A Study of Medicalizing Management
Mikael Holmqvist

For more information about this series, please visit: www.routledge.com/Routledge-Advances-in-Sociology/book-series/SE0511

The Field of Water Policy
Power and Scarcity in the American Southwest

Franck Poupeau
Brian F. O'Neill
Joan Cortinas Muñoz
Murielle Coeurdray
Eliza Benites-Gambirazio

LONDON AND NEW YORK

First published 2020
by Routledge
2 Park Square, Milton Park, Abingdon, Oxon OX14 4RN

and by Routledge
52 Vanderbilt Avenue, New York, NY 10017

Routledge is an imprint of the Taylor & Francis Group, an informa business

First issued in paperback 2021

© 2020 Franck Poupeau, Brian F. O'Neill, Joan Cortinas Muñoz, Murielle Coeurdray and Eliza Benites-Gambirazio

The right of Franck Poupeau Brian F. O'Neill, Joan Cortinas Muñoz, Murielle Coeurdray, and Eliza Benites-Gambirazio to be identified as authors of this work has been asserted by them in accordance with sections 77 and 78 of the Copyright, Designs and Patents Act 1988.

All rights reserved. No part of this book may be reprinted or reproduced or utilized in any form or by any electronic, mechanical, or other means, now known or hereafter invented, including photocopying and recording, or in any information storage or retrieval system, without permission in writing from the publishers.

Trademark notice: Product or corporate names may be trademarks or registered trademarks, and are used only for identification and explanation without intent to infringe.

British Library Cataloguing-in-Publication Data
A catalogue record for this book is available from the British Library

Library of Congress Cataloging-in-Publication Data
A catalog record has been requested for this book

ISBN: 978-0-367-19259-4 (hbk)
ISBN: 978-1-03-208287-5 (pbk)
ISBN: 978-0-429-20139-4 (ebk)

Typeset in Times New Roman
by Deanta Global Publishing Services, Chennai, India

Contents

Acknowledgments		vi
Preface: when the river flows again		vii
Abbreviations		ix
Introduction: a sociological perspective on water policy		1
1	Engineering the arid West: the emergence of hydrocracies	27
2	Supporting the economic order: urban sprawl and coalitions for growth	58
3	Reinventing water conservation: institutions for sustainability	85
4	Sharing flows: new professionals with old methods	117
5	Implementing water policy: instruments and their social uses	139
	Conclusion: dealing with scarcity	165
	Annex 1: Revisiting the Law of the River	174
	Annex 2: Statistical analysis	184
	Bibliography	207
	Index	226

Acknowledgments

This collective survey of the protagonists of Southwestern American water policy has been realized thanks to the support of the joint international unit iGLOBES (National Center for Scientific Research (CNRS)/University of Arizona). Colette Doressoundiram has been a fantastic administrator throughout the project, allowing the unit's members the full time they needed to dedicate themselves to research activities.

Many other collaborators have helped us during the many years leading to the completion of the project. First among them are Ed Curley, with his vast knowledge of environmental issues in the American West, and Evan Canfield, who took us to where it all started – where the Santa Cruz River flowed again …

Many other people have encouraged the unit iGLOBES' activities or participated in them: Rebecca Bernat, Anne-Lise Boyer, Leandro Del Moral, Pierre Deymier, Regis Ferrière, Claude Le Gouill, François-Michel Le Tourneau, Pierre Lucas, Pierre Meystre, Lala Razafimahefa, Eduardo Rios, Marie-Blanche Roudault, Joaquin Ruiz, Claire Zucker, Rositsa Yaneva. At the INSHS (CNRS), Patrice Bourdelais and Pascal Marty have also strongly supported the unit. At the Udall Center, Chris Scott and Robert Varady have always collaborated positively.

This research has been supported by the ANR BLUEGRASS, the OHMI Pima County, which is part of the Labex DRIIHM (ANR-11-LABX-0010), by the UMI iGLOBES (UMR 3157 CNRS/University of Arizona), and by the CREDA (UMR 7227 CNRS/Paris III).

Any possible errors, or misunderstandings in this book, remain the sole responsibility of the authors, however.

Preface

When the river flows again

You have to hear the water flow in the bed of the Santa Cruz River near Tucson, Arizona, to realize that something is happening in the field of water policy in the American West. After being exploited for decades for sanitation and drinking water, agriculture, surface and subterranean mining, and urban development, the water course that the historian and legal scholar, Robert Glennon, described, oxymoronically, as the "dry river" (2002: 36), is now benefiting from the work carried out by Pima County, near the Mexican border, to restore ecosystems and conserve water resources. In a state as politically conservative and as focused on development, both economic and in terms of real estate, as Arizona, the emergence of green approaches to water policy may be surprising. In a sense, then, this book is an attempt to explain such a paradox: how can a process of "ecologization" (Poupeau et al. 2018) be generated in adverse conditions corresponding to a king of a worst-case scenario.

It would be easy to attribute this perhaps unusual state of affairs to the drought currently being endured by the American West. Its effects, it might be argued, have left the various state governments of the region with little choice in the matter, and Arizona, the state furthest downstream of the source of the Colorado River, would clearly be the hardest hit by water shortages. Beyond the impact of an external factor like the drought, the development of an explanatory framework describing water stress represents a real challenge for sociology. The task at hand is to demonstrate not only the impact of human activity and approaches to managing water, but, more importantly, to describe the social causes of water scarcity affecting the region, and the way in which institutions approach the problem. In the end, the aim is to develop a perspective adapted to predicted scenarios and the emergencies of the moment.

With this objective in mind, a specifically sociological approach had to be developed in a research area that had already been largely defined by hydrologists and geographers (Poupeau et al. 2016). Within a short space of time, the idea that water policy in the American West should not be analyzed as an ensemble of local situations, but that, instead, measures taken in a specific area could have ramifications for other areas not necessarily linked to it in an obvious way, led us to consider how policies were applied in a systematic way, and to examine their coherence. Consequently, the notion of the "field," rarely applied to public policy viii *Preface*

(Bourdieu 2001; Dubois 2014; Hilgers & Mangez 2015; Albright et al. 2017), emerged as an exploratory tool capable of encompassing the relational and systemic dimension of water policy in the American West. At this point, the problem was to define which field we were talking about – if the notion of the field even made sense (Cortinas et al. 2017). The various states in the region are characterized by a wide range of ecological, agricultural, and urban situations (Pincetl 2011; Cortinas et al. 2017). There are thousands of water service operators, and regulatory institutions are at once numerous and sector-based. Consequently, the development of a sociological approach describing the field of water policy represented a kind of challenge for the discipline.

At the same time, the team conducting the survey of approaches to adapting water policy to the drought – an issue from which this book takes its inspiration – was exploring other theoretical and methodological frameworks for analyzing conflicts over water in the Americas. An application of the Advocacy Coalition Framework, coupled with Network Analysis, made it possible to explore more circumscribed areas associated with water access (Poupeau et al. 2018), while taking into account their systemic and relational character (De Nooy 2003; Singh 2016). In a certain sense, local analyses of systems of relations implicit in various networks served as a gateway to the larger field of systems involving the protagonists of the management of water resources and urban services, while at the same time providing a form of methodological balance with the field analysis approach. The survey of conflicts concerning the management of the drought in Arizona has made it possible to grasp a relatively coherent and autonomous subspace – a fraction of a field – and to understand its principal properties, while simultaneously articulating them with the water policy system in the American West as a whole.

This book is the product of a somewhat extravagant enterprise that has taken a rather modest form. It approaches a "major subject" using "small objects," which are both empirical and circumscribed, and capable of revealing how systems operate. It aims at understanding the social conditions of emergence of water alternatives, and more generally the process of ecologization of environmental policies. Against the background of the vast literature on water and the environment in the American West, its objective is to make a specific contribution by emphasizing, in an empirical fashion, the importance of the social characteristics and trajectories, both professional and academic, of the protagonists of the water sector, so that the sociological notion of the field can be applied with a view to developing an intelligible model that is at once exploratory and explanatory.

Abbreviations

ACF	Advocacy Coalition Framework
ACWA	Association of California Water Agencies
ADWR	Arizona Department of Water Resources
AMA	Active Management Areas
AWBA	Arizona Water Banking Authority
CAGRD	Central Arizona Groundwater Replenishment District
CAP	Central Arizona Project
CAWCD	Central Arizona Water Conservation District
DOI	Department of the Interior
GMA	1980 Groundwater Management Act
IID	Imperial Irrigation District
INA	Irrigation Non-Expansion Areas
LADWP	Los Angeles Department of Water and Power
MET/MWD	Metropolitan Water District of Southern California
ROD	Record of Decision
SDCWA	San Diego County Water Authority
SGMA	2014 Sustainable Groundwater Management Act
SOI	Secretary of the interior
SRP	Salt River Project

Introduction

A sociological perspective on water policy

The drought in the American West as a social process

"*We are in a drought*": any tourist visiting Disney World or Universal Studios in California can read this information on the door of his motel bathroom. Having been told this, he is enjoined to save water by not sending the towels from his room to the laundry service. This kind of injunction has been generalized to most institutions in the Western United States, as if this were the most important answer to the current threat of water shortages. In such a prestigious part of the world – representing the "new frontier" of economic growth, urban sprawl, and technological civilization – this kind of moralized recourse to small individual initiatives seems rather pathetic.

The problem with this kind of prescriptive invitation ("*We are in a drought, save water*") does not only owe to the, in fact, dramatic scale and length of the drought in the Western United States, or the disproportion of the proposed solution for resolving it (a sum of individual, optional measures), but rather the very formulation of the problem: the concealment of all the social logics that have generated the problem itself. Indeed, drought is not just a natural phenomenon linked to a decrease in rainfall or to a decline in water flows in rivers due to climate change and changing rates in glacier melt upstream. It is associated with a broad range of social factors related to land use and water provision (Lynn-Ingram & Malamud-Roam 2013; Mount et al. 2016). In the USA, the states located to the west of the 100th meridian are drier and subject to higher variations in precipitation than are the states to the east of this line. However, the vast swathes of farmland located in these areas require substantial irrigation systems. Most water still goes to agro-industry: 77% in California, 79% in Arizona, 90% in New Mexico, etc. (Howitt et al. 2015). Moreover, the expansion of urban areas and the economic activities carried out in those areas, many of which are located at a substantial distance from sources of water supply, demands the construction of large water storage and transport systems, as well as an intensive use of groundwater (Glennon 2004). Water outages have already affected a number of states, causing, for example, the governor of California to declare a "state of emergency": "The Colorado River (…) has been gripped since 2000 by the worst drought in over a century of record-keeping" (Grant 2008: 964). Since the 2000s, watersheds including the Colorado

2 Introduction

River Basin have experienced not only low levels of rainfall and snowmelt, but also high temperatures, with a negative impact on the balance between supply and demand (Barnet et al. 2008).

While measures introduced in cities have succeeded in minimizing the effects on retail consumption, the agricultural sector has proven to be more vulnerable. In 2015, farmers in the Central Valley in California saw their provision of surface water decline by 50%. In all states, competition for available water resources has generated disputes, sometimes even leading to litigation. State institutions and the federal government are also on the front line. The federal government, as owner of most of the land in the American West, on behalf of which it financed mega-infrastructure projects throughout the 20th century, provides agriculture support programs and climate risk funds. There are, in all, more than 20 federal agencies involved in drought management, including the Federal Emergency Management Agency, the Department of Agriculture (including the US Forest Service), the Department of Commerce, the Environmental Protection Agency, the Army Corps of Engineers, and the Department of the Interior (encompassing the Bureau of Indian Affairs, the National Park Service, and the Bureau of Reclamation).

The water crisis in the American West constitutes a unique opportunity to understand the implementation of environmental policy. First and foremost, the region's spectacular desert landscapes are the very incarnation of the wilderness, considered as an ideology that structures the relationship between North Americans and their natural environment (Nash 1967). These landscapes represent a "frontier," an external territory that society attempts to circumscribe by introducing parks and conservation policies. While the American West is a desert, it is nevertheless an inhabited desert. Inhabited, or, in other words, prey to a growing urban expansion throughout the 20th century, an expansion coupled with the effects of climate change. As Edward Abbey wrote in *Desert Solitaire*, one of the founding works of political ecology:

> Water water water ... There is no shortage of water in the desert but exactly the right amount, a perfect ratio of water to rock, of water to sand, insuring that wide, free, open, generous spacing among plants and animals, homes and towns and cities, which makes the arid West so different from any other part of the nation. There is no lack of water here, unless you try to establish a city where no city should be ...
>
> (Abbey 1968: 130)

As the ultimate site of ecological nostalgia and conservationism (Jacobi 2003), the West is also the birthplace of American anthropology; in the 19th century, as unknown lands were explored and cartographic missions were organized, an interest developed in local native populations (Fowler 2010). Information gleaned in the various exploratory missions to the Colorado River, the Green River, and the Grand Canyon, undertaken by John Wesley Powell around 1879, was later used in the planning of major hydraulic projects in the region on the basis of a form of governmental science piloted by the federal government (Worster 1991). In the

Introduction 3

following decade, Powell was appointed director not only of the US Geological Survey, but also of the Bureau of Ethnology at the Smithsonian Institution in Washington DC, where his position was somewhat weakened by the maneuvers of Senators defending "local interests" against federal projects. He was probably the first to define the West as an "arid region" that needed to be regulated at a time when the area still represented a "frontier" and a dream of freedom. As Wallace Stegner (1953: 226) explained:

> In general, American Law was based on English Common Law. But the Common Law, accumulated out of the experience of a rainy country where water was no problem, affirmed only what were known as riparian rights to the water of streams. The man who owned the bank could make any use that he pleased of the water, but he had to return it to the stream when he was through with it. That worked for running grist mills, but it did not work at all for irrigation, which used the water up instead of taking advantage of its passage. In the West, before and since Powell's time, there have been heads broken with irrigation shovels because of someone's attempt to apply riparian law upstream, and take uncontrolled advantage of the water. In an irrigating country, appropriation becomes an essential criterion, and delicate refinements about more or less beneficial uses, and priority, and dipping rights, and a great many other complications still unheard when Powell wrote. There was nothing wrong with the riparian law for the West except when downstream bank owners sooner or later found themselves with riparian rights to a dry creek bed. Water is the true wealth in a dry land; without it, land is worthless or nearly so. And if you control the water, you control the land that depends on it. In that fact alone was the ominous threat of land and water monopolies.

Therefore, the American West raises a series of questions concerning the impact of aridity on natural resources and the use to which they are employed, as well as on ways of living and the institutions that regulate economic and social life. How did people who had taken possession of the land adapt to such difficult ecological conditions? Achieving that promised freedom correlated to a desire to transform nature:

> Those five centuries of learning about the Colorado (actually most of the learning was concentrated in about five decades) seem almost never to have raised in people's minds a simple question: What changes in society would be required to master the Colorado's course? Only Powell gave the matter much consideration; he recommended that both big government and big business stay away from the river, that ordinary settlers be encouraged to organize themselves into "cooperative commonwealths" and set about in their own way to make use of the watershed. Had his suggestion been followed, development would have been confined to the smaller side streams and upcountry valleys, for the main river was too strong for any local group of settlers, with limited capital and expertise, to harness.
>
> (Worster 1982: 67)

4 *Introduction*

The West was a frontier to be conquered by organized and autonomous communities of smallholders incarnating the "American Dream." But, it ultimately proved to be shaped by the megaprojects advanced by the federal government and powerful economic forces – agro-industry, the military, high technological industry, and real estate companies.

In fact, it is generally acknowledged that the major projects of the 20th century were not managed by self-organized smallholders, for the simple reason that they did not have the capacity to finance such infrastructure, particularly the construction of the various dams along the 2,300 km course of the Colorado River.[1] These projects were designed to regulate the flow of a river running through the arid and semi-arid areas of several states (Colorado, Utah, Nevada, Arizona, California) before being reduced almost to a stream, before it arrived at the Gulf of Mexico. In 1994, the completion of the Central Arizona Project Canal, begun in the 1960s in order to meet the irrigation needs of the agriculture of southern and central Arizona, also contributed to meeting the growing urban demand of the Sun Corridor (Phoenix and Tucson). In the end, the development of the Colorado River not only enabled California – notably the Imperial Valley and Los Angeles (Leslie 2005) – to expand throughout the 20th century, but also made possible the expansion of the entire area to the west of the Rockies (Summitt 2013), a region less desert-like than it first appeared and, in reality, largely structured by agricultural irrigation. No more than small farmers, agribusiness did not on its own have the resources required to build such infrastructure. Toward the end of the 19th century, large-scale farmers had to call upon the federal government (Reisner 1985) in order to mobilize and accomplish the ideal of the "American Dream" in the frontier. In so doing, however, it prompted a number of conflicts over rights to the use of water.

While, in a semi-arid environment, irrigation reduces uncertainties linked to natural factors, a high degree of institutional regulation is nevertheless required in order to resolve conflicts about access to water between different groups of farmers. The political ideal of autonomous community organizations managing water supply, presented as the most effective solution in terms of guaranteeing economic development, cooperation, and social justice, echoed Jeffersonian ideology, according to which agricultural smallholders constitute the heart of American democracy – as if the civic virtues allotted to them, supported by the pastoral mythology of their communion with nature, enabled them to embody the role of regulator. With growing urbanization affecting the desert lands of the West, and the New Deal period destined to provide a remedy for the Depression, approaches to economic development were indissociably linked to the federal government, which became the manager and main contractor of major water projects at the national scale (Pisani 1984). The predominant role played by the driving forces of

---

1   The Hoover Dam and the Glen Canyon Dam, completed in 1946 and 1964, respectively, are the most famous of Western U.S. infrastructures but, in reality, several thousand dams and canals were built throughout the region within a period of a few decades.

economic development (large-scale farmers, San Francisco investors, and the Los Angeles elites) undermined the democratic hopes of the previous period (Reisner 1985). Although they may have changed scale, conflicts over the use of water persisted. Disputes now involved not small farmers, but the states of the West, which fought against California for a share of the Colorado River in order to boost their economic prosperity.

The region is, therefore, more than a natural context colonized by man, as in the semi-mythical stories about "how the West was won." Indeed, it forms a complex socio-ecological system, marked by the presence of social organizations and institutions actively working to transform and regulate nature (Ostrom 2009). This process generates the "outgrowths" represented by the cities of Las Vegas, the tourist destination located in the Mojave Desert (Nies 2013), and Phoenix, an "unsustainable" city in the Sonora Desert (Schipper 2008; Ross 2011). The West is located at the crossroads of a series of needs and desires: the conquest of new demographic spaces and pressures; the influence of federal bureaucracies and local authorities; demand for agricultural activity to guarantee food supply and exports, etc. It is, therefore, all the more difficult to reduce the development of the US desert to an ineluctable process of population increase and economic development, especially in that the "American Dream" was used to legitimize a wide variety of approaches, including economic modernization through agribusiness. The symbolic construction of the desert, nourished by various narratives concerning the conquest of the West – ranging from paeans to "modernization" to catastrophist critiques of that same process – should, first and foremost, be analyzed from a historical and sociological perspective (Walton 1993; Teisch 2011; Carroll 2012).

Indeed, *contra* the enchanted vision of the "American Dream," it is, of course, possible to highlight the destruction engendered by the construction of the West and, like Marc Reisner in *Cadillac Desert* (1985: 481), to question whether it was really necessary to build such large dams rather than off-stream reservoirs, or to irrigate relatively unfertile land instead of developing a less extensive form of agriculture. This environmental, and even civilizational catastrophism – as indicated by the title of Reisner's final chapter, "A Civilization, If You Can Keep It" – nevertheless leaves unanswered the question of what logic there is underlying the approaches at play, which remain to be addressed sociologically. Reisner's narrative of the various agents offers a vision of a somewhat absurd field devoid of meaning or, more exactly, of motivations. Politicians, administrators, engineers, and landowners fighting for or against major projects are cast either as cynics corrupted by power and money or as "political idiots" who fail to understand the implications of their actions, namely the construction of infrastructure and the kind of economic development that it enables. They are either traitors to the "American Dream" or fanatics for technological modernization. The end of *Cadillac Desert* shows the brute, and indeed brutal, force of economics, but gives little understanding about how the management of rivers and dams is also a symbolic construction that involves, beyond mere personal interests, collective struggles over the principles that inform a legitimate vision and division of the world

6 *Introduction*

and its development. The desert narrative provides a dramatic vision of the environmental history of the West, which is a history of conflicts, violence, and spoliation, but it does not explain how these relations of domination are articulated to the social logics that make water into a scarce resource. Nor does it explain how such a tormented history is today able to create a wide consensus in terms of deciding the objectives and the instruments of water policy (Davis 2001: 538). The production of consensus is one of these key components, as can be seen with the consistent movement toward collaborative and negotiated efforts and away from legal cases. Therefore, while there is still a struggle in policymaking, it has taken a novel form, namely that of the struggle to reach consensus. This consensus over areas of potential disagreement means that as time passes, the struggle becomes less and less a matter of "taming the waters," as in the first part of the century, and more one of working within the confines of the established management model in the Colorado River Basin and then in each state.

Throughout this history, it can be seen that the model of managing water in the West has been a consistent movement away from what might be considered more traditional forms of conflict such as litigation and court action. These actions have created novel institutional tools within the Western states, but also within Arizona, a state that has much to lose from long-term drought conditions because of the wider model for the management of the Colorado River Basin's water resources. Furthermore, Arizona has created a unique model for itself, which stresses cooperation and consensus over conflict, an emphasis borne of the concern to avoid repeating history all over again. Much past study of water involved extensive research into the hydrologic cycle or issues of who/what should govern and at what scale, from the local to the state or federal levels. Many more academic and newspaper articles as well as op-eds espouse the notion that there is a drought crisis in the West. But how is this situation different, and what framework of empirical investigation can be applied to it? If the current situation of scarcity and drought is important, this is not just because it is the most severe in recent memory. It is because there is a risk of a break with the past. A consensus has been built up, which has allowed for the unequal sharing of water, and this has created clear social and political divisions. But it is also a consensus that has created a norm of collaboration and an obligation to obtain agreements. Therefore, it is plain to see that water management is not only a matter of managing flows (and their economic benefits). Rather, it means managing trust, it means managing people, and it means managing power: water policy refers not just to engineering, but to politics.

The politics of scarcity

The question of managing scarce natural resources is central to the study of "adaptive capacity" to climate change (Delli Priscolli & Wolf 2009; Markard et al. 2012; Varady et al. 2016). This involves both an analysis of the conflicts generated by the appropriation of these resources (Barraqué 2011) and an examination of policy strategies adopted, at their different levels of action, by the institutions

Introduction 7

concerned (Lorrain 2008). In pursuing such a study, the social sciences dispose of analytical tools that are capable of taking into account the systemic character of environmental issues and providing existing approaches with an analytical framework that integrates different factors that are generally studied separately, such as the management of resources, the distribution of network services, and the elaboration of public actions. The objective of this study is to construct an approach to water policy based on the notion of the "field," such as has already been applied in a wide variety of case studies (Bourdieu & Wacquant 1992; Martin 2003; Fligstein & Kluttz 2016).

The notion of the field can be understood and applied in a number of ways. As a tool for the description of the social world, it is inscribed within a historic vision of the transformations of differentiated contemporary societies (Lemieux 2011), within the emergence of an autonomous economic field (Polanyi), and within the gradual empowerment, in the relevant timeframes, of other microcosms of social life (Bourdieu 2012), including the cultural, literary, artistic, scientific, and legal fields (Bourdieu 1977, 1991; Lebaron 1997; Sapiro 1996; Duval 2006). In this perspective, it is possible to study an environmental field objectively, meaning the system of agents and institutions involved in addressing the issues of contamination, the management of natural resources, and sustainable development (Dezalay 2007). The notion of the field can also be used to describe the organizational spaces of corporations and their strategies of action (Fligstein & MacAdam 2011). But this notion also serves a more original, exploratory, end, as an analytical model. This involves two epistemological constraints in order to construct a scientific object. On the one hand, it encourages a focus on the relational aspect of the object studied, with systems of properties that classify, consolidate, and contrast the elements of which it is composed. On the other, it casts these systems of relations not only as objective distributions (fields of force), but also as issues in – and instruments of struggles between – groups that position themselves in regard to those systems and attempt to impose principles of vision and division of social spaces that they see as conforming with their positions and interests, and with the strategies they intend to develop (field of struggles).

While there have indeed been studies on housing (Bourdieu & Christin 1990), cultural action (Dubois 1999), and publishing (Bourdieu 1999), public policy has rarely been addressed as a "field." Yet this notion could

> help us to see as a whole what the division of scientific labor in standard analyses tends to separate, namely the structure and functioning of the bureaucratic field, the systems of relations that constitute the state and its power, and public policies defined as practices and positions taken within these relational structures.

More pertinently, the notion of the field invites us "to take into account not only the specific social spaces of public action, but also, more broadly, relations between distinct social spaces, in that social action is founded on those relations and helps give them structure" (Dubois 2015: 14–15). In this sociology of water

8 *Introduction*

policies, an attempt will be made to link the intervention of the public authorities to social relations of domination.

Water policies regulate a particular market, the water market, which is largely controlled by the public authorities (at the global level, only 6% of the market is in the hands of private companies). France is an exception to this rule, with 65% of the market controlled by delegated management contracts, as compared, for example, with the United States, where "investor-owned operators represent under 10% of the market" (Lorrain 2011: 3–4). While the globalization of the sector that began in the 1980s contributed to an extension of privatization, with the intervention of major transnational companies, international engineering firms, development banks and investment funds (Bakker 2010; Barraqué 2015), the market remains an economic sector largely controlled by individual states and their regulatory authorities, whose relations with operators have undergone realignments over the course of the contemporary period.

Indeed, the unified management of a technological network by a single operator, whether public or private, is linked to a political and industrial tradition that has, since the 19th century, entrusted the entire local water cycle to the expertise of the engineering corps (Mollinga 2008; Molle et al. 2009; Fowler 2010; Teisch 2011). Consequently, calling the territorial monopoly of the operator into question implies taking into account all the "protagonists of the water sector" (Lorrain & Poupeau 2016) involved in the management of technical systems. A relational approach to water policies based on the notion of field makes it possible to take into consideration not only private distribution companies, but also organizations operating in the water sector and contributing to the elaboration of public action: governments and regulatory administrations, interstate commissions tasked with negotiating how water and water rights are to be shared, consumer groups (economic farming lobbies and small citizen associations, etc.), NGOs and think tanks producing expert reports, and industrial companies active in the engineering and construction sector, "clean tech," and similar spheres. (Lorrain 2011).

This ensemble, which has the air of a genuine "nebula" (Topalov 1999), helps to make water policy a relatively autonomous space of action, complete with its own formal and informal rules articulated around specific issues. These latter include the definition of price structures and decisions on the kinds of measures to be taken in the face of natural disasters (flood, drought, contamination, etc.). Therefore, the field of water policy can be considered as the provisional objectivization of the structural state of the power relations involving the various protagonists of the water sector. Seen from this angle, *the sociology of water policy is part of a sociology of domination*, from different perspectives: the making of water policy can be considered as an "object of government" (Carroll 2012) and a manifestation of the power of "water bureaucrats" (Molle et al. 2009), whose competencies are now disputed by new models of management (Poupeau et al. 2016a); furthermore, water policy involves the construction of major technical systems that have been used to construct agro-industry and contemporary metropolises, but that have also generated environmental conflicts that have, in return, influenced those policies (Walton 1993; Espeland 1998). Finally, the study of the

Introduction   9

field of water policy makes a contribution to the *sociology of the market* in the sense of a socially constructed space, or series of spaces, "in which firms, suppliers, clients, employees and government interact with one another" (Fligstein & Dauter 2007: 3). In this perspective, "action strategies" and their "instruments" (Fligstein & Calder 2015: 11) should be linked to the system of positions occupied by the various protagonists in the field and to the positions they adopt in consequence (Bourdieu 1977). The challenge for the research presented here is to apply this sociological approach to the water policy that has been implemented in the face of the drought that has been affecting the American West, and, more particularly, the Colorado River Basin, since the early 2000s. The analysis focuses on the instruments that regulation has designed to try to avoid water shortages (Taylor et al. 2012) and sets them back in the context of their "modes of appropriation" (Lascoumes & Simard 2011). Basing itself on an analysis of water policy instruments, considered as a system of positions taken by various institutions, this approach aims to provide an understanding of the factors that impact institutional responses to the drought.

First, the instruments developed to face the drought are linked to a number of strategies designed to reduce the risks of water outages: "technology to augment existing supplies and conservation to extend them are only two methods for coping with future water shortages. A third method is to reallocate water from less productive to more productive areas" (Grant 2008: 984). In their study of cities in the United States, Hess et al. (2016: 808) focus on the first two factors. On the one hand, the option is to develop new supply sources (new surface infrastructure to transport water, new wells, the acquisition of use and storage rights, restocking aquifers for future use and/or improving water quality, and building desalination plants). On the other, they emphasize reducing demand (measures designed to conserve supply sources and aquifers, recycling wastewater in most cities, etc.). Hess et al.'s research question consists of defining the kinds of conflicts over water supply strategies cities are faced with, and what kinds of institutional logics are at work (2016: 809). This dichotomic approach marginalizes not only the issue of the resistance of communities to water transfers (Ingram & Oggins 1990), but also the process of implementing those transfers (water markets), which have been the object of inter- and intrastate negotiations. In order to understand the various ways in which water policies are appropriated, this study has opted to take into account all major categories of instruments and place them in their current context, where all parties consensually accept the need to manage water in a sustainable manner, and each individual institution makes its own specific adaptations to this need. Indeed, at the turn of the 2000s, due to the effects of the drought, the need to secure water resources had begun gradually to exert an influence on water policies and change the very nature of water conservation measures.

The hypothesis underpinning the research of this book is that even if the protagonists of the Colorado River Basin water sector are not all in contact with one another, they are linked both by the same problematic (managing the effects of the drought and the decreasing volume of water from the Colorado River) and by

10   *Introduction*

shared norms (concerning the need to guarantee a sufficient supply of water for human activities). These two factors define the framework of water policy and the conditions of its application by individual institutions within the limits of their territorial remits (Summit 2013; Fleck 2016). Obviously, water policy primarily consists of managing water flows and infrastructure and finding sources of water supply capable of supporting economic development. But water, like other goods necessary for social life, is an "object with two faces, one economic, the other symbolic, [...] at once a commodity and a meaning" (Bourdieu 1999). Managing water flows involves managing a power that is not limited to the financial capacities generated by the water market, but that implies the imposition of a vision of the social world within which water policies take on their full meaning. In particular, these policies involve defining the privileged mode of economic development and, therefore, determining which models to adopt in terms of both priority objectives and tools for action. Consequently, the various protagonists of the water sector fight to impose a definition of water policies as close as possible to their own position within the system of institutions concerned. And they do so as a function of their own capacity for action. Clearly, these struggles are linked to the relative power of individual institutions, whether in terms of priority rights to water, their lobbying and negotiating capacity in terms of federal and state rules, or the available funds (and this can be a constraint on strategies that focus on building and maintaining major infrastructure designed to diversify supply). On the other hand, they are also linked to the development of small water conservation structures (individual water reuse systems, etc.).

To these objective variables, the sociological approach adds the study of the social characteristics of the water professionals involved in drought management: that is, the dispositions that are required in order to act like a manager. Struggles over the imposition of a legitimate model for water policy are also influenced by the professional itineraries of water professionals, for example their academic background (engineering, law, economics, environmental science, etc.) and their careers in various institutions, which can impact their fields of competence and, consequently, their capacities for action. In his foundational study on water policy in the American West, the environmental historian Robert Gottlieb observed the transformations that were beginning to affect the sector:

> the public water agencies are the mainstay of the water industry. Their local leaders, members of their boards, are often drawn from the business and political elite in their communities. Some but not all of these figures have a direct interest in the activities of their industry while most have ended up making a career out of participation in water matters [...]. The leaders of these public agencies have often tended to be middle-aged or elderly white men. Many of them have held their positions ten years or more, some as long as thirty or forty years. Agency managers, also nearly exclusively white and male, have largely been engineers, though both lawyers and those with a financial background have played more of a role in recent years.
>
> (Gottlieb 1988: 247–248)

Introduction 11

While such transformations in the water sector were only at the gestation stage when Gottlieb was writing about them, the challenge now is to understand how these modes of domination have persisted into the present, and to analyze the degree to which they have been impacted by the context of water scarcity. The fact that the expertise of engineers and the instruments they promote have each been called into question is likely to affect the way in which the water market functions as an institutionally framed and regulated sector. The relations between the characteristics of the institutions in this industrial sector, the socio-professional characteristics of their leaders, and the instruments that they employ in order to deal with the threat of water shortages, are at the heart of this research. The construction of the relational space of the protagonists of the water sector makes it possible to define the variables relevant to an analysis of the positions that these institutions take – and the reasons why they take them – in their struggle to impose a legitimate model for managing water from the Colorado River.

If this sociological perspective has never been applied to environmental policy, the research presented here cannot ignore the large range of frameworks developed for the purposes of understanding the stalemates of water policy in the Western United States. One of the epistemological challenges of field theory is thus to integrate these previous works on drought management into a coherent approach, within one explanatory model. These approaches can be differentiated as a function of their epistemological content and the levels of action at which they are situated: from a focus on the development of water policies as systems of domination to the analysis of bureaucracies specializing in water management and the power-knowledge relations they institute, and the examination of beliefs and cause-based coalitions. It should be added that such approaches take into account both institutional architectures and public policy networks. For all these approaches, whose contributions this research attempts to incorporate and apply, the American West works as a research laboratory.

Beyond the hydraulic society

In his *Rivers of Empire* (1986), the environmental historian Donald Worster studies the American West as a "hydraulic society" in which power and influence are held concurrently by a private sector dominated by wealthy farmers, and a public sector composed of bureaucratic planners and politicians. His work is often presented as a simple transposition of the perspective of the despotic states of Asia developed already by Wittfogel to the vast landscapes of North America (Banister 2014; Bichsel 2016). According to Wittfogel, given the organization of labor and capital required to build the necessary infrastructure, agricultural irrigation would lead to a centralization of political power. Worster nonetheless stands in contrast to Wittfogel in that his interest is broader in scope; indeed, he focuses on an original definition of the hydraulic society and the power structures that developed in the American West: "a social order founded on the intensive management of water. That regime did not evolve in isolation from the industrial system, of course, but all the same it was a distinctive emergent, reflecting the

12   Introduction

geography and arid climate of the state" (Worster 1992: 55). This is an almost exact return to the ideas of Max Weber in *Economy and Society*, who, long before Wittfogel, referred to hydraulic and "royal" bureaucracies in Asia and the Middle East, stating that irrigation and the corresponding water management regime was a question of winning land back from the desert, i.e. the imposition of natural forces strongly correlated to a bureaucratic state (Foster and Holleman 2012). Yet, Worster differs and builds on both these past approaches. His emphasis is less on the omnipresence of a centralized state constituted through approaches to water management, and more on the impact of relationships of domination that traverse all the social groups concerned. Worster outlines the implications of the social and ecological transformation of California, which enabled it to strike a balance between the ideals of the West (freedom, democracy, individualism) and its mythical history (the saga of men and women leaving civilization to dig a means of subsistence from the bowels of nature with their own hands, the story of liberation from the East, from tradition and control, and the tales of cowboys and other intrepid adventurers). Veering away from a conception of the West as a simple colony of the East – as described by Cronon (1992) – he suggests that the concept most suitable to defining its specificity is that of "empire." This empire emerged in the 19th century with the transformation of a desert region into a verdant, prosperous territory: the introduction of major hydraulic projects oriented a fast-developing California toward the export of agro-industrial products. This empire was structured around a politico-bureaucratic elite from the metropolises of the East Coast and wealthy local farmers, motivated by a shared desire to transform an arid desert into a fertile oasis and a source of profit.

In this framework, the manipulation of rivers led not only to the introduction of new models of human interaction, but also of new relationships of domination. Worster provides a review of the principal approaches to water management characterizing the history of irrigation, based on specific criteria such as the scale of water networks, the type of managerial authority that operates them, and the goals pursued by the irrigators. In the American West, the approach to water management characteristic of the capitalist state was accompanied by the emergence of a social order within which power and influence were held by both a private sector and a public sector supporting one another in regard to the elaboration and control of water resources. He argues that this created a hierarchical society in which workers were used as instruments of environmental manipulation, while, at the same time, rivers became a means of control over the workers. In such a hydraulic society, in which the action of the capitalist state is guided by the constitution of an empire, water is no longer thought of as a biological necessity, as it would be in the kind of subsistence economy characteristic of traditional societies. Water here becomes a commodity, the value of which is assessed in function of what it is capable of representing (an irrigated parcel of land, kilowatts of energy) or producing (bales of cotton or truckloads of oranges).

Worster shows that in seeking to transform a sterile desert into an economic commodity, the capitalist state granted pride of place to engineers, whose technological expertise made it possible to build gigantic dams. The centralizing elites

Introduction 13

of the irrigation sector belonged to a new generation of administrator-engineers who were in a position of strength in the government, who had little belief in democracy as a social remedy, and who defended the idea that only a technical elite could guarantee national growth. During the course of the transformation of the rural spaces of the American West into a vast agro-industrial complex, California was the site for the emergence of a form of domination based on the parallel and combined accumulation of two types of resources, namely capital in the form of land owned by wealthy farmers, and the technical expertise of federal officials. According to Worster, there was nothing democratic about irrigation management, which was structured around quasi-governmental districts originally designed to regulate access to property and plots of land that could be irrigated. Few smallholders took part in a decision-making process largely dominated by influential representatives of the private sector elected to the board of directors, and by expert managers suspicious of communitarian participation that might present a risk to the maximization of technological and economic efficiency. The ongoing transformation of a desert into a commodity presupposed large-scale irrigation, and to be able to consume ever more water, new regional alliances were needed. After the depression of the 1930s, the federal state became the indispensable partner of agro-industry in the American West, which required its expertise. Indeed, the actions taken by this "service bureaucracy" protected the position of the regional elites. From the 1940s, the emergent hydraulic society was the result of a convergence of instrumental forces: farmers harvested a profusion of cereals, with no other aim in mind but accumulation; federal technicians, tireless in their reorganization of natural basins, rendered reasonable what they saw as irrational. The development of this large-scale hydraulic engineering approach enabled the American West to occupy a triumphant position. In an arid environment in which water was becoming scarce, the private sector found it hard to prosper without external aid. It therefore called upon the state to help it pursue its logic of accumulation in spite of the growing scarcity of water.

According to Worster, the main reason why the centralizing elites promoted an irrigation program was to boost the wealth and influence of the country in order to serve their own interests: they represented a new generation of administrator-engineers who enjoyed a powerful position within government, who had little belief in democracy as a social remedy, and who defended the idea that only a technological elite could contribute to national expansion. In this regard, Worster disagrees with those historians who see in the legal and institutional concretization of this conception (the 1902 Act and the setting up of the Bureau of Reclamation), a victory for ordinary people, who were provided with the right to own land and accrue wealth. For Worster, the federal agency's decision to make land available represented, above all, an opportunity for speculators to get rich quick by purchasing plots of land, not with the intention of exploiting them, but with a view to selling them on as soon as access to water had been guaranteed. Indeed, that decision also reinforced the position of previously established landowners. On occasion, the state's involvement in the reorganization and development of a valley was not carried out entirely to the advantage of private interests. In this schema of national

14   *Introduction*

expansion, for large, established landholders, "federal water" was a real godsend (Coeurdray et al. 2015). On the other hand, for small farmers who had migrated to the West, working on public land that had never previously been exploited was associated with hard manual graft and debt. In these conditions, the hoped-for mass immigration of endless waves of people who had previously lived in rented accommodation and who were willing to leave overpopulated cities behind in order to become landowners did not really take place. Rather, the conquest of the West was structured around a relationship between a national political-administrative elite and a regional economic elite. It is thus unsustainable to maintain that the West was developed by an omnipotent federal government, as in Wittfogel's analysis; Worster suggests, on the contrary, that the effects of a composite *field of power*, made up of coalitions established at multiple administrative levels, are to be sought in the sphere of the control of resources.

In this regard, Worster himself shares in the fierce critique elaborated by Arthur Maas in *Muddy Waters* (1951). Professor of political science at Harvard, director of the Harvard Water Program from 1955 to 1965, and consultant to a number of public sector environmental agencies, Maas denounced the unbridled power of a federal elite, the US Army Corps of Engineers, that he defined as an insubordinate, exclusive "clique," with little concern for public well-being. Linked to the senators of the West and the economic forces that they represented, this lobby, one of the most powerful in Washington, composed of around two hundred officers from the upper echelons of society (controlling nearly 50,000 engineers on the ground), was responsible, according to Maas, for preventing the needs of the region from sufficiently being taken into account. In the early 20th century, the expansion of the American West was threatened by a problematic ecological situation owing not only to repeated droughts, but also to a lack of sufficient capital for constructing the irrigation systems needed by small, family-run farms. The conquest of the desert demanded large-scale irrigation that could not be managed unaided by small farmers, but that presupposed a new mode of control and organization.

The main contribution of Worster's sociological research is to demonstrate that an emphasis on the opposition between market and state is not the most effective approach to describing the power structure in the American West, where capitalism had to adapt to specific ecological conditions. In an arid environment in which water was scarce, the private sector found it hard to prosper on its own, and called for state action to overcome this problem and allow it to pursue its own logic of accumulation. The hydraulic society to the west of the Rockies was built on restricted environmental foundations, those of aridity, producing an integrated system of power including both the state and the private sector in a relationship of interdependence, a system that made it possible to exploit every river and creek in the region in the cause of increasing the wealth of the West and of America in general. This power structure gradually established itself, accompanying regional industrial transitions and encouraging the creation of future desert metropolises through the creation of an unprecedented water infrastructure. But as the legitimacy of this empire was increasingly called into question at end of the

Introduction 15

20th century, the state was charged with achieving contradictory goals: promoting the accumulation of private wealth through the augmentation of the availability of a scarce resource (water), while maintaining social harmony via its equitable distribution. Meanwhile, the federal state had privileged a logic of accumulation incompatible with its redistributive function. The question of justice, in its various forms, was raised more and more frequently: protests against the introduction of new dams; juridico-political debates on limitations on land allocations seen as an attack on the freedom to do business or as a form of democracy prejudicial to economic growth; strikes led by agricultural workers against agribusiness; claims made by native populations in regard to water rights dating from the 19th century. This dissension revealed that the hydraulic society was more fragmented and fragile than had previously been thought. Alongside technological feats and the accumulation of profit, it had also generated growing levels of inequality: the elaboration and scope of irrigated agriculture was accompanied by the exploitation of proletarianized immigrants; the Bureau of Reclamation did not hold to is promise of an equitable redistribution of land making access to property and prosperity possible for the greatest number (particularly for the urban proletariat of the East); the management of water rights suffered from a democratic deficit; and farmers were increasingly unhappy about federal control over their ability to acquire land. Public criticism of major hydraulic projects, considered economically unjustifiable and harmful to ecological systems, highlighted the need for an alternative society focusing on the conservation of nature. These criticisms also marked the emergence of a new struggle over the empire's legitimacy, a struggle not only concerning the validity of modes of administration, but also about the principles used to define that legitimacy and, consequently, the legitimacy of the domination of the water sector by a coalition of agribusiness and the federal administration.

If Worster's approach has been criticized for reducing water policy to an instrument of domination, his perspective nevertheless reveals the impact of water bureaucracies and the influence of the federal system in terms of the development of major hydraulic systems (Coeurdray et al. 2016a; Poupeau et al. 2016b). François Molle et al. (2009) has explored the structuring role of these "hydrocracies" and, above all, the kind of engineering expertise promoted as a universal management model, not only in the United States and Europe, but also in India and China. In seeking to transform a sterile desert into an economic product, the capitalist state thus accorded a privileged role to the knowledge and expertise of engineers, whose technological prowess made it possible to build gigantic dams. The main protagonist in the development of water infrastructure in an arid environment (the state) appears less as a body echoing the voice of the people, and more as the product of an elite motivated by a spirit of conquest and power. The hydrocracy approach was applied by Patrick Carroll (2012) in his study on the development of the "techno-scientific state" in California, in which he shows how water governance profits from the contributions of scientific engineering, to the point that it forms an "engineering governmentality" encompassing all the issues associated with water in the sphere of public action (irrigation, flows, drainage,

16 *Introduction*

salinity control, urban supply, etc.). While Carroll's analysis of these hydrocracies emphasizes the shifting borders between science and policy and their impact on technical systems, it nevertheless remains somewhat vague with regard to their conservationist commitments. Taking a different tack are approaches based on analyzing coalitions. Most of these approaches are articulated around qualitative surveys focusing on the protagonists in the water sector, and they have the objective of entering into detail about how such policies are elaborated.

Coalitions for water policy and institutional networks

The Advocacy Coalition Framework (ACF) examines the degree to which a problem is defined as political and susceptible to institutional remediation. In this respect, the ACF focuses on various forms of appropriation (cognitive appropriation, protests, etc.) effected by different social groups (Jenkins-Smith & Sabatier 1993). In spite of its limits (Bergson et al. 1998), this approach is of particular interest in the case of a collectively shared problem like that of the drought in the American West, where a substantial number of organizations, bureaucratic bodies, and private actors are engaged in institutional debates and involved in coalitions. Sabatier and Jenkins-Smith (1993: 212) draw attention to

> the utility of focusing on advocacy coalitions as critical means of simplifying the hundreds of actors involved in policy change over a decade or more. An advocacy coalition consists of actors from a variety of governmental and private organizations at different levels of government who share a set of policy beliefs and seek to realize them by influencing the behavior of multiple governmental institutions over time.

In order to unravel the institutional entanglements that can be observed within the management of the drought, the ACF reframes public policy in the context of transformations occurring over relatively long (10-year) periods, the idea being that these policies mirror systems of belief (Sabatier & Jenkins-Smith 1993: 118–120). The ACF is thus located at the level of subsystems that not only encompass institutional bodies making policy decisions, but also all the agents participating in the process, from members of official organizations to journalists, consultants, and scientists.

Another characteristic of the ACF approach is that it focuses on the beliefs and values thanks to which coalitions are able to implement their public action programs (Jenkins-Smith et al. 1991). Members of subsystems are in agreement about a central core of normative actions, as well as about a series of secondary elements made up of instrumental decisions and strategic policies, which support those axioms within the subsystem. But if shared axioms are resistant to change, other levels of belief are more flexible. Policy changes therefore derive either from events that occur outside the subsystems (changes in socioeconomic conditions, public opinion, etc.), from events that occur within them (transformations within political parties, election results, etc.), or from lessons drawn from past policies ("policy-oriented learning"). This is revealed in the research carried out by John

Munro (1993) on water policy in California and the conflict over the building of the Peripheral Canal south of Los Angeles. Here, the dominant coalition, made up of agro-industrial groups, experts, and federal civil servants, politicians, and state administrators, came under attack in the 1970s from an ecological coalition favorable to the introduction of water conservation measures. Munro shows that, in spite of the efforts of a policy broker– the governor of the time – to mediate, and of the fact that the beliefs of the existing coalitions were little considered, a compromise solution in favor of water transfers between territories nevertheless gradually emerged thanks to a policy learning process. This learning process concerned not only environmentalists, with the emergence of a new generation, which had a deeper knowledge of economics, but also the water professionals of the Imperial Irrigation District, faced with the legal obligation to reduce water consumption by 55% and to sell unused surplus to Metro Water District in Los Angeles. As "a direct consequence of both forced and unforced learning, water markets are evolving into policy options that lie within the acceptable policy space of both developmentalist and protectionist advocacy coalitions" (Munro 1993: 124).

In this perspective, the ACF approach is also particularly well adapted to analyzing how the drought, which has been affecting the American West since around 2010 and which concerns all the states that, to varying degrees, depend on the Colorado River for water supplies, constitutes an "external factor" capable of transforming water policy, without, however, being the only explanatory factor (Cortinas et al. 2017). The study of environmental governance as a "process by which stakeholders articulate their interests" in order to take decisions (Furlong & Bakker 2008: 3) can help us understand the mechanisms by which public policy develops. Governance models can encompass a policy of water conservation inscribed less in a technical perspective than in a long-term and collaborative vision. This latter entails criteria for sharing responsibilities and accountability that in turn define norms. This makes it possible to avoid simply having to rely on the good will of the institutions concerned. A distinction should, then, be made between strategies implemented at the federal and regional levels (price regulation, monitoring performance, benchmarking, financial transparency, coordination, etc.) and at the municipal level (cost recovery principles, economic steering, community participation, etc.). However, while this analysis of governance enters into the details of usable instruments, it nevertheless presents two disadvantages. First, it fails to articulate different levels of action; and, second, more importantly, it does not take into account the impact of the protagonists in the water sector as a social and professional group, whether in regard to their relational networks or to the institutional architecture by which their actions are framed.

Insofar as networks are concerned, the study of relations between institutions and public policies is based on a hypothesis according to which power, far from being a unique reality, depends on connections between actors and resources (Le Naour 2012; Massardier 1997). Most of this research is inscribed within the framework of the analysis of coalitions: "coalitions must in part reflect prior relationships and collaborations" (McClurg & Lazer 2014). More precisely, writing about the introduction of the California Marine Life Protection Act in 1999,

18 *Introduction*

Weible (2005) reveals the degree to which shared beliefs and, to a lesser extent, the perceived influence of certain organizations, help to explain the development of active networks in the field of environmental policy. Moreover, these networks are more like coordination than information networks (Weible & Sabatier 2005) and are studied at an interorganizational level. The "ecology of water management games" model developed by Lubell et al. (2014), based on the management of the coastal areas of San Francisco Bay, shows that coordination networks are supported by federal or state agencies whose collaborative objectives go beyond territorial frameworks. In fragmented systems, those agencies have the resources (political, economic, technical, etc.) to implement a system of "polycentric governance" capable of coordinating network policies. However, one problem with network analyses is that, while they are able to explain the development of cause-based coalitions, they are less effective when it comes to explaining the strategies that various groups deploy with regard to public policy instruments (Cortinas et al. 2017). Furthermore, while this kind of research explores systems of interaction between institutions and groups within a single territory, it does not take into account "invisible" protagonists, who do not belong to the same space of territorialized conflict, but who nevertheless influence the strategies of various actors. For example, it is impossible to understand the policy developed by the Central Arizona Project in terms of the conservation of water from the Colorado River unless one takes into account the contractors and operators in the neighboring state of California who possess most of the prior appropriation rights, and who are therefore able to ensure that most water shortages are borne by Arizona.

With regard to institutional architecture, the study of water management in the American West reveals a complex system in which the range of institutions involved effectively renders the issues invisible. After all, until recently the residents of cities, like everyone else in the USA, had been accustomed to a cheap and copious supply of water (Pincetl et al. 2016). A detailed analysis of the various types of organizations involved in water distribution in California, basing itself on the areas they supply and the interdependence of their supply flows, highlights the degree to which the system is fragmented. For it involves a substantial number of different institutions, public, private, municipal, and cooperative, organized by commissions that monitor infrastructure and prices. Alongside contractors who import water from the Colorado River via the State Water Project Canal, there are wholesale operators, like the municipal water districts who purchase water from contractors, and retailers, small operators who sell directly to consumers. But, curiously, an insistence on the fragmentary nature of the spatial distribution of the service tends to obscure the power relations between the various institutions, and to downplay the importance of the contractor, the Metropolitan Water District of Southern California, which supplies 37 operators, and accounts for 12% of the annual consumption of 4.5 maf[2] imported from the Colorado River. The rich and

2 An acre foot is a unit of volume equal to the volume of water one acre (0.405 hectare) in area and one foot (30.48 cm) in depth; 43,560 cubic feet (1233.5 cu m)

Introduction 19

detailed description of the system provided by Pincetl et al. (2016), based on an analysis of this system's opaque elements and the problems associated with local governance, does not however explain the link between institutional architecture and the spread of water conservation policies. Yet this fragmentation impedes a successful adaptation to new conditions of water scarcity.

If we want to make use of the contributions made by these various approaches, as we study the system of institutions involved in determining water policy in the Colorado River Basin, we can use the concept of field as an exploratory model. Here, field is used as an operative notion, a model of understanding, more than a fixed and closed theory. The study of a field follows three steps (Bourdieu & Wacquant 1992; Grenfell 2014): (1) determining the relation of the considered field to the field of power; (2) mapping out the different competing agents; and (3) analyzing their habitus and the system of dispositions involved in the field. In order to apply this methodology, built for the purposes of studying more homogeneous social groups (artists, intellectuals, editors, etc.), it is necessary to determine to what extent water policy constitutes a field. This demonstration involves not only determining the existence of a "common issue" over which the field agents supposedly compete (i.e. there is some minimal agreement as to the object of their disagreements), but also the existence of field effects that simultaneously define the boundaries of the field, which are frequently the object of symbolic struggles. If we are to define a common issue that constitutes the field of water policy, we must first determine what the social agents are really competing about, and thus pay attention to their practices. As has earlier been explained, managing water is not only a matter of building technical systems (tunnels, canals, dams, urban networks, etc.) and regulating flows: rather, it also involves managing technical and professional skills (engineering), economic markets (development of the service, prices, contracts, etc.), and water rights and how they are shared. Finally, to manage water is to manage power: power over the city, over the power of producing goods, collecting taxes, etc. When people and groups struggle to impose a model of water management in their city or in their region, they are also competing to determine what skills are appropriate to implementing this model, whatever that model might be. Many analysts advance the hypothesis that water managers utilize what is referred to as "best practices" in order to realize the "common good"; but a sociological frame of analysis leads to the idea that water managers above all try to implement strategies to define a water policy that corresponds to their own practices and their capacities. As a consequence, the imposition of a legitimate model of water management helps them to maintain their power and the power of their organization in the field of water policy. However, the field of water policy is not a homogeneous microcosm with social agents interacting at the same level of action, but rather a complex and hierarchical world involving various levels (from the federal to the municipal). Thus, a different process of autonomization emerges in relation to the field of power, as a function of the dominant water policy coalitions' real level of action. That is the reason why conflicts related to the distribution of the Colorado River waters in the Western US during the "mega-drought" affecting the region since the beginning of the 2000s (Fleck 2016), constitute a

20 *Introduction*

key point of entry to understanding how water policies are shaped in relation to the field of power. This mega-drought is not only a natural disaster, but also the result of the historical transformations that have affected the West for more than a century.

The Colorado River Basin: determining the limits of the field

Situating the analysis of water policy at the level of a river like the Colorado is not the same as defining a territorial unit – the river basin – as something "natural." The choice of river basins as a unit of management and governance is the product of a political construct that has made it possible to articulate various water issues around a series of relatively unified policies in the United States, Europe, and their colonies since the 19th century (Molle & Wester 2009). The study of "river basin trajectories" is situated at the level of

> long-term interactions between societies and their environments, with a focus on the development and management of water and associated land resources. A basin trajectory encompasses human efforts to assess, capture, convey, store, share and use available water resources, thereby changing waterscapes and turning parts of the hydrological cycle into a "hydro-social cycle." It also includes human efforts to deal with the threats posed by particular "shock events," such as droughts, floods and contamination incidents, and to achieve a degree of environmental sustainability. Lastly, a basin trajectory includes institutional change and the shifting relations of power that govern access to, and control over, water resources.
>
> (Molle & Wester 2009)

The notion of "river basin trajectories" made it possible to set inextricably linked environmental and social factors that contributed to a definition of water use and its potential exhaustion ("basin closure") at the center of the analysis. Seen from this perspective, the study of the Colorado River Basin makes it possible to set the territorial unit, generally used as an analytical framework, back within the relational space of the institutions that define it as a territory to be administered.

Starting in the Rocky Mountains of the state bearing the same name, the Colorado River crosses seven states on its journey to the Gulf of California in Mexico. It supplies almost 40 million inhabitants with water and electricity, and it irrigates 1.2 million hectares of agricultural land (Kennery 2009). Since the late 19th century, water from the river has helped to transform this arid and semi-arid region, through the development of major technological systems (dams, canals, reservoirs, etc.) that have been central to the promotion of economic growth (Summit 2013). The water (surface and groundwater) was first used in intensive agriculture, which required substantial quantities of this resource, before it was gradually transferred to urban uses. These latter uses went hand-in-hand with a labor market that was increasingly oriented toward the production of manufactured goods and services, and to dealing with the demographic explosion of the

Introduction   21

region's cities (Pincetl 2011). Throughout the 19th century, the conquest of new frontiers was fueled by a desire to transform the arid lands of the West into the "bread basket" of the East Coast (Cronon 1992) and then into an "oasis in the desert" (Gober 2006; Logan 2006; Ross 2011). This phenomenon is at the heart of what the directors of the Arizona Department of Water Resources (ADWR) and the Central Arizona Project (CAP) describe as a "structural deficit" (Davis 2014) between the growing demand for water linked to human needs and a decrease in available water caused by a decline in snowmelt. The drought affecting the American West since the early 2000s is thus framed by the environmental and social factors that characterize the use of water from the Colorado River.

The Colorado River Basin (see *Figure I.1*) is a complex technical and normative system whose most impressive structures are the Hoover Dam (completed in 1936) and the Glenn Canyon Dam (completed in 1967), which stock water in Lake Mead and Lake Powell, respectively, the Colorado River Aqueduct, which supplies the Metropolitan Water District in Los Angeles, the All-American Canal (1942), which supplies Imperial Valley in California and the Yuma region in Arizona, and the Central Arizona Project (completed in 1992), which transports water over a distance of 600 km to Phoenix and Tucson, both in Arizona (Cortinas et al. 2016a). A large number of additional infrastructure projects (20 dams, thousands of kilometers of diversion canals, etc.) make the Colorado River one of the "most controlled, controversial and litigated rivers in the world" (Southern Nevada Water Authority 2012). This technical system is regulated by the "Law of the River" (see Annex 1), a phrase used to describe a corpus of interstate agreements (including the Colorado River Compact of 1922), federal laws and regulations, decrees, legal rulings, and contracts that define how the estimated 16 maf taken annually from the Colorado River is shared between states (O'Neill et al. 2016). For example, the Boulder Canyon Project Act (1928) allocated 4.4 maf per year to California, while Arizona, allocated 2.8 maf per year, did not sign an agreement until 1944. The legal configuration made the secretary of the interior the "water master" for the water and irrigation districts of the Basin.

In California, the Seven Party Agreement (1931) defined the volumes of water to be shared between contractors (Palo Verde Irrigation District, Yuma Project, Imperial Irrigation District, Coachella Valley Irrigation District, Metropolitan Water District, and the City and County of San Diego). While the Imperial Irrigation District received almost 70% of the water from the Colorado River allocated to California, the Metropolitan Water District was allowed to use, for Los Angeles and its operators, water that other states had not consumed from their quotas. Consequently, California received over 5 maf per year for several decades, until restrictions were imposed due to the current drought. Faced with the emergence of these two major protagonists – agro-industry and urban development – Arizona's situation is more straightforward. The Arizona vs. California decree (1964) defined the amount of water allocated on an annual basis to Arizona (2.8 maf per year). Meanwhile, the Colorado River Project Act (1968) ratified the construction of the Central Arizona Project, while at the same time regulating water service interruptions between states in case of drought and limiting CAP

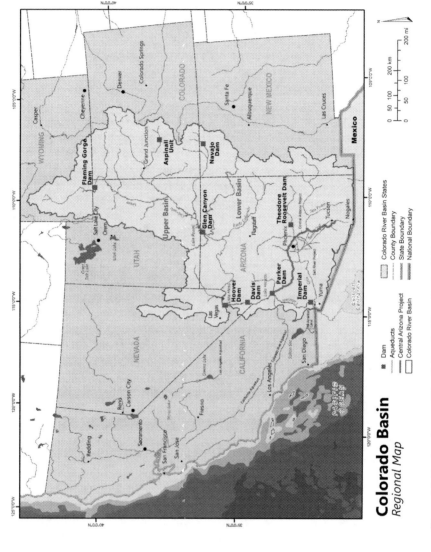

Figure 1.1 Regional map of the Colorado River Basin. © Rositsa Yaneva.

supplies to zones that were already irrigated. In the 1970s, the construction of the CAP was subordinated to the implementation of a measure designed to regulate the use of groundwater, namely the Groundwater Management Act (1980), which gave the state agency, the Arizona Department of Water Resources, a considerable amount of power (Coeurdray et al. 2016a, 2016b). The state's agro-industrial sector is seen as a sort of buffer zone, reducing the number of water outages. In California, certain irrigation districts (Palo Verde, Imperial Valley) have priority rights (the "Present Perfected Rights" backed by the Supreme Court in 1979). The position of urban agencies thus became increasingly fragile in prolonged drought situations, especially in that the Metro Water District was able to use unused surpluses, thereby accentuating the inequalities created by the overestimation of the Colorado River flows at the outset of the agreements (16.5 maf annually instead of 15.5 maf) (Lynn-Ingram & Malamud-Roam 2013).

The effects of climate change on water are magnified by another factor, namely urban expansion. And it is Arizona and California that have seen the highest rates of urban expansion in the United States (Ross 2011; Benites et al. 2016).[3] In the early 2000s, California was roundly criticized by other states for its excessive water consumption and, in 2003 the secretary of the interior forced it to limit its consumption to an allocation of 4.4 maf. In 2009, the Water Conservation Act was passed with a view to a 20% reduction in the urban consumption of water supplied by operators by 2020. In spite of these measures, the levels of Lake Mead and Lake Powell, the main reservoirs serving the Lower Colorado Basin, continued to decline. They decreased to 37% and 51% of their capacities, respectively (Byrd 2016). In Arizona, the increasing numbers of Drought Management Plans also bear witness to a growing awareness of the finite nature of water resources (Pima County 2014). Indeed, major cities, including Phoenix and Tucson, are now introducing water conservation measures (Hess et al. 2016; Benites et al. 2016). State agencies (Natural Resources Agency, Fish and Wildlife Agency, etc.) contribute to this new "conservationist crusade" (Hays 1999). The secretary of the interior's authority over Colorado River water is thus supported by a large network of institutions operating within restrictive legislative frameworks. Article 10, paragraph 2 of the Californian Constitution, defines water supply norms according to "reasonable uses" and the "protection of ecosystems" that urban operators and irrigation districts must respect (Cortinas et al. 2017). In Arizona, water law defines how water from the Central Arizona Project is shared and determines the use limits of groundwater resources (whose management is regulated by the Groundwater Management Act, see above).

A huge number of organizations, acting at various levels from the federal to the local, are involved in the distribution of water from the Colorado River. Their involvement corresponds to relationships of institutional dependence. Agencies deal with issues of water quality and decide on who to allocate use permits to

---

3   On urban growth in the United States, see Benites et al. (2016): http://www.cairn.info.inshs.bi b.cnrs.fr/revue-francaise-de-sociologie-2016-4-page-735.htm.

24 *Introduction*

(State Water Resources Control Board of California, Arizona Department of Water Resources); others deal with environmental questions (protecting flora and fauna); while yet others take care of canal infrastructure (State Water Project, Central Arizona Project). In California alone, over 2,000 organizations have responsibilities in the water sector. They all have their own level of competence, and, consequently, a certain degree of autonomy. Furthermore, the institutional architecture of water management varies from state to state. This is an extremely decentralized model characterized by state institutions whose power focuses essentially on incentives and the definition of management guidelines, rather than on a capacity of constraint and coercion of all the protagonists in the water sector. Thus, planning is the essential tool available to the California Department of Water Resources. This consists of defining the objectives for all institutions supplying water to various users. It does not have a power of coercion, but it can introduce incentive measures – essentially by means of subsidies – in order to convince various agencies to respect norms. On the other hand, the very dense legislation on water in Arizona gives state institutions a major role in terms of providing a framework for the water management approaches taken by individual agencies. A focus on the Colorado River Basin also makes it possible to consider the institutions concerned with processing and distributing water from the river as a system whose constituent parts, while they are not all in direct contact with one another, are nevertheless interdependent. They are, in fact, linked by laws, legal norms, and inter- and intrastate agreements about water distribution and guaranteeing property rights (Davis 2001; Jacobs et al. 2007).

Organization of the book

This introduction has presented both the political and scientific focuses of the book. It has provided new insight into drought management in the American West, as an extreme situation impacted by two general factors: the insufficiency of water supplies and the continuing urban growth of the region. It has moreover called into question the dominant narratives or scholarly frameworks in water policy studies on the arid West. Instead, it has presented the specificity of this book's own sociological approach: the adaptation of Bourdieu's field theory to water policy. This framework has several requirements: the definition of a common issue on which all the protagonists of water are fighting for, and a determination of the limits of the field, which points to the need to explore the social logics of its historical formation and their impact on the contemporary structures of the field. The field analysis is thus developed in several stages, each of them being the object of a chapter.

Chapter 1 represents a historical detour, but one that is necessary for understanding how the field of water policy operates in our own present. Water management has moved away from the rationality of engineers toward more political-, legal-, and business-oriented processes. In dealing with these themes, this chapter also importantly presents the social logics that water policy has for economic development. This includes mega-projects realized by federal engineers and

Introduction 25

federal funds, but also disputes on the water flows and evolution toward legal solutions that have now progressed to emphasizing cooperation and a general discourse of consensus.

Chapter 2 discusses how policy was slowly transferred to the local level. The book moves into interpretations and conclusions drawn from empirical fieldwork, rather than the perhaps better-known, although sometimes obscure, historical references of the opening chapters. At the local level analyzed here, economic forces (often in the real estate sector) remain decisive, despite the conflicts this poses for environmental norms. In addition, it broadens the analytical depth and breadth of the field analysis by showing how both issues of economic management and environmental presentation are combined in the thinking of water professionals. This will be important for a discussion of the *habitus* of the water professionals, a key step in a comprehensive field analysis.

Chapter 3 explores the case study of Southern Arizona, usually known as a bastion of Republican values, to investigate the paradoxical emergence of a conservationist coalition, especially between local institutions (like Pima County) and state regulators. This coalition is not a mere product of the drought affecting the region, but the result of several social logics structuring the strategies of adaptation to future water shortages. First, the institutional architecture of water management in Arizona creates an interdependence between the protagonists of the water sector in order to implement their policy instruments; consequently, the more central institutions need minor institutions to ensure that their policies are implemented, appropriating what are, a priori, the most improbable ideas (water conservation in Arizona). Second, the common academic background of the main water professionals makes possible the conditions for a common dialog beyond the differences of interests and beliefs. This perspective is capable of filling certain lacunae in the sociology of the process of production of public policies. It aims to demonstrate that a subsystem of institutions in which interdependence and the absence of a regulatory monopoly exerted by any one of them produces such a degree of uncertainty about the results that conflicts are, in practice, either marginalized or ignored in order to produce consensus and agreement, which is all the more vague and flexible in that it is based on instruments that can be used by everyone (drought action plans, for example). On the other hand, the introduction of new variables, for example academic backgrounds and career paths, which have mainly been addressed from a qualitative point of view in this chapter, suggests a potential for an analysis of the social determinants of systems of action – particularly the role of engineers and strategies designed to convert their technical skills to the sphere of water management.

Chapter 4 focuses on California, a state that has for many years held a dominant position in the field, both in terms of the positions of its institutions and the influence of its professionals. Conservation policies are embedded in complex economic strategies and reveal different coalitions as an inverted phenomenon to that which is observed in Arizona. The chapter shows empirically though, how instruments such as desalination reveal a transformation in water policy in the state. New professionals are exhibiting what might be considered as old technical

26   *Introduction*

methods, that of promoting mega-projects, just as they did before the 1970s. Yet, rather than a return to the mega-project, as many are now proposing in water policy studies, this case study shows that these managers and professionals are not the same as they were 30 years ago, as business and management academic backgrounds seem more and more necessary to get an influential position, and yet, still there is a lag in the instruments they are willing to use to make the desert bloom.

Chapter 5 presents an extensive survey on water institutions and professionals in Arizona and California. It takes the reader through the determination of a relevant sample of effective institutions in drought management allowed for the analysis of the relational space of the field (type of institution, characteristics of the managers, etc.) and the position takings, which were characterized in terms of instruments of water policy (water reuse, water markets, desalination, adjustment of tariffs, etc.). The analytical framework adapted to the study of water policy goes beyond visible interactions between protagonists in the water sector in Arizona and California and takes into account all the variables affecting the emergence of conservation and the consensus about its implementation. Such a field reveals links between a number of networks that function as so many empirical points of entry for research. The construction of the relational space of the institutions involved in drought management makes it possible to define the variables relevant to an analysis of the positions, and the reasons for those positions, taken by these institutions in their fight to impose a legitimate model of water policy for the Colorado River Basin. The statistical analysis based on this database reveals the principles structuring the implementation of water policies, whose instruments depend as much on the characteristics of the institutions concerned as on those of their leaders.

Finally, the conclusion gets back to the initial question of the study: how to deal with drought and water scarcity, and what does it mean for the water protagonists involved in the struggles for the definition of water policy and of its instruments. It becomes possible to understand how the same policy instruments for water conservation, which are the apparent product of a general consensus among water protagonists, take in fact different political meanings in Arizona, where engineers still contribute to the application of environmental norms, and in California where water business remains the structuring force of the sector.

1 Engineering the arid West
The emergence of hydrocracies

Water for a "new America"

Few regions are associated with such idealized images as those linked to the desert landscapes of the American West. However, it is not an uninhabited desert, as it has been prey to a growing urban expansion throughout the 20th century, and this expansion is now coupled with the effects of climate change. The worsening drought situation forces water professionals to try to find a way to keep water reservoirs high in order to avoid future water shortages in the West and satisfy the competing needs of man and nature. Indeed, this continuing attitude toward regulating water deficit stress on the local population can be surprising in some aspects. One might think that the building of the federal mega-irrigation infrastructures along with huge water reservoirs could have been the ultimate technological solution to cope with drought cycles in the West. However, a social history of water policy shows that the regulation of water resources has been complex, especially due to the fact that it implies a number of levels of decision-making – municipal, regional, state, interstate, and federal – and often that of a decentralized nature. Furthermore, both the tensions and articulations between different levels have not only fashioned water policies but also carried forward a certain idea of the economic development of the West. It is, therefore, difficult to understand the stakes of water management in such a region without taking into account the historical and social forces that have contributed to the construction of large technical systems for this very purpose. More specifically, this poses the need to consider the approaches taken by the economic, political, and administrative teams that have struck opportunistic coalitions in order to advance their interests and their vision of the world, and thereby promote their view of what role the federal government should play in the regulation of resources in general and the development of the American West in particular. An examination of the social origins of these water policies reveals that many of the contemporary questions addressed by water management and decision makers are not new. They touch, for example, upon old conflicts between Arizona and California, as well as the recurrent issue of drought, and the need for adapting to an area of constant scarcity.

The scientific perspective developed in this chapter is based on a social history of water policy. Its goal is to examine the social logics underpinning what

28   *Engineering the arid West*

the current paradigms of political studies on water governance present as novel issues, and to do so by paying attention to the social conflicts sparked by water policy in the American West. It aims to understand why and how the management of water and drought in the American West today relates to a decentralized and multilevel institutional structure, which itself corresponds to the lack of national planning in terms of water use; an instrumental vision of water as a vector of economic growth; and a political field heavily influenced by local and regional forces. To that end, a distinction will be made between three phases of water policy in the West of the United States. The first, which began in the late 19th century and lasted until the 1920s, corresponds to the genesis of federal policy, whose advocates and structuring effects we will here identify. The second phase encompasses the 50 years between 1920 and 1970 and is articulated around the battle between Arizona and California for the water of the Colorado River, the legal resolution of which led to the elaboration of the Central Arizona Project (CAP) as the main source of supply for Arizona. This phase makes it possible to shift focus from the federal to the regional level and to shed light on the third phase – as exemplified by the conflict over water quality that broke out in the city of Tucson in 1992. This research, based on secondary information and data, the archives of these conflicts' protagonists, constitutes the first step of the analysis of the disputes over water, the logic that underpins them, and their social effects. It pays specific attention to the emergence and transformation of coalitions for water policy, as they contribute to the constitution of a social field.

Taming nature and economic survival

The first federal water policy was introduced in the United States in the form of the Reclamation Act passed by Congress in 1902. This legislation was the result of a project promoted and steered by the economic powers of the West in conjunction with business lawyers, well connected not only to agro-industrial and industrial circles but also to Washington politicians. Its objective was to foreground problems concerning the distribution of water. It was those same economic agents who, a few years before, had fought against Powell's power and influence. In 1890, they introduced a new strategy designed to address two new series of constraints: on the one hand, the economic structure of the West as constituted in the 1860s, and, on the other, the effects of climatic conditions, notably drought, on the way in which that structure functioned.

By the end of the 19th century, most of the land in the West was in the hands of railway companies, banks, and other large landowners. However, the land was later sold to farmers. This period witnessed the transformation of subsistence agriculture into commercial agriculture, in which the exchange value of agricultural products was the basis of producers' existence (Hofstadter 1955: 39). These producers were strongly oriented toward the market, taking enormous financial risks in order to mechanize their farms in a context in which the railway companies charged sometimes extortionate prices for transporting goods. The third structuring element of the economy of the West was its speculative character: land changed hands on a regular basis, a phenomenon promoted not only by large landowners, but also by farmers, who saw their land as a commodity (Hofstadter 1955: 43–54).

This speculative dimension of the economic structure of the West reached its apogee between 1870 and 1887. It was during this period that land prices increased exponentially. The bubble burst in 1887: the existing economic structure collapsed due to the drought in the winter of that same year, which affected a third of the West. The fall in the price of farms destroyed the confidence underpinning the speculative market (Hofstadter 1955: 57). In consequence, land prices dropped in an unprecedented manner, people left the country for the city in droves, and many farmers found themselves unable to repay their debts. This explains why the region's economic powers (banks, railway companies, large-scale manufacturers, and suppliers of products consumed by farmers) began to promote federal irrigation projects. The railway companies in particular supported these projects with a view to increasing the value of their land and increasing rates of traffic. Aware that mining, despite its profitability, was not enough to ensure their continued expansion, they viewed the arrival of new occupants as the most effective way of transforming the West into a new economic El Dorado (Worster 2001: 483).

San Francisco's financial leaders saw in these irrigation projects the chance to develop a planned economy protected from economic crises and climatic fluctuations (Pisani 1984: 296). Other industrial producers and suppliers in the West, like the National Board of Trade, the National Businessmen's League, and the National Association of Manufacturers, were part of this coalition of interests. These economic actors used the services of two highly thought of business lawyers based in the West who had close connections with the region's business milieu and political elites. In 1897, the first, George H. Maxwell, became the founder and leader of the National Irrigation Association, an institution that lobbied Congress on behalf of the advocates of federal irrigation projects. The second, Francis G. Newlands, a congressman since 1893, would use his position to promote a federal irrigation policy.

George H. Maxwell, a reformist in the field of water

George Hebard Maxwell is a typical example of a reformist who played a key role in the Progressive Era by generating a substantial number of ideas that were taken up by politicians. Reformists of this kind were professional men from the urban middle class: local business leaders, entrepreneurs, and professionals outraged at the economic power wielded by Wall Street, industry, and the railway companies. These men invested in a broad range of different areas, including the replacement of sub-standard housing, the regulation of working conditions, and social insurance. Their reforms were designed to regenerate an America that they thought of as suffering from moral decadence. Some of these reformers, including Maxwell, were to attain important social roles in this struggle for their political ideal. Maxwell was born in Sonoma, California in June 1860. After being educated in public schools in Sonoma, San Francisco, and San Mateo, he became a lawyer in Arizona

30 *Engineering the arid West*

in 1882. He specialized in disputes concerning water management in California and was particularly sensitive to the problems of small farmers faced with the major landowners. In 1896, he helped to develop federal irrigation projects in the American West, before going on to join the National Irrigation Congress, where he promoted federal, rather than state and private projects. In 1899, he set up his own organization, the National Irrigation Association. At that point, he abandoned his legal career to focus on promoting legislation favoring a national water policy. He achieved his goals in 1902 when Congress approved the Reclamation Act, a document he helped to draw up.

From this date on, his professional career was informed by two main commitments. On the one hand, he was actively involved in managing the water projects that emerged in the wake of the Reclamation Act. He was the Executive Director of the Pittsburg Flood Commission from 1908 to 1911, Executive Director of the Louisiana Reclamation Commission from 1912 to 1913, and member of the Ohio State Water Conservation Board from 1931 to 1942. On the other hand, he promoted the reformist ideal close to his heart by encouraging the development of a West made up of small communities of farmers, functioning as an alternative to the saturated urban centers that he considered to be a source of social problems. In 1907, he became a founding member and the Executive Director of the American Homecraft Society, an organization that defended the interests of small farmers. He promoted a large number of projects based on the ideal of homecraft in Arizona, Massachusetts, Minnesota, and Indiana. However, like many of the reformers of the time, Maxwell's political influence waned and died as the Progressive Era came to an end in the 1920s.

Maxwell shared the ideas of middle-class urban reformers involved in crusades aimed at solving the issues of deteriorating living standards and values in industrial cities – notably the decline of the family, the spread of disease, and urban overpopulation. They believed that if this situation was left unaddressed, it may have led, if not to a proletarian revolution, then at least to social unrest (Hofstadter 1955; Topalov 1988). Maxwell's grand idea was a new America of small landowners based on the concept of "homecraft" developed by the Cadbury brothers (Lovett 2000): an America where each family would own its own home in a healthy environment and in which workers would be motivated by contact with the land and the development of the family farm. In Maxwell's view, this notion of America, or more precisely, of the West, as an Eden for small landowners, offered a solution to the problems of the army of jobless people from the country's major cities, whose revolutionary potential the economic and political elites of the period so feared.

We believe that, as a Nation, we should be less absorbed in Making Money, and should pay more heed to raising up and training men who will be Law-Abiding Citizens: that the welfare of our workers is of more consequence than the mere accumulation of wealth and that stability of national character

Engineering the arid West 31

and of social and business conditions is of greater importance to the people of this country as a whole than any other one question that is now before them.

(Maxwell, in Pisani 2002: 28)

Newlands, on the other hand, was less interested in defending the ideas of a reformist movement than in promoting an alternative approach to irrigation. He had, indeed, already tested this alternative. In the late 1880s, he had promoted the Truckee Irrigation Project, a private initiative that had failed for a number of reasons, among them a failure to ensure agreement between the divergent interests of multiple landowners (Hays 1999: 12). Furthermore, for Newlands, the only way to develop the economy of his state, Nevada, was through agriculture and cattle rearing. But in the end, like Maxwell, his approach led to the emergence of a coalition of economic groups and institutions that contributed to the development of water policy.

The Reclamation Act of 1902

The lobbying campaign led by the coalition between these successful lawyers and the large landowners of the West found a favorable echo in Congress: the Reclamation Act of 1902 led to the setting up of the Reclamation Service, which, in 1923, became the Bureau of Reclamation. Making water management issues a public problem, or, more specifically, a recognized problem taken into account in the elaboration of a water policy, was linked to two factors. The first, and most important, concerned the bureaucratic arena. The early part of the 20th century, which has been defined as the dawn of political capitalism (Kolko 1963), witnessed the emergence of a strong alliance between, on the one hand, the economic power of big business, and, on the other, the political power of Congress and the federal government. Their alliance was designed to confront the "dangers" that could imperil each of them.

> There were disturbing groupings ever since the end of the Civil War: agrarian discontent, violence and strikes, a Populist movement, the rise of a Socialist party that, seemed, for a time, to have an unlimited growth potential. [...] The political capitalism of the progressive Era was designed to meet those potential threats, as well as the immediate expression of democratic discontent in the States. National progressivism was able to short-circuit state progressivism, to hold nascent radicalism in check by funding the illusion of its leaders – leaders who could not tell the difference between federal regulation of business and federal regulation for business.

(Kolko 1963: 285)

In the West, the sudden expansion of populism that had first emerged in 1880 threatened not only the economic elites, but also the two established parties, i.e. the Republicans and the Democrats (Lash 1991). This party/movement was successful in the states of the West, where farmers were experiencing enormous difficulties due to the instability in the prices of agricultural products, high rates of debt linked

32 *Engineering the arid West*

to the purchase of their land, and transport problems that prevented them from effectively distributing their merchandise. These farmers and ranchers, who were seriously in debt, with products and livestock that were losing value on the market, gave their support to the party most likely to defend their interests against those of the banks and railway companies, accused by farmers of being the source of all their ills (Hofstadter 1955: 64). But beyond the local economic power directly targeted by the propositions of populists, it was the hegemony of the Republican and Democrat parties that was being contested. In order to diffuse the threat of the populist movement, the two parties adapted a catchall strategy with a view to appropriating the issues on which its popularity was based (Hofstadter 1955: 94–130). An alliance was struck between the financers of Maxwell's campaign and the political elites of Congress and the federal government with a view to introducing the Reclamation Act, designed to mollify the populists of the West by limiting the size of government-funded farms to a maximum of 160 acres. The dominant interests of the political sphere thus chimed with those of the economic power brokers of the West, who were seeking to increase land values after the land-price bubble burst in 1890. The idea was to promote irrigation projects that could only be funded by the federal government. Federal intervention in the West would have the effect of shoring up both the political and economic power brokers of the region. Thanks to the gradual incorporation of Western states into the Federation in the 1880s – Idaho, Montana, North Dakota, Washington, and Wyoming – these power brokers wielded an ever-increasing degree of political power.

The content of the law that gave birth to the Reclamation Service in 1902 was based on reformist ideals that favored small farmers. Irrigation projects run by the Reclamation Service were linked by law to farms that, in order to promote the development of smallholdings, were limited in size to 160 acres. Furthermore, the law included measures designed to preclude speculation on land designated for irrigation projects (Hays 1999: 12). A water management system was also set up by the users of these irrigation projects. The system was made up of districts tasked with setting up associations to regulate irrigation within the geographical limits of water basins. However, the idea of small farmers was not debated in the draft law, which demonstrates that it was not considered to be the most important political issue at play. There was a consensus among the participants about the need to develop a model of economic expansion capable of resolving the economic crisis that had ravaged the country. But within this consensus there was disagreement between those who thought that water policy was key to economic expansion and those who believed that a different approach, including, notably, the conquest of overseas markets, was the best option. Worster (1985: 163) describes debates in the Senate and Congress in the following terms:

> What they really were wrangling over was the wisdom of the traditional American policy of economic expansion and its future direction in the new twentieth century. Did the country need more farmland in production? Was the westward movement now outmoded? What impact did expansion have on older settled regions? Was it wiser to expand overseas or at home?

Engineering the arid West 33

The law proposed by Newlands made it possible to meet the needs of economic expansion by convincing a majority of people that a water policy based on the irrigation of the West was, in the long term, the only viable solution: "Newland's bill passed, whether it was constitutional or not, whether there was a national need for it or not, because it promised to augment American wealth and muscle" (Worster 1985: 165). The dominant coalition that presided over the implementation of the major water projects can thus be understood in terms of convergent interests and shared beliefs.

The failure of the America of small farmers

However, it quickly became clear that the water policy of the first two decades of the 20th century had failed to usher in the new America of small agricultural landowners described in the promulgation of the Reclamation Act. This failure unfolded at several different levels. First, in the period 1900–1920, very few projects were developed and the number of hectares irrigated was small (Pisani 2000a). Second, after farmers abandoned their land *en masse*, the West of smallholders and small farmers came to be largely dominated by large-scale agribusiness (Pisani 1984). These two setbacks were associated, in particular, with a lack of political links among Reclamation Service directors in the West. In fact, their profile as civil engineers was unsuitable to the region's economic and social structures, and they found it difficult to deal with local elites, speculation associated with the sale of land, and the requirement to take local needs into account.

The Reclamation Service was directed by Frederick H. Newell between 1902 and 1915, and by Arthur Powell Davis between 1915 and 1923. As engineers who had spent their entire careers working for the US Geological Survey, their professional specialization was the construction of reservoirs (Carpenter 2001: 331). They were both "New Engineers," products of the boom in the profession that occurred between 1880 and 1920. Their training was based on a vision of the discipline that emphasized a mastery of nature and technological development to the detriment of the political, social, and economic aspects of public projects. These "New Engineers" considered technical expertise based on the laws of nature as a tool for getting around economic interests and class conflicts. They believed that science stood above politics and business, and, as such, beyond discussion (Pisani 2002: 24). They therefore focused entirely on the laws of physics and paid little or no heed to the problems that the beneficiaries of irrigation projects would encounter prior to project completion, and they failed to spend time establishing the kinds of links with local power brokers that would have been required to ensure the projects' success. Unlike Maxwell and Newlands, Newell and Davis shared a vision that focused strictly on the construction of dams and reservoirs; such a vision marginalized soil analysis and drainage, and it failed to provide support for new agriculturalists and farmers in land irrigated by federal projects (Pisani 1984; Carpenter 2001: 327).

Frederick H. Newell and the New Engineers
Frederick H. Newell, head of the Reclamation Service from 1902 to 1915, was one of the "New Engineers" who emerged during the boom in the

34 *Engineering the arid West*

profession. Between 1880 and 1920, a substantial number of engineering schools were founded, leading to a dramatic rise in graduates. Trained in the belief that technology, of which they regarded themselves as the masters *par excellence*, would enable them to apply natural laws to governing the world more effectively, they thought of themselves as standing above politics. Their professional ethic was based on the notions of organization, efficiency, rationality, and expertise, and not on democratic ideals. Their technical knowledge earned them recognition from their peers and the professional prestige required for brilliant careers in public service, in a period in which reformist ideas informed policies concerning the management of natural resources. Nevertheless, Newell shared the ideas of the advocates of the Reclamation Act, according to whom small communities of farmers had to be developed in the West in order to regenerate an America whose decline had manifested itself in the social revolts of the 1890s. All that had to be done was to complete useful engineering projects and introduce planning for infrastructure to transport water to the communities of this regenerated America. His attachment to the Jeffersonian ideal can be linked to his social trajectory.

Newell was born in 1862 in Bradford, a poor, rural town in Pennsylvania. He went to public schools and, thanks to his impressive academic results (and to the fact that he was able to live in his grandfather's house), he was accepted by the Massachusetts Institute of Technology in 1880. In 1885, he graduated with an engineering degree, and in 1888 he met John Wesley Powell, who advocated a water policy based on small irrigation projects managed by consumers in small farming communities in the West. Powell hired him to work on the study he was conducting on potential irrigation projects, thus giving him a place in the most prestigious geological institution of the time, the US Geological Survey. Belonging to this institution opened doors to other scientific establishments and provided Newell with political contacts that eventually enabled him to become the head of the Reclamation Service in 1902. He joined the Great Basin Lunch Mess, a think tank made up of the leading experts of the time in the field of natural resources. He later joined the National Geographic Society, the American Geographical Society, and the American Forestry Association. Thanks to his contacts, he became President Roosevelt's adviser on natural resources. Like many people whose reforming activities reached their apogee during the Progressive Era, Newell's professional career trajectory began to trend downward in the late 1920s. During this time and until the end of his life, in 1931, he spent an increasing amount of time teaching and conducting research in universities.

Furthermore, the knowledge required to ensure the success of irrigation projects in the West (soil analysis, planning, and the building of canals) was part of the remit of the Department of Agriculture and the Army Corps of Engineers. However, cooperation between these organizations was reduced to a strict minimum due to

Engineering the arid West 35

a conflict between the men heading the two, and, more broadly, the engineers of the Army Corps and those of the Reclamation Service. Moreover, few of these engineers were from the West. This meant that the majority of them were unfamiliar with the region and its soil characteristics. Although irrigation systems were an obligatory subject, the reality was a long way from the specialist areas of the universities from which they had graduated (Carpenter 2001: 335).

Irrigation projects were confronted with other social obstacles associated with the position of engineers within the state bureaucracy. These latter belonged to federal agencies that enjoyed a large degree of autonomy with regard to the federal government. Between 1902 and 1914, the Reclamation Service was not obliged to answer either to Congress or to the President of the United States; it had its own budget, which it could use as it saw fit, with only the secretary of the interior to review it. During this period, the problems that derived from the Reclamation Service directors' conception of its role became more serious, due to the way in which its administration was organized. The Reclamation Service – later known as the Bureau of Reclamation – was part of the Department of the Interior, which at the time had 12 divisions tasked with overseeing the Service and dealing with certain aspects of its work. In regard to legal questions, all decisions had to be authorized by the assistant of the Department's advocate general; all expenditure was overseen by the finance section. The size of the administration and the way in which tasks within it were organized meant that it took the Reclamation Service an inordinate amount of time to put its projects into effect. The Service was thus slow to react to problems in the field. Beyond this form of organization, based on an extreme division of tasks, a further problem was its hierarchical aspect; the Reclamation Service had to wait for the signature of the Department's lawyer, which often took months. As an example, such bureaucratic delays deprived the Nevada farmers of water for an entire season (Carpenter 2001: 333).

Ultimately it was the entire territorial structure of political power in the United States that reared up in anger against the Reclamation Service, thereby contributing to an unforeseen increase in the cost of the first reclamation projects. Poor calculations about the cost of drainage, the quality of water supplied to irrigated properties, the yield of irrigated land, and, consequently, about the potential capacities of new farmers to reimburse the Service for the cost of their properties prompted congressmen to question the competence of this federal agency, whose autonomy came to an end in 1914 when Congress took control of the its budget. Furthermore, the method applied to calculating the value of the land to be purchased by the Reclamation Service for the development of its projects left too much room for negotiation with landowners. These landowners' speculative attitudes caused a considerable increase in the cost of land purchased by the Service. Even these unforeseen costs would not have had such a great impact if the Reclamation Service had been able to recuperate its outlay in the form of bank drafts paid by the beneficiaries of its irrigation projects. However, in the first two decades of the 20th century, most of the occupants of irrigated plots of land vacated them without settling their debts. The increase in construction costs led to

36 *Engineering the arid West*

an increase in the price of the projects, and this had a knock-on effect on incoming farmers, making it even more difficult for them to succeed.

Another problem that made the job of the Reclamation Service more difficult during this period was the territorial political divide between the federal government and individual states and local centers of power. Individual states were unhappy at the idea of what they saw as their water being used to irrigate land in other territories:

> An even more troublesome problem confronted the Reclamation Service: water in one state often could most efficiently irrigate lands in another. Yet the transfer could rarely be accomplished. In Nevada, for example, Newlands and others waged an unsuccessful campaign to obtain water from Lake Tahoe in California to irrigate lands in the lower Truckee Valley in Nevada. Newlands had hoped that the federal government could plan for full development of interstate streams by retaining the freedom to locate reservoirs and irrigable lands irrespective of state lines. Yet, the Reclamation Service met great resistance from local people who wanted to use the water in their own state and complained of federal interference with state rights.
>
> (Hays 1999: 18)

In spite of these issues, the First World War gave a second wind to the dream of a new America of small farmers. Migration from the country to the city increased (the number of urban employees rose thanks to the war industry), while, at the same time, there was a need to provide jobs for veterans. Contemporary fears over the "Yellow Peril" in California also contributed. However, one of the projects of the Reclamation Service during this second youth, the Yuma Project, itself suffered from the same ills as most of its predecessors. Of the 173 farms set up by the Service in the Yuma area, 68 were abandoned in 1910, 17 in 1911, 10 in 1912, and 4 in 1913. A second project, the Klamath Project, met the same end, largely because it was located on the border with Oregon in a region far away from agricultural markets. A third initiative, the Orland Project, was also confronted with problems associated with speculation, the lack of experience of new farmers, and technical problems regarding the distribution of water. These problems led to the breaking of contracts between the Service and recently settled farmers, which caused serious disputes over conditions of payment for farm properties. The most visible consequence of this state of affairs was that farms were abandoned, and debts left unpaid.

During this initial period, very few projects were completed. Indeed, one might legitimately question what impact the Reclamation Service really had in its efforts to promote a new America in the West in the first two decades of the 20th century. In 1920, only one major project was actually completed, the Arizona Salt River Project. Others reached 80–90% of their capacity, while yet others, such as Newlands, Klamath, and Shoshone, barely reached 50% (Reisner 1985). Even with the impetus provided by the First World War, fewer than half of the 60,000 government project farms were irrigated; only 3%

Engineering the arid West 37

of the public land in those projects was cultivated, while private land was unused. In 1925, a sixth of all government farms were vacant, and less than 10% of irrigated land in the West was exploited by the federal government (Pisani 2002: 293). The cumulative effect of these factors was to usher in a new period, which began in 1928 and became truly established with the advent of the Great Depression in 1929. The era of irrigation projects, based on a law that attempted to promote the interests of smallholders, had come to an end. Hitherto there had reigned an alliance between economic and political institutions managed by engineers who believed in the power of science as the primary instrument for running the country. This alliance was now confronted by new political forces affecting the way in which the capitalist system was organized in the Western United States.

A new model of water management emerges

Figures such as Powell, the Cadbury brothers, and others had believed in a West that would be built on an emphasis on communal spirit. Yet despite the social failure of this unrealized West, the Reclamation Act did enable the implementation of a new model of management of natural resources, as illustrated by the case of the Salt River Project (SRP) in Arizona. SRP is the name used to refer to two entities that provide water and electricity to Phoenix, one of the most sprawling urban centers in the Western United States.

Created in 1903 as a land-based organization, the SRP model generally raises questions about its capacity to meet the needs of urbanizing communities (Logan 2006). The way in which this model responded to the concern of communities experiencing rapid population growth and new patterns of living has facilitated a shift from a rural use of water resources to urban uses. This adaptation issue has to be understood in the light of a broader historical context of water use. Indeed, water managers in Arizona emphasize that their know-how in addressing water scarcity has not come out of the blue, but is instead based on broad-ranging experience gained over the last century, which is the very basis of their professional legitimacy – a collective accumulation of practical skills and science based on decision-making, and the test of experience through the implementation of the SRP.

In order to understand the sustainability of the SRP model, it is necessary to analyze how and why the technical system implemented in Arizona responds to specific constraints, at the intersection of ecology and economy (Mann 1963; Kupel 2003). As one first step, it is important to examine the social context, dating back to the early 20th century, that generated such a utility (first for local agro-industry, then for urban growth). Indeed, so doing provides relevant and valuable insights into the role of various coalitions in the establishment of SRP in the region. Yet this historical perspective is not enough to capture the whole picture of this pioneering model. It must therefore be cross-linked to a sociological analysis of specific practices geared toward combining a large set of factors: standards of technical systems; contracting and pricing issues; and the environmental

38 *Engineering the arid West*

constraints for sustainable growth in a context where urban sprawl has been constantly increasing (Abbott 1981, 1993).[1]

The National Reclamation Act included a provision for landowners related to federal assistance for dams and irrigations works, which also applied to those living in the Salt River Valley around Phoenix. In Maricopa County, the construction of a dam and reservoir on the Salt River, located 65 miles northeast of Phoenix, was promoted by investors from the city that also got a hearing in Washington (Zarbin & McCabe 1986). To qualify for this federal assistance, landowners – namely farmers and ranchers – were obliged to create a water users' association, which would have contractual liabilities to the government such as: buying up canals that were owned by the Arizona Water Company, a private company; settling the issue of water rights; and ensuring the complete reimbursement of building work to the government. The Salt River Project therefore paved the way for the numerous multipurpose projects to come, which were not only designed to irrigate arid lands but also to electrify the country. They thereby contributed to regional development. The construction of water reservoirs went hand in hand with the construction of power plants, which not only had the function of responding to the increasing demand for electricity from small municipalities around Phoenix, but also had the financial function of allowing the federal government to be reimbursed for the cost of the dam through the sale of electricity to taxpayers.

The power of the Salt River Project
The SRP is not a usual company – it refers to two separate entities:

The Salt River Project Agricultural Improvement and Power District (the District) is an agricultural improvement district organized in 1937 under the laws of the State of Arizona.[2] It operates the Salt River Project (the Project), a federal reclamation project, under contracts with the Salt River Valley Water Users' Association (the Association), by which it has assumed the obligations and assets of the Association, including its obligations to the United States of America for the care, operation and maintenance of the Project.

(SRP 2014: 6)

SRP's Power District is a public utility and a political subdivision of Arizona whose board members are elected by landowners within its territory. It owns and operates an electricity system that generates, purchases, and distributes energy and provides an electricity service to residential, commercial,

---

1 For a history of the Salt River Project, see: www.srpnet.com/about/history/water.aspx. For a presentation of the Salt River Project's water rights, see East Valley Water Forum: http://evwf.org/wp-content/uploads/2015/01/AppendixC-WaterSuppliesAvailable.pdf.

2 The legal entity of the Association was initially designed to be both a company (corporation) and a cooperative (Smith 1972: 15). Then the Salt River Valley Water Users' Association was designated to represent owners to the government.

industrial, mining, and agricultural users in the city of Phoenix and its neighborhoods. The Association is a private water company that manages a system of dams and reservoirs; it is responsible for the construction, maintenance, and operation of a supply system to deliver raw water for irrigation and municipal treatment purposes. The Association provides the water supply for an area within the major portions of the metropolitan area of Phoenix, its surrounding cities (including Glendale, Mesa, Tempe, Chandler, and Scottsdale), and the Gila River Indian Community. It administers the water rights of SRP's 375 square mile water service area, and it operates and maintains the irrigation and drainage system. The members of the Association's Board of Governors are also elected by the landowners within the water service territory. Operating revenue from retail electricity and other electricity is $2.6 billion in 2014, whereas the Association declares $14 millions of benefits in 2014, for a covered population of 983,745 users (SRP 2014: 27). With a profit of $14.4 per capita/year, it is no exaggeration to say that the water service is almost free, and that the costs of the service are covered by the sales of electricity. The interdependence of the Association and the Power District allows such a low-cost distribution, but the declared investments of electricity benefits into SRP activities are $62,184,000 ($6.32 per capita/year).

The Arizona Water Company, a New York-based private company, was the owner of the surrounding canals through which water was sold to farmers and ranchers. This company had a contractual relationship with the Pacific Gas and Electric Company, a Californian company, which resold electricity generated by the water from the dams to inhabitants of Phoenix. Farmers and ranchers had a strained relationship with the Arizona Water Company, as they were dependent on it for water to irrigate their land. By the early 1880s, the construction of a dam along with the creation of a reservoir was considered to be key to economic growth in the Salt River Valley. The problem was that the price of such a dam was very high, estimated at between 2 and 5 million dollars; and the United States forbade the territory of Arizona, which was still not part of the Union, to incur such a debt (Fudala 2001). Despite the advanced irrigation system enjoyed by the Valley, however, an assured water supply was still critically important for growing crops and raising livestock because of the repeated droughts that the landowners endured.

For over a decade, private companies and local communities tried unsuccessfully to finance a dam. A special event speeded up the process for change. At the time, a national movement for local water recycling projects funded by the federal government was developing (Carpenter 2001; Pisani 2002). The lawyer George H. Maxwell became the leader of an alliance of economic interests and promoters of federal irrigation projects in the states that existed at that time. In Phoenix, the businessman Benjamin A. Fowler quickly assumed leadership among local stakeholders. Beginning in 1901, Fowler went to Washington DC to represent the interest of the Salt River Valley and to lobby Congress on behalf of Arizona. He worked along with Maxwell, the Republican Francis G. Newlands of Nevada, and Senator Henry Hansbrough of North Dakota on a bill that would provide a way for

40 *Engineering the arid West*

local organizations to create a pool of water as well as to implement projects for supply services (Shermer 2013). The bill won the support of Theodore Roosevelt, for whom the future of the West could not be separated from the management of its natural resources, including water. Roosevelt signed the National Reclamation Act on June 17, 1902.

The SRP did not exactly fit with the National Irrigation Act guidelines of the Reclamation Act. Indeed, in the Salt River Valley, all the land potentially eligible for federal aid belonged to the private sector. The National Irrigation Act's purpose was, however, to make public land available to settlers, facilitating agricultural work by irrigation systems. Envisioning this difficulty, two Phoenicians who were also members of the National Reclamation Association successfully advocated for an amendment to the Act, allowing private landholders to jointly collateralize their lands to guarantee repayment of construction costs (Needham 2014: 37). Through the passing of this amendment, additional motivation arose for the creation of the SRP. The choice of the Salt River Project was driven by several main factors: the perfect location for the dam, the organizational capacities of landowners, and the unfailing support of the National Reclamation Association, led by Maxwell. In the end, the success of the project would give impetus to the national irrigation movement (Zarbin & McCabe 1986: 44).

The Association was incorporated in February 1903. In 1904, the home affairs secretary gave his support to the contract with the Association for building the Roosevelt Dam. Before obtaining the necessary federal loan, members of the Association had to use their land as collateral to prove to the Department of the Interior that the reservoir and dam construction costs would be repaid. The owners of over 200,000 acres in the Salt River Valley formed the backbone of the Association where the share of holders varied according to the area of land owned. The Association took the form of an "unnamed company," which included landowners in the decision-making process of irrigation plans. The major representatives from the Association (the Board of Governors) were elected by an electorate of owners who had committed their land values into the irrigation project. The legal entity of the Association was initially designed to be both a company (corporation) and a cooperative (Smith 1972: 15). Then the Salt River Valley Water Users' Association was designated to represent the owners to the government. The businessman Benjamin A. Fowler, who had defended the project in Washington, became the first president of the Association. Shortly after, the dam on the Tonton Basin site was one of the first five projects authorized under the Reclamation Act.

Nevertheless, for Washington, the implementation of the project was still a problem, as the prior water rights remained to be settled. Where there were disputes over water rights, the government would incur no expense. According to Washington, a court had to identify what land would be irrigated, in order to determine the amount of water available to be distributed to the land selected for refunded infrastructure costs. The problem was that in the Salt River Valley farmers were fighting among themselves – and with the owners of canals, including the Arizona Water Company – to settle who had the right to water and the amount they could use. The attorney of the Association filed a lawsuit in the

Engineering the arid West 41

Arizona Superior Court in Maricopa County to adjudicate the rights of all people using or diverting the water flow of the Salt River, and to select complaints from water users asserting the oldest priority claims. In March 1910, the verdict of the trial led to the Kent Decree, which determined that almost 240,000 irrigable acres in the Salt River Valley had a right to water for agricultural purposes (Zarbin & McCabe 1986: 113–114). The Kent decree draws on early principles of prior appropriation whereby the party who was first able to beneficially use the resource held the rights to it. Importantly, it allowed for the land to be seen as having value only when there was water associated with it. The right to the appropriation of water was based upon beneficial use (prior appropriation doctrine), and the right of appropriation depended upon a supply of water (as a common good). The Kent decree regulated the right to water for more than 200,000 acres in the Salt River Valley. These rights are still applied by SRP managers in the 2010s, for want of the completion of the Gila River Adjudication.

Mega-projects as a remedy for the Depression

From the late 1920s, and to a greater degree from 1933 with the arrival of the Roosevelt administration, the federal government's water policy entered a new phase in terms of its objectives, resources, and beneficiaries. The idea was no longer to use irrigation projects to create a new America of small farmers, but rather to help America clamber out of the Depression. Mega-water projects based on the construction of large dams were not only designed to develop irrigation projects but also to generate electricity and control river flows. This period was also characterized by an increase in the number of water projects. From 1902 to 1933, the average annual budget for the Reclamation Service/Bureau of Reclamation's projects was $9 million, as opposed to $52 million between 1933 and 1940. Between 1902 and 1928, the agency completed 36 irrigation projects, as against 228 in the following 30 years (reservoirs, lakes, canals, dams) (Reisner 1985: 165). This period was characterized by the rise of agribusiness and the cities. These latter were the leading beneficiaries of water projects, over and above the initial plans for a water policy designed to favor small farmers.

Above all, this period marked a new phase in capitalism. Now the focus was to re-establish the national economy following the collapse of the financial system and to quell social tensions. This was to be achieved with the aid of a federal investment program in which major projects played a key role. In this quest for new foundations for economic growth, water was an important factor:

> Hoover argued [that the federal government] should not merely regulate business and referee economic disputes; it should direct, promote, and sustain economic growth. It should integrate and rationalize the nation's economy, making the marketplace as orderly and predictable as possible. Without water management, there could be no planned economy. And without a planned economy, the United States would remain vulnerable to boom and bust cycles.
> (Pisani 2002: 244)

42 *Engineering the arid West*

For the purposes of overcoming the economic and social consequences of the Depression, the federal government was obliged to act at the level of individual states. The American economy of the 1930s was much more interdependent than it had been at the turn of the century (Pisani 2002: 252), with the effect that crises and natural disasters in one state also impacted on the economies of other states. The nature of the new initiatives, which principally took the form of large hydroelectric plants that also controlled the flow of the great American rivers, enabled several states to benefit from a single project.

These transformations had repercussions in Congress with, in particular, the approval of the first two laws of the new period: the Flood Control Act and the Boulder Dam Bill. These two laws were passed in 1928 after having been blocked in Congress for several years. The Boulder Dam Bill had been presented in 1922 by Phil Swing, congressman for Imperial Valley in California, and California Senator Hiram Johnson. This proposal was refused by Congress in 1922, 1924, and 1926, largely due to the opposition of the states of the northern basin of the Colorado River, which did not share the same interests. At the same time, the states of the Pacific Northwest supported a different project to build a dam in the Columbia Valley. Similarly, the states of the Midwest and the South had no particular interest in the Boulder Dam. "The old mercantilist view that one state or region's gain was, inevitably, another's loss remained powerful during the 1920s" (Pisani 2002: 259). This view was mirrored in the irrigation projects of the original Reclamation Service, which promoted initiatives focusing on a specific territory within a single state. This was an approach that exacerbated tensions with other states, provoking opposition in Congress. On the other hand, the new policy of the late 1920s focused on the large-scale production of electricity using hydroelectric power sources that were not confined to a single state.

Congress's approval of the Boulder Dam project in 1928 was linked to its acceptance of the Flood Control Act, passed in the same year in the wake of the floods caused by the Mississippi breaking its banks in 1927. These floods wrought massive damage along the entire course of the river and provoked economic and social disaster in the states of the Midwest and the South composing its watershed. A policy designed to control the flow of rivers then emerged as the only way to protect these states from further catastrophe. The representatives of the West promoting the Boulder Dam decided to negotiate with the states concerned with the Flood Control Act, offering their support for the law in exchange for a vote in favor of the Boulder Dam Act. This episode marked the emergence of much broader coalitions for water policies than had been the case with earlier irrigation projects. It was thanks to this association between representatives from the Midwest, the South, and the West that the Flood Control Act was passed.

In regard to the Boulder Dam, the representatives of California needed the votes of the states of the Colorado River's northern basin. Electricity constituted a key element of the water policies of the period. The Boulder Dam was a hydroelectric project designed to generate energy for a large part of the West. During the 1920s, private electricity companies began to lobby against the Boulder Dam in order to avoid a situation in which most electricity was produced and controlled by government agencies. These companies formed a powerful trust, just as the railway companies had done at the turn of the century. The states that had formerly opposed the Boulder Dam understood that a vote against the project would mean that a key resource like electricity would fall under the control of private interests, implying a loss of political control over future economic development in their territories. It was this shared interest, created by the emergence of electricity as an object of new water policies between the different states of the West, which made it possible to move beyond opposition based on particular interests, and led to the states of the West casting a majority vote for the Boulder Dam Act in Congress in December 1928 (Pisani 2002: 253–262).

This change in approach to water policy was also made possible by non-political factors, and particularly by transformations in American agriculture. Little publicly owned land was available for the creation of new communities; agriculture demanded increasingly more knowledge and equipment and therefore more investment; cities, meanwhile, became more attractive in terms of living conditions. On the one hand, the difficulties of the 1920s (the drought of 1925 and the Depression) widened the gap between large landowners, who were able to ride out such problems, and smallholders, who were forced to give up their land to those landowners. On the other hand, the increase in the Californian urban population that started in 1900 encouraged the development of agribusiness. The state's urban population grew by 89% from 1900 to 1910, by 58.5% from 1910 to 1920, and by 78.8% in the 1920s (Pisani 1984: 452).

Until 1914, decision-making in the sphere of water projects was shared by the Department of the Interior, its technical agency (the Reclamation Service), and the White House. Presidents could leapfrog Congress and green-light the federal budgets required to develop the West. This coalition can be explained with reference to the fact that Congress, strongly represented by the elites of the East at a time when the states of the West were constructing their legitimacy, saw no interest in voting through budgets for projects that did not directly affect their constituencies. A series of water projects was therefore authorized, primarily to the advantage of California, which had achieved statehood in 1850. This situation created tensions with other, younger states in the West, including Arizona (founded in 1912), that fought against the federal government to protect the control of their natural resources, while at the same time aspiring to economic development. From the 1930s, the more delegations from the states of the West organized themselves and gained influence, the more decision-making powers they acquired. The battle to obtain federal funding took place in the Congressional arena, in the House of Representatives and the Senate, in which representatives of the states of the East and the West engaged in debates about the wisdom of initiating major projects such as the construction of dams. Some Arizona elites understood this and, in order to promote the development of water projects, attempted to develop a united front instead of systematically opposing the federal government.

The growing influence of Congress was accompanied by bureaucratic change. In the early years of the century, the Reclamation Service's irrigation projects still focused on specific territories within single states, an approach that

44 *Engineering the arid West*

exacerbated the tensions between state interests in Congress. The new policy of the late 1920s continued with the New Deal through a focus not only on irrigation systems but also on the large-scale production of electricity and controls on river flows. This generated effects far beyond the territorial power structure, encompassing interstate relations within the federal government. This situation presupposed compromise and consensus in Congress. The change in policy also had an impact on bureaucratic practices. In order to provide a framework for multipurpose regional projects, bureaucracies needed to enlarge their zones of influence to the national level in order to gain legitimacy. Other transformations of a sociological order should also be taken into account. Between the 1940s and the 1960s, the Bureau of Reclamation was not only a breeding ground for engineers, but also employed a considerable number of assistants who provided a link with congressmen. Some of these assistants were promoted to the level of directors. During this period, the Bureau was no longer able to count on the support of the secretary of the interior and the White House in the promotion of its technical projects, since it was Washington politicians who now held decision-making powers. But the Bureau did also combine its technical resources with political support. It courted politicians less because of their party affiliation than because they shared a common interest, namely the development of the West.

But while the decision-making process was now associated with Congress, in contrast with the preceding period, the Supreme Court had also become an institutional actor, and its verdicts influenced the authorization and implementation of water projects. Negotiations in Congress did not always succeed in smoothing tensions between states confronting one another over river access rights. The legal battle between Arizona and California that lasted from 1931 to 1968 is an exemplary illustration of the importance of the "law of the river," and therefore of the Supreme Court, in arbitrating relations between the states represented in Congress and the federal administration. It was in these three spheres – the political, the administrative, and the legal – that the issues of the decision-making process with regard to water projects played out.

Struggles in sharing the Colorado River: Arizona vs. California

In Arizona, support for the CAP had its origins in a struggle between individual states, anxious to develop their economies, for a share in the Colorado River. The New Deal period is considered to have greatly aided the expansion of California, notably thanks to the policy of building dams to irrigate agricultural land. The completion of the Hoover Dam on the Colorado River in 1936 consolidated the legitimacy of the federal government's approach to developing the state. However, the American West neither begins nor ends at the Californian border, and other states had a major interest in controlling and exploiting the river that Reisner (1985) called the "American Nile." Arizona elites envied California's economic prosperity, while at the same time accusing it of overexploiting the Colorado River.

Engineering the arid West   45

In Arizona, the struggle with California over access to the Colorado River manifested itself in various ways depending on whether the elites concerned were state leaders or advocates of the interests Arizona in Washington. The conflict can also be interpreted with reference to two general characteristics of policies on the West, namely, on the one hand, political individualism, which emphasized local interests, and, on the other, political pragmatism, which rejected ideology in favor of an approach based on problem-solving (Thomas 1991: 9). The opposition between these two approaches has been described as an expression of the "political paradox of the West" or, in other words, "the political manifestation of the contradictions between the myth and the reality of western development" (Thomas 1991: 14). This took the form of certain Western political elites' denials that financial aid from the federal government had indeed played a part in the region's development. As we shall see, this paradox tended to dissipate as the objectives of the CAP became increasingly better defined, and as elites attempted to reconcile individualism and political pragmatism.

When, in the 1930s, against the backdrop of the New Deal, the Department of the Interior decided to sign a contract with the Californian water distributor – the Metropolitan Water District – to build the Parker Dam in Arizona, Benjamin Baker Moeur, the Democrat governor of the time, informed federal officers that if Arizona's rights in the matter were not clearly defined he would oppose the deal (August 1999). In effect, he considered that a dam could not be built to divert the Colorado River without the consent of his state. When the project was given the go-ahead, Governor Moeur declared martial law on the site, bringing in the Arizona National Guard and accusing the federal government of calling Arizona's sovereignty into question. Since any negotiations with the State of Arizona were doomed to fail, the federal government took its case for building the Parker Dam to the Supreme Court. The dispute took an unexpected turn when the Supreme Court ruled in favor of Arizona, ruling that the federal government had failed to demonstrate that the dam had been authorized. But, shortly after the verdict, Congress authorized the dam's construction.

This conflict between Arizona and California is one episode among many. Indeed, on many occasions in the 1930s Arizona used the Supreme Court as an arbiter to impose its sovereignty and legitimacy over the Colorado River. Considering itself poorly treated in regard to water resources (Hundley 1975: 289), the state refused to ratify the Colorado River Compact, designed to regulate water distribution between the river's Upper and Lower States. However, the Supreme Court declined to uphold Arizona's complaints about California, preferring instead to emphasize the rights of the federal government to elaborate water policy in the watersheds of the American West.

This tension between the defense of a state's sovereignty and a federal approach to regulating the Colorado River was not the only factor defining the opposition between Arizona and Washington DC. Senator Carl Hayden, Arizona representative in DC, called into question the attitude of the elites in his state, notably that of Governor Moeur (August 1999), just as he had in the previous decade in regard to Democrat Governor George W.P. Hunt. Hunt was also hostile to the Colorado

46   *Engineering the arid West*

River Compact and had not helped Hayden obtain compromises favorable to the State of Arizona when federal legislation concerning the Colorado River was being drafted (Hundley 1975: 240). From Hayden's point of view, Arizona's cause could only be furthered by changing political tactics. It was his belief that decision makers, at whatever level they operated, should unite over a project – in this case, the CAP – that not only served their interests, but also echoed the logic underpinning the federal government's approach.

Mark Wilmer, lawyer for Arizona against California. Law of the River v. prior appropriation

Mark Bernard Wilmer was born in July 1903 in Wisconsin. The son of a farmer, he grew up in the small town of East Troy, essentially a community of farmers, dairy workers, and shopkeepers. Attracted to literature and to the new, increasingly urban America, the embryonic growth of which he saw every morning on his way to Burlington College, he developed a genuine desire for mobility, a desire encouraged by his father, who wanted his son to continue his university studies. In 1926, he gained a place at the College of Law at the University of Georgetown in Washington DC. Two years after graduating in 1929, he qualified for the State Bar of Arizona in May 1931.

In the early days of his career in Phoenix, his first legal case concerned disputes between Roosevelt Water Conservation District and the Salt River Project. He did not yet know that water would become an important part of his legal career. Indeed, the complex problem of regional rights, going beyond the merely local context, placed him at the center of the political, environmental, and legal history of the West in the 20th century. At the time, the dispute between Arizona and California was only just beginning, and he was still to establish a professional reputation. In the 1930s, his legal portfolio was essentially made up of criminal cases. He was a litigator. The skills he displayed in the local courts impressed the region's more politically minded judges. He was invited by the District Attorney of Maricopa County and the Attorney General of the State of Arizona to help them in their work. During this period, he met Frank L. Snell, a well-known, well-established attorney, a graduate of Kansas School of Law, based in downtown Phoenix, with whom he set up the Snell and Wilmer law firm.

Between 1940 and 1950, the Snell and Wilmer law firm became one of the largest in the American West. It provided a wide range of services and expertise and considerable resources to its clients, with 400 lawyers in six offices in Arizona, California, Nevada, Colorado, and Utah. Due to its size, the firm helped to shape Arizona's political and economic agenda. And when Governor McFarland of Arizona went in search of the best litigator in the state, at a time when the legal battle against California seemed to have been lost, the Association of the Bar of Arizona and the legal community as a whole recommended Mark Wilmer. In 1957, at the height of a remarkable legal career, Wilmer accepted the challenge of defending Arizona's case against California, which he did until the Supreme Court delivered its decision in

Engineering the arid West 47

1963. By accepting the case, Wilmer entered a world defined by water (or the lack of it), as well as by culture and tradition. He familiarized himself with the legal case, the rulings of the courts, and cross-border conflicts, imbibing as much information on the state's most valuable resource as he could and defining his relationship with those against whom he applied his defensive strategy.

In the field of law, Arizona's Spanish heritage was reflected in the Latin principle *qui prior est in tempore, potior est in jure*, which means "he who is earlier in time, is stronger in law." This doctrine of prior appropriation remained valid throughout the Mexican period (1881–1948), during which it was applied to regulate uses of land and water. When the Territory of Arizona was set up in 1863, the Howell Code passed by the Legislative Assembly incorporated Spanish and Mexican customs of prior appropriation. As more and more colonists gradually arrived in the Territory, and periods of flooding were repeatedly followed by severe drought, competition for land and water intensified, giving rise to numerous legal battles. In regard to the Salt River, Judge H. Kibbey of the Territory's Supreme Court was invited, in 1882, to resolve disputes between water consumers and the canal company (Salt River Valley Land). The court's ruling reasserted the doctrine of prior appropriation: water belonged to the land rather than the canal companies and, therefore, could not be sold as a separate commodity. The Kibbey Decision linking land and water was used as the basis of water law in Arizona. Around 20 years later, on March 1, 1919, Judge Edward Kent, of Maricopa County, who worked in the Territory of Arizona, followed the Kibbey Decision in the Hurley versus Abbott case (1910). This case opposed the owners of land irrigated by the Salt River Users Association, which (under contract with the government) owned canals to the north of the river, received surplus water from those canals, and the individual owners to the south of the river who had no contractual relationship with the federal government and who claimed the right to access water. The Kent Decree reaffirmed the doctrine of prior appropriation concerning cultivated plots of land, including all of the Salt River Valley connected to the Salt River. The Kent Decree was the key element in terms of water law and the administration of Arizona at the moment that it ceased being a territory and became a state in 1912.

The legal heritage of Spain and Mexico that gives primacy to *prior appropriation* was not exclusively applicable to Arizona and did not only govern local water supplies. Wilmer quickly realized that this legal doctrine was an issue for the states of the West who coveted the Colorado River, and led to serious disputes, notably between Arizona and California, whose explosive growth at the beginning of the 20th century constituted a regional threat in terms of rights to the Colorado River. He discovered the degree to which California was an organized entity capable of influencing the water policies of the West; indeed, the Imperial Irrigation District was one of Wilmer's most powerful legal adversaries. In 1911, Phil Swing, Imperial Valley's lawyer, who later converted his legal influence into a seat in the House of Representatives, along with the real estate developer, Mark Rose, set up

48 *Engineering the arid West*

the Imperial Irrigation District (IDD), which lobbied Congress and the secretary of the interior to develop water projects (notably, the All American Canal). This was part of a race to secure California as many prior rights to the Colorado River as possible. The coalition between the IDD and the federal department set alarm bells ringing in the Arizona parliamentary delegation and alerted other states with an interest in the river. Meanwhile, the City of Los Angeles attempted to secure increasing volumes of water to fulfill needs associated with its rapidly expanding population. Like Arizona, the Upper Basin States – Wyoming, Utah, Colorado, and New Mexico – saw Southern California, with its urban centers and agricultural users, as a threat to their future development. Prior appropriation had to be fought.

As Mark Wilmer discovered in the Congress archives, the tensions between California and the other states of the West were at the origin of legal actions that led to the promulgation of the Colorado River Compact of 1922 and the Boulder Canyon Act of 1928. During this period, the governors of Arizona were strongly opposed to this legislation, which they regarded as overly favorable to California. They took legal action against the federal government and the Golden State in order to defend state rights to the water of the Colorado River. Forty years later, however, Wilmer used the legislation as a guideline in his legal strategy in favor of Arizona at the Supreme Court. In spite of the fact that the legislation sanctioned the construction of the Hoover Dam, it abrogated the principle of *prior appropriation* and provided annual allocations of water from the Lower Colorado River Basin as follows: California, 4.4 million acre-feet; Arizona, 2.8 million acre-feet; Nevada, 300,000 acre-feet.

These "laws of the river" were made up of legislation voted by Congress. These laws, exclusively concerned with the distribution of water from the Colorado River (excluding its tributaries), provided the cornerstone of Mark Wilmer's legal defense. Wilmer attempted to convince the Supreme Court by using arguments derived from legislative history and previous debates. California, which denied Arizona any legal right over the Colorado River, took the position that the desert state already benefited from water from its tributaries (the Gila River and the Salt River). California's lawyer, Northcutt "Mike" Ely, based his case on legal history, citing the Supreme Court's decision of January 5, 1922, on a dispute between Wyoming and Colorado concerning a tributary of the Colorado River, applying the priority rule to rivers running through two states. Finally, on June 3, 1963, the Supreme Court endorsed Mark Wilmer's case:

We are persuaded by the legislative history while that the Act was not intended to give California any claim to share in the tributary waters of the Lower Basin States. [...] Where Congress has exercised its constitutional power over waters courts have no power to substitute their own notions of "equitable apportionment" for the apportionment chosen by Congress.

(August 1999: 89)

A new coalition for a new project

After the Second World War, the New Deal's legacy was apparent in the way in which natural resources were managed. The development of the West was still envisaged in terms of the construction of more and more dams; electricity generation was considered a surefire bet, in that it had helped to produce the ships and planes that secured victory against Germany, while the creation of irrigation systems helped agribusiness. It was in this post-New Deal, postwar context, favorable to large-scale water projects, that the CAP, initiated by the State of Arizona, took shape. Indeed, at the time, Arizona was experiencing unprecedented demographic growth, a fact that encouraged the state's elites to find solutions to problems associated with the seasonal migration of significant numbers of "Snowbirds" who consumed water and used air-conditioning in a region in which aquifers, still the main source of water, were gradually drying up due to the demands of agriculture.

In order to ensure the legitimacy of the CAP, the elites of the State of Arizona sought federal funding, which presupposed authorization from Congress. After the ratification of the Colorado River Compact by Arizona in 1944, concrete initiatives were taken to develop a political consensus: an approach that contrasted sharply with the conflict-ridden period of the 1930s. In 1946, the CAP Association (CAPA) was set up by local decision makers (farmers, bankers, lawyers, companies working in the general interest) who shared the belief that water from the Colorado River was of fundamental importance to the future of Arizona's economy. From the outset, the Association was closely linked to the Arizona Congressional Delegation, notably in terms of the legislative activities of the two Democrat senators, Carl Hayden and Ernest McFarland, in favor of the CAP.

The CAPA was involved in setting up hearings on early legislation about the authorization of the CAP, which Senators Carl Hayden and Ernest McFarland presented to the Senate Subcommittee on Irrigation and Reclamation. In 1948, the Association was behind the creation of a state agency, the Arizona Interstate Stream Commission, whose aim was to advocate on behalf of the state's claims to access to the Colorado River in Congress and at the courts (Mann 1963: 128). Wayne Akin, president of the CAPA, was appointed president of the Commission by Governor Osborn. This appeared not to be a neutral choice in that, through the Association, Akin could count on the advice of the most influential local decision makers in the state (Johnson 1977). Moreover, since graduating in the 1940s, he had been a member of the League of 14. Made up of two members from each of the seven states of the Colorado River Basin, the League's objective was to bring together decision makers in the water sector to discuss shared problems and, where possible, to resolve their differences.

This initiative was perceived as having the potential to contribute to building a consensus around the CAP project. Furthermore, Wayne Akin could also count on Charles Carson, legal adviser to Governor Osborn and the Arizona Interstate Commission, and also a member of the Board of the Phoenix Chamber of Commerce, who had sought Akin out when the CAPA was first set up, and who later supported the legislative efforts of Congressmen Hayden and McFarland.

50   *Engineering the arid West*

Independently of the CAP, this form of lobbying is best understood if we bear in mind that, in the West, political participation was not structured exclusively around the parties, which were considered weak, but also focused on interest groups that attempted to influence public policy in their own particular fields (Thomas 1991: 165). In the case of the promotion of the CAP in Congress, the CAPA interest group and a handful of Arizona politicians decided to put their differences to one side and work together, thus strengthening their influence relative to California, which was both strongly represented and highly organized.

Carl Hayden, Western lawmaker: from the Salt River Project to the Central Arizona Project

The use and distribution of water is central to the public career of Senator Carl Hayden. Born in Arizona in 1877, Hayden enjoyed a 57-year career as a congressman and senator. After spending ten years as a local politician, he represented the brand new state of Arizona, first in the House of Representatives, from 1912 to 1927, and then in the Senate, from 1927 to 1969. Although he is famous for the part he played in developing the American West by means of the CAP, Carl Hayden was a product of the legendary conquest of the "frontier."

Hayden's father, Charles Trumbull Hayden, was born in Connecticut on April 4, 1825. He was one of the pioneers who left the East to make their fortune out West. While working the region to the north of Salt River Valley as a manufactured product salesman, Hayden saw the potential of this arid and hostile territory. His ambition was to transform Salt River Valley into a canal-irrigated agricultural empire. In the mid-1870s, the irrigation community in which he lived – based in the south shore of Salt River – assumed a pioneering role thanks to a variety of rapidly expanding firms (grain fields, mills, orchards, etc.). As well as this family success, Hayden recalls that at the time his parents' farm was repeatedly hit by drought and flooding. The farmers and businessmen of the Valley asked the government for aid to halt the flooding and provide water storage facilities. These environmental problems occurred in the context of the irrigation movement of the 1880s, led by its promoters, Maxwell and Smith, who organized meetings dedicated to the "conquest of arid America," which Charles Hayden attended. Distributing tracts and magazines at conferences, he introduced the young Carl to the problems of his community and other territories in the states of the West. His family spent considerable sums of money in the cause of preserving the rights of these territories, winning and losing cases along the way.

During his time at California's Stanford University, one of the West's pioneering academic institutions, a career in law and politics with a focus on water issues seemed an obvious choice to Carl:

I want to make water law a specialty not only because it is a new and open field where the prizes are large to the winner, but also because through it I can have a greater power for good and evil than at any other branch of the

Engineering the arid West 51

law. I know that the law of water is not taught in schools nor found in books, but that is all the more reason why it will be so valuable when known. [...] I have no fear of not getting along in this world. Just let me train rightly for the right thing and the result is not in doubt. I am going into politics – I shall make honest water laws and see that they are honestly executed.

(August 1999: 24)

The project was somewhat delayed by the death of his father: he spent a number of years successfully running the family business. However, he did not give up politics, which he considered useful in solving local problems. Later, he gradually left his business interests to one side, starting out in politics at the local level, where he immediately sought aid from Washington to develop water distribution networks. He subsequently started campaigning in state, and later federal elections. His Washington ambitions can be explained with reference to a series of factors: aware of the economic potential of Roosevelt's new federal policy, Carl Hayden and other local leaders encouraged the development of water projects with a view to enticing people to set up in arid areas. On March 4, 1903, the Salt River Project, for which he was the spokesman in Washington, was the first of 26 projects authorized by the Department of the Interior in the first decade of the national irrigation program. This successful experience was the starting point for his runs for Congress. Having arrived there, he dedicated the best part of his political career to issues concerning the development of water distribution in the West.

During the 14 years he spent in the House of Representatives, he witnessed a transformation in American society. When he entered Congress in 1912, America still defined itself in terms of Jefferson's agrarian ideal of small communities, decentralization, and competition. By the time Hayden became a senator in 1927, the Progressive Era was tracing out a new America that was more urban, more centralized, more industrialized, and more secular than ever before. The development of the Colorado River became a major issue in the 1920s, dominating the agenda of the politicians of the American Southwest. Hayden was already involved, taking part in negotiations over the Colorado River Compact in 1922. He remained active in the field up to and including the passage of the 1968 Colorado River Basin Project Act, which, among other things, authorized the CAP. With the development of the Colorado River, Hayden was confronted by other issues. Instead of advocating an irrigation project centered on a river in a single state, as had been the case with the Salt River Project, he was responsible for resolving the problem of how to share a river crossing seven states of the Southwestern United States and part of Mexico. Hayden also had to resist the All American Canal project promoted by California and, along with it, the advocates of the Imperial Valley. While he supported a regional conception of the development of the river, he opposed California's desire to obtain the exclusive right to access water from the Colorado with the help of the federal government,

52   *Engineering the arid West*

with the sole objective of increasing the prosperity of the Imperial Valley: "you are now coming to Congress asking that an extraordinary thing be done by the passage of his legislation and Congress must look to the development not only of the Imperial Valley, but the Colorado River Valley as a whole, and that can only be fully developed by storage" (ibid.: 76).

Carl Hayden also fought against leaders in his state, particularly Governors Hunt and Moeur, and Senator Fred Colter, advocates of a state-based approach to rights concerning the development of the Colorado River. In 1923, promoting a federal approach, Hayden announced his support for the ratification of the Colorado River Compact.

Any fair-minded person must conclude that Arizona alone cannot undertake the development of the great river without the consent of the United States, and without understanding with the other states of the Colorado River Basin, all of which leads to the conclusion that sooner or later the Colorado River Compact must be approved by the State of Arizona.

(Ibid.: 92)

According to Hayden, the main partner in the development of the Colorado River was the federal government. In the 1940s, a change of governor in Arizona combined with increasing urbanization within the state, created a new situation that, in turn, led to the emergence of a new approach to water policy. Senator Hayden introduced the first legislation on the CAP, a process that brought him up against Californian interests and the alternative projects promoted by Arizona. Nevertheless, legislative negotiations about how water from the Colorado River was to be shared culminated in the authorization of federal funding for the CAP, crowning the senator's political career.

By the late 1950s, Arizona's economy had reached a turning point. With demographic expansion concentrated in the "Sun Corridor" (Phoenix and Tucson), agriculture was no longer the main source of wealth. Indeed, there was a proliferation of new jobs in other industries (Sheridan 2012). In 1961, this context forced the Association to adopt a new approach to promoting the CAP, which recognized the demands for water from industry and the cities (Johnson 1977). At the same time, the Arizona Interstate Stream Commission ordered the Bureau of Reclamation's local agencies to re-evaluate water use in areas outside the distribution zone originally designated by the CAP, including, notably, an extension of the aqueduct toward Tucson. As part of the quest for national unity in the face of Congress, the aim of this new approach was to demonstrate that the CAP did not exclusively serve the water needs of the city of Phoenix. This provided a tactical advantage in terms of undermining the validity of California's argument, according to which the CAP was essentially intended for agricultural purposes. In 1966, the members of the Arizona Interstate Stream Commission and the CAPA joined a task force designed to support the efforts of the Arizona Delegation to Congress, a process that culminated in the authorization of the CAP in 1968.

Engineering the arid West 53

However, if they were to have a chance of making their voice heard in Congress and successfully defend the CAP in the face of opposition from California, Arizona's elites had to present a united front. However, within Arizona itself, water policy went through a radical change with the election of Sidney Osborn (Democrat) as governor in 1940. Osborn signed the Colorado River Compact in 1944, ratifying a regional vision of water distribution in spite of strong opposition from the state's utilities, as well as from the Arizona Highline Reclamation Association (an organization promoting the interests of the state and irrigation projects in each of the state's counties and districts, whose president was the Democrat Fred Tuttle Colter), and from two other senators and six congressmen (Hundley 1975: 299). In so doing, Osborn distanced himself from the kinds of conflicts that characterized the Arizona political scene in the preceding decades, in particular the tradition of systematic opposition established by the preceding Democrat governors, George W.P. Hunt and Benjamin Baker Moeur. In effect, having exhausted all legal possibilities, the State of Arizona had practically no chance of satisfactorily settling its differences with California (Hundley 1975: 299).

This policy change also reflected a growing awareness of the potential consequences of long-term economic growth in the state, particularly in and around Phoenix and Tucson. Not only did this growth prefigure Arizona's urban development in the following decades, but it also posed the question of water supply in a state that had already experienced water and energy crises in the droughts of the 1930s and 1940s. Governor Osborn's new political orientation, represented in Washington by Senator Hayden, was also part of the effort to develop the consensus that the State of Arizona needed to pass the CAP in Congress (August 1999). However, in the 1960s, the politico-legal disputes over the CAP led to the formation of new coalitions among the nation's senators.

Legislative compromises and environmental pressures

Between the Supreme Court's 1963 decision in favor of Arizona in regard to sharing the Colorado River with California and the confirmation of that ruling by Congress in 1968, the federal administrators and representatives of the states of the Colorado River Basin began to elaborate a regional plan for the development of the West. While debates in Congress primarily focused on the CAP, in 1963 a new project, the Pacific Southwest Water Plan (PSWP) was promoted by the new secretary of the interior, Stewart Udall. He had been appointed to this post two years previously by President John F. Kennedy, to whom he was close (Johnson 2002). Eschewing a concept focused on national borders, and, instead, promoting a regional approach to water needs, the objective was to unite the interests of Arizona and California without passively accepting the energy policy of the moment. The proposal presented by Stewart's half-brother, Morris Udall, included the construction of two giant dams (Bridge Canyon and Marble Canyon) near the Grand Canyon National Park.

The Democratic congressman for Tucson, Morris Udall – a lawyer by training and profession – emerged as the mediator of opposing interests. For Senator

54   Engineering the arid West

Carl Hayden, the main advocate of the CAP, the PSWP was a competing and contradictory legislative initiative (August 1991). The senator regarded the PSWP as a stalling tactic on the part of California, designed to delay the authorization of the CAP. Paul Fannin (Republican), elected governor in 1958, also thought of the PSWP as "a conspiracy against Arizona born in California." He defended Senator Hayden's approach, which consisted of promoting the idea of the CAP in a separate legislative proposition. This vision was rejected by Morris Udall, who favored a more regional approach to the CAP. However, in Arizona, the influential *Arizona Republic* condemned Udall's future political career in Arizona by accusing him of being beholden to the California water lobby represented by James Carr, the undersecretary of the Department of the Interior.

The administration's preference for a regional approach to developing the Colorado River, in the form of the PSWP, enabled Senator Hayden to gather support. In 1966, the Arizona Task Force got behind the legislative effort by uniting the main sources of expertise on water of the time (the Arizona Interstate Steam Commission, the Arizona Public Service, the CAP Association and the Salt River Project). Moreover, the CAP had the support of powerful allies in the Senate: Senator Henry Jackson (Democrat, Washington), head of the Senate Interior Committee, and Senator Clinton Anderson (Democrat, New Mexico), president of the Power and Reclamation Subcommittee of the Interior Committee. In their struggle in favor of the CAP, these Democrat senators supported Carl Hayden against his Californian Republican opponents, i.e. Thomas Kuchel, member of the Senate Committee on Insular and Interior Affairs, and Claire Engel, who had helped torpedo the CAP project in the House of Representatives in 1951. For the real battle for the CAP was, in the end, the one waged in the House Interior Committee and the Irrigation and Reclamation Subcommittee directed by Wayne Aspinall (Democrat, Colorado). Aspinall was very wary of California (and Arizona) and what he saw as their expansionist aims, and was concerned at the idea that the Upper Basin states, especially Colorado, might not obtain their due from the Colorado River Compact. Hayden also clashed with John Saylor (Republican, Pennsylvania), a member of the House Interior Committee. Saylor, a conservationist, opposed the construction of dams included in the CAP; he was opposed to the continuous development of public sector electricity generation schemes. His position earned him the respect of those of an ecological persuasion.

In the end, the Colorado River Basin Act of 1968 integrated the projects supported by the representatives of different states. This result, produced by a compromise between the various forces at play, was based on pork barrel politics, according to which Congress's allocation of public funds served the interests of the legislators' constituencies rather than the national interest. With the CAP and the Pacific Southern Water Plan, what was at issue was not only the economic development of the West, but also political careers and reputations. This meant that everyone had to take into account the needs of their respective constituencies in terms of new projects and the allocation of sections of the Colorado River. While, for example, California lost the legal battle, it nevertheless obtained a

Engineering the arid West 55

guarantee of 4.4 million acre-feet of the Colorado River in case of drought, which later turned out to be more than useful in countering the water crisis of the 2000s.

If coalitions were to be able to hope that their needs could be fulfilled, they had to find a point of agreement. And they also had to take external pressures into account, particularly from environmentalists. These latter were fundamentally opposed to the construction of new dams that might have risked flooding the Grand Canyon – one of the jewels of the West – and instead favored alternative energy sources. In the 1970s, the rise in the number of environmentalist votes changed decision-making processes; authorization for major water projects was not only based on economic viability and technical reliability, but also, increasingly, reflected a new problematic that sought to reconcile economic growth with environmental protection. Furthermore, a new legislative framework had also been introduced in 1970, the National Environmental Policy Act. During this period, a number of dam construction projects were abandoned in favor of projects based on alternative energy sources, and it is not by chance that this coincided with the emergence of a new generation of bureaucrats and politicians. These latter were much keener on adapting to the emergence of new and different values than had been their predecessors, motivated exclusively by economic considerations. And it is also probably not by chance that, also during this period, Congress's authorization for the federal funding of major water projects was accompanied by the requirement for the states concerned to meet certain legislative imperatives, notably in regard to the protection of their natural resources.

Up until this point, Congress and the Bureau of Reclamation had championed the development of the West. The need to incorporate environmental concerns was expressed by a new generation of Arizona elites, including Stewart Udall, then secretary of the interior. They were doubtless helped in this by their legal background and their experience as lawyers. By suggesting that, in order to support the CAP, the Bureau of Reclamation should become a shareholder in a coal-powered electricity plant, Stewart Udall managed to echo the concerns of the environmentalist movement (to which he had dedicated a book, *The Quiet Crisis*, in 1963), while at the same time promoting the economic ambitions of the elites of the West. Finally, on September 30, 1968, the Colorado River Basin Act was passed by Congress and signed by President Lyndon Johnson; among other projects supported by Congress, it authorized the CAP. It was as if, thanks to the authorization of the CAP, tensions between the states over how the Colorado River should be shared had been politically neutralized, and a new equilibrium established in the balance of power between the fierce advocates of economic development, the promoters of dams, and the inveterate defenders of the environment.

Stewart Udall, a lawyer from Arizona promoted to Washington DC: between the pioneer spirit and the environmental cause

Stewart Udall was born in Arizona on January 31, 1920. He spent his childhood in the Mormon community of St. Johns, growing up in an arid milieu in which water management was part of basic education and irrigation seen as a way of life and a scientific principle. The Mormons were known at the time

56 *Engineering the arid West*

for their ability to transform previously arid areas into fertile agricultural land by building dams and small canals. Beyond his familiarity with water issues, the sense of justice inculcated by his mother, and the public service ethos associated with his father, who had been president of the Arizona Supreme Court, also informed his interests. Over the course of his professional career, Udall attempted to reappraise the heritage of the pioneers, reconciling it with the law and the democratic ideal.

After graduating with a degree from Arizona in law in 1948, Stewart set up a law firm in Tucson with his brother Morris to fight against segregation in the city. Along with his legal activism, he harbored political ambitions. He was elected vice president of the Central Committee of the Democrat Party, then treasurer of the Legal Aid Association of Pima County. He was also elected three times to the House of Representatives in Washington DC. When John F. Kennedy announced that he was running for president, Stewart was one of his most fervent supporters, recruiting delegates from Arizona to help him. In 1961 this link with Kennedy helped him gain promotion to Washington DC as secretary of the federal Department of the Interior, managing 65,000 employees and a budget of 800 million dollars, allocated to regional development and water management. During the eight years that he occupied this post, he bore witness to the end of the Golden Age of water projects and the emergence of the environmental movement: "I began with the idea that dams were probably a good thing." [...] "I presumed that if anyone, the Corps of Engineers, the Bureau of Reclamation, wanted to build a dam, it was a good thing. I ended up thinking that we ought to be highly skeptical of any dams" (Johnson 2002: 31). This point of view accurately reflects the attitude he took in negotiations over the CAP between 1963 and 1968: while ensuring the adoption by Congress of the Colorado River Basin Compact authorizing the federal funding of the latest major water project, he also campaigned for sources of energy alternative to dams, thus incorporating the environmentalist cause into federal water policy for the first time.

In public debates in the 1960s, the most controversial CAP legislation concerned dams. The idea that an alternative source of energy was required to pump CAP water to central Arizona provoked a reappraisal of approaches to the project. These environmental concerns were promoted by the Sierra Club, whose president, David Bowyer, had made a name for himself in the 1950s for his anti-dam campaigns in the Grand Canyon and his promotion of coal as an alternative source of energy for transporting water. Moreover, the need to find an alternative to dams was made more urgent by the fact that, at the time, pressure for environmental issues to be taken into account in water projects was growing. This trend was given concrete form by President Johnson, whose administration set up the National Environmental Protection Agency in 1969, which forced federal agencies to evaluate the environmental impacts of water projects. Having won the legislative battle in 1968, the advocates of the CAP had to take into consideration this new institutional framework. It allowed social groups that had previously been excluded from the decision-making process to express their concerns, and obliged federal agencies to take notice of them. Winning battles in Congress no longer guaranteed local support: it was probable that the electors concerned no longer systematically represented the interests of the Eastern allies of the federal agencies.

From the 1970s, water projects in the West were targeted by congressmen from the East and Midwest, who criticized them on the grounds of regional favoritism and a lack of economic efficiency. At the same time, these projects were increasingly unpopular with local people. President Carter attempted to shut down the CAP project, whose promoters were forced to adjust their position. To ensure that the CAP was not eliminated from the federal budget, the senators of the State of Arizona had to abandon construction work on the most controversial dams. Meanwhile, federal agencies were told to find alternative approaches to funding the storage of local water and providing flood control for the project. The implementation of the CAP in Arizona was therefore dependent on legal reform in regard to the management of groundwater. In contrast to the period 1940–1960, this was the end of a political era dominated by pork barrel politics that, in terms of water projects, had been structured around stable coalitions between a few key congressmen from the West, the Bureau of Reclamation, and the interests of farmers and promoters of local development who shared a desire to see the West prosper. New sources of influence and coalitions emerged, based on an idea of politics defined by a respect for formal rules and the protection of the environment. This took place at a time when an increasingly urbanized American West was now confronted with water shortages resulting from its economic success.

2 Supporting the economic order
Urban sprawl and coalitions for growth

Urban development and conflicts over water

This chapter describes the logic that seems to underpin all struggles for water – the economic order of things. But understanding how "*water flows uphill to money,*" as the now overused axiom goes, does not mean it is necessary to think only in terms of the force of capitalism: it implies the need to look for systems of relations that make up water policy as a field, and, therefore, homologous logics and struggles that articulate between the federal, state, regional, and municipal levels as society struggles for the legitimate definition of growth and indeed "sustainability" that the Central Arizona Project (CAP) is said to provide.

The arrival of the CAP in Tucson illustrates how local coalitions form and, indeed, can be undone by the necessity of a resource. The repercussions of its arrival, which are still being felt, had a profound effect on the water professionals in the region. The event marked a new stage in water policies, described by Marc Reisner in the following terms:

> the farmers got established in the central part of the state because of the Salt River Project. The cities grew up in the middle of the farmland. The real estate interests, the money people – they are all in Phoenix and Scottsdale and Tucson. They didn't want to move. So we're going to move the river to them. At any cost.
>
> (Reisner 1985: 305)

From the 1920s onward, the spatial expansion of American cities had been promoted by coalitions of developers keen to boost the real estate market, helped in this not only by the growth of the automotive industry, but also by policies designed to subsidize consumption and by federal support for social housing (Gonzales 2009). What changed was the political influence of the cities on the coalitions formed around water issues. Responsibility for water distribution, which had initially been guaranteed by private companies in the late 19th century had since passed to public administrations run by city mayors whose goal was to extend the networked infrastructure and guarantee quality of delivery and supply. After the Second World War, the growing needs of the cities meant that other

Supporting the economic order 59

sources of supply were required, a situation that implied federal aid. Thus, in 1946, at a time when groundwater was increasingly being used to supply expanding cities, mainly Phoenix and Tucson (Kupel 2003: 153), the Central Arizona Project Association was founded. To the degree that drawing off water destined for agricultural purposes, especially in regard to the Salt River Project serving Phoenix, was a delicate strategy, local politicians became fervent advocates of the CAP, in spite of federal norms and pressure exerted by environmentalist movements. The CAP would eventually come to be billed as a sustainable supply by its purveyors and today the logic of sustainability remains intimately tied to economic growth.

The Groundwater Management Act of 1980 (GMA) in Arizona reorganized the distribution of water in several zones referred to as Active Management Areas (AMAs), not only instituting an innovative style of managing groundwater based on basins, but also introducing limits to the expansion of irrigation. However, the system was difficult to implement: each new urban development located in one of the zones had to have an "assured supply" water for a period of 100 years. Very often, the CAP could provide this directly, or CAP water could be sent into the aquifer for potential later use. The later introduction of the Central Arizona Groundwater Replenishment Districts (CAGRDs) in the 1990s gave real estate developers the chance to introduce subdivisions in places in which there were no direct connections to CAP water (Valdez-Diaz 1996; Blomquist et al. 2001: 662). These districts were given extended powers in 1999 with the aim of supporting real estate activities in Arizona (Avery et al. 2007). They functioned as water banking tools for developers, enabling them to access CAP water and guarantee supply. Thanks to the GMA, developers could purchase rights to a quantity of CAP water covering needs for 100 years, even though they could not sell that water immediately. Often, due to costs associated with building the infrastructure required to create subdivisions, the water had to be "stored," which necessitated drilling groundwater wells. This CAP water could therefore be used to feed the aquifer. Nevertheless, a new problem emerged (a problem that was still troublesome in the years around 2010) in that an unevenly depleted aquifer was created at the site of subdivisions due to the fact that water was not directly injected into the more vulnerable hydrological zones from where it was pumped. The words of the crafters of the GMA are illustrative on these points, and also indicate how difficult it often proves to protect the environment from the perpetual necessity for economic growth, a sentiment not uncommon among water professionals as this is one of the key structuring dichotomies of their careers. The below quote comes from someone who was a sort of "right hand" of Babbitt's in this process:

> Truly the primary goal of reducing withdrawals is conservation because we were never able to get everyone to agree on something more drastic. And you can only do so much by conservation, but if you say to the cities, you can't grow without an assured water supply, then it forces them to find other sources of water other than groundwater. And you can't use groundwater to demonstrate an assured water supply. So, it has been a huge, huge tool in

60 *Supporting the economic order*

forcing cities to do other things to serve new uses. Unfortunately, in the mid … when was it, I think it was in the 90s, largely at the request of developers, the Legislature created something called the Groundwater Replenishment District. And this District is supposed to recharge water; it basically helps developers who don't have access to anything other than groundwater. So, they can join this District and then the District has to recharge and it allows them to pump groundwater. I think that is … I've never liked that piece of legislation. I think it's kind of been an end run on assured water supply provision to a certain extent.[1]

The GMA has had far-reaching and significant historical effects that still can be felt, and it has been an area of intense debate. Another measure introduced by the GMA was the creation of the Arizona Department of Water Resources (ADWR) to replace the Arizona Water Commission. At the time, the ADWR was directed by a committee of seven members elected by the citizens of Arizona, while the director was appointed by the state governor. This ensemble of institutional and economic measures, introduced by the State of Arizona and its governor, Bruce Babbitt, encouraged the Department of the Interior and the Bureau of Reclamation to make the CAP one of its priorities in the 1980s (Colby & Jacobs 2007). These new approaches to water management help to explain how the arrival of CAP water in Tucson marked a displacement of conflicts at the city level and why it did so much to reshape local political coalitions.

Bruce Babbitt: new visions for Arizona and America
Bruce Babbitt is one of the foremost characters in Western environmental politics. Born into a ranching family in Flagstaff, Arizona in 1938, he rose quickly to prominence with his election as governor of Arizona in 1978 after being attorney general of Arizona since 1975. He would stay in this position until 1987 when he ran on the Democratic ballot for president. He became President Clinton's secretary of the interior from 1993 to 2001. His tenure as secretary has proven to be his most lasting impression on American politics and he is considered to be one of the most successful to hold that position because of his extensive conservation efforts through use of the Endangered Species and Antiquities Acts in addition to his ability to "reach bipartisan compromises on issues whenever possible" (Leshy 2001: 199).

Babbitt maintained a strong environmental ethic throughout his political career. His father was one of the founders of the Arizona Wildlife Federation as well as the Arizona Game Protective Association. Following interests

---

1   In addition to the many interviews conducted by our research team, we also engaged in various kinds of historical research, from hard-to-find newspaper and other records to archived internet source material. We were very grateful for a series of publicly available transcripts that have been organized at this link: https://www.cap-az.com/about-us/oral-history-transcripts. The above quotation refers to the interview with Kathy Ferris.

Supporting the economic order 61

in the natural world, he received a degree in geology from the University of Notre Dame and then moved on to the University of Newcastle, United Kingdom, to receive a MS in geophysics, and finally to Harvard Law School before entering his political career. About the time that he became the secretary of the interior, Babbitt was extensively considered for a position on the US Supreme Court as well (Terrain.org 2006).

Indeed, throughout his career, he exhibited an uncanny ability to see the big picture. As Leshy states:

Babbitt has been the most nationally focused of them all [referring to the legacy of various SOIs]. From the Flagstaff of his youth, his worldview was leavened by years at Notre Dame and Harvard, by graduate school in England, by much travel around the country and abroad, and by an inquisitive mind and voracious reading on many subjects.

(Leshy 2001: 201).

Additionally, Leshy goes on to say that it was his ability to engage with the details that was

a technique he had mastered soon after becoming governor of Arizona, when he almost literally locked representatives of major water interests in his office for months while, under his strong direction, in 1980 they hammered out the first meaningful groundwater management law in the state's history.

(Leshy 2001: 203)

It is in this context that it is possible to see yet another example of strong leadership in order to promote consensus to prevent future problems.

Today, Arizona's Groundwater Management Act of 1980 is thought of very highly for its success and ability in compensating for the damage that had been done to Arizona's aquifer's by placing limits on the amount of groundwater that could be withdrawn from certain areas, unlike its predecessor, the Critical Groundwater Code of 1948 (Connall Jr. 1982: 314). It has been argued that *Farmers Investment Company v. Bettwy* (558 P.2d 14, 113 Ariz. 520, 1976) was the event that set the actions of Babbitt and others into action. This case involved pecan growers in Arizona (south of Tucson) and the Anamax Mining Company. The copper mine needed water and the company was drilling wells in the Sahuarita-Continental Critical Groundwater Area with the intention of then moving the mined water outside of the Critical Management Area as defined by the 1948 statute previously mentioned. In many ways, we still see these same issues arise, although remedies such as the CAGRD were made possible by the implementation of the GMA, despite some adverse effects (Avery et al. 2007). This case proved fundamental because it applied the reasonable use doctrine as prohibiting the transportation of groundwater away from the land from which it was extracted. Major Arizona cities like Tucson as well as the mining community stood to lose a great deal from this type of legal application because cities were transporting

62   *Supporting the economic order*

water from wells that were a great deal outside their service areas (Pearce 2007: 42).

Bruce Babbitt, as governor of Arizona was able to recognize the potential implications that this case had for cities and, instead of going again to the courts, he was able to successfully enact the GMA, which helped cities and allowed for new development opportunities, but in a way that was more secure than in the past. The GMA has had implications for Arizona beyond what anyone could have anticipated. It allowed for Arizona to craft a unique model of management in the state built around the consensus of interested parties instead of having to deal with large-scale courtroom action. Importantly, the GMA set the stage for a whole host of legal and institutional tools that would shape the way Arizona manages its water for years to come. By instituting proactive measures in the last 20 years to conserve water, Arizona (especially Tucson) feels that it is well positioned for future shortages on the Colorado River.

The federal government and new local leaders

While the CAP was associated with the struggle between two states, Arizona and California, over the Colorado River, the project was finally given the go=ahead thanks to its positioning within the balance of power between federal authorities and local elites concerning the regulation of groundwater. It seems that the CAP obtained federal funding because the dominant idea among the advocates of the project was to build a consensus over the need for it for the sake of well-understood interests, namely the economic prosperity of the state, guaranteed by the development or reinforcement of agriculture, industry, and tourism.

In Arizona, the territorial constitution of 1864, the Howell Code, which declared that surface water was public property, made absolutely no mention of groundwater (Mann 1963). In the 1930s, due to the growing efficiency of pumping mechanisms, the increase in the price of cotton, and the availability of cheap electricity, groundwater was increasingly used for agricultural purposes. The question of its extensive use became a feature of political debate. But it was above all the federal CAP project that triggered legislative action in Arizona between 1948 and 1980. The 32 years between the promulgation of two legal frameworks regarding the CAP can be interpreted as the transition from one coalition to another, a transition rendered possible by the emergence of a new political configuration.

In the 1940s, the Department of the Interior declared that the CAP would only be approved if the State of Arizona committed to a legislative plan to restrict agricultural irrigation methods involving the pumping of groundwater. Under the aegis of Governor Osborn, the Groundwater Code was passed in Arizona in 1948. The Code forbade the expansion of agriculture irrigated using groundwater without resolving existing problems regarding the pumping of water, the quantity of water allocated to landowners, or the overexploitation of groundwater. In spite of federal pressure, the successive governors of Arizona were confronted by strong opposition within their state from mining companies, farmers, and city

Supporting the economic order   63

governments, which were unhappy about rigorous legislation and who claimed exceptional rights to administer their own water. This coalition had every chance of success in a context in which the Supreme Court swayed between contradictory decisions (groundwater as public property *versus* rules governing the use of groundwater according to the needs of landowners). Legislators were constrained to a "policing role," which created a legislative impasse, because of a lack of political unity regarding the issue. Although he had supported the CAP as a congressman a few years before, Governor McFarland (Democrat), elected in 1954, introduced no legislation on the subject (Mann 1963), as if he were somehow echoing dominant interests, which had little time for federal grievances.

However, the more support the CAP gained in Washington, the more local decision makers were obliged to legislate on the subject of groundwater. This development threatened the very existence of the project. In the context of the 1970s, increasing criticism of major projects, especially with regard to their impact on the environment and their prohibitive cost, was enough to call federal funding into question. Moreover, the continuing urbanization of Phoenix and Tucson exacerbated the competition for water between farmers, mining companies, and cities. A coalition of new local elites inclined to the mediation of old conflicts encouraged the State of Arizona to change its policy on groundwater, which was the *sine qua non* for the CAP to benefit from federal funding. This change was, doubtless, also rendered possible by the fact that states in the federal system were becoming increasingly influential in terms of controlling and implementing water policies at a time when federal funding was increasingly hard to come by as policies announcing the end of the welfare state were introduced. These structural transformations affecting political power in Washington, where the beliefs of the dominant coalition were undermined by the environmentalist cause and the all-conquering advances made by neoliberalism, created the preconditions for a realignment of existing coalitions within the field of a local power configuration that was itself characterized by new urban problematics.

The Groundwater Code did not address the issue of supplying the two cities with water. In the late 1960s and early 1970s, differences persisted in approaches to the question. While the pumping of groundwater was generally limited to the area covered by a single supplier, the resource was sometimes pumped beyond these parameters to urban areas for both industrial and domestic uses. This kind of water distribution created tensions that were resolved between 1969 and 1974 in a series of legal cases brought against the City of Tucson and arbitrated by the Supreme Court of Arizona. Tucson was also forbidden to transport groundwater from wells in the Avra and Alter Valleys, designated as critical areas. For the Supreme Court, property rights over groundwater were linked exclusively to rights of use. Those rights were limited to "reasonable use" and were not associated with ownership of the resource.

The issue was not limited to Tucson, and other disagreements between local farmers and mining companies soon emerged. In 1976, the Farmers Investment Company (FICO), a large pecan producer located in the Santa Cruz Valley to the south of Tucson, brought a case against the copper mining company, Anamax, in

64 *Supporting the economic order*

the Arizona Supreme Court (Doyle 1983). This case has often been considered the trigger for the Groundwater Management Act of 1980. In effect, the problem was that several mining companies to the south of Tucson pumped water from an area considered as critical (Sahuarita-Continental Critical Groundwater Area), transporting it to their own sites outside that perimeter. FICO, which owned nearly 7,000 acres of farmland located in that area, took the view that the mining companies were not respecting the law and had broken rules governing the use of water and its transport beyond authorized areas. The mining companies argued, on the contrary, that it was necessary to precisely define the area from which the water was pumped, since the water they used came from the same aquifer as the water used by the farmers.

The mining companies also claimed that pumping groundwater did not cause aquifers to diminish as long as the water was used and replaced. The City of Tucson also got involved in the controversy, claiming that FICO and the mining companies were polluting the groundwater of the basin from which the city extracted most of its water. The mining companies countered that, contrary to regulations, the City of Tucson transported groundwater a long way from its basin of origin. Citing rights of use, the Arizona Supreme Court found in favor of FICO and against the mining companies, but nevertheless ruled that it was incumbent on the legislature to define rights based on economic interests and decide whether it was in the interest of the state to encourage mining to the detriment of agriculture. It was based on this ruling that the mining companies and the City of Tucson formed a coalition against the farmers with a view to encouraging the legislature to undertake a legal reform of regulations governing the transportation and use of groundwater.

In the past, the mining companies and FICO had often clashed in Tucson over water management, but it seemed that interests had evolved (Connall 1982). Mining companies and City Hall both wanted to change the way in which water was transported. For example, the monopolistic position of farmers (who consumed 89% of water supplies) encouraged City Hall to take a conservationist stance. On the other hand, farmers criticized the mining firms and the cities for being openly hostile to agriculture. During the arduous negotiations organized with a view to resolving these problems, each party was represented by a different legal point of view: agriculture by Jon Kyl (the Salt River Project's lawyer), Mark Wilmer (FICO's lawyer), and Brock Ellis (a lawyer from Phoenix). The mining companies were represented by James Johnson and James Bush (from Phoenix) and Thomas Chandler (from Tucson). Furthermore, the spokesmen for the cities were Jack DeBolske, Director of the League of Arizona Cities and Towns, and Bill Stevens, a Phoenix lawyer.

Legislative activity was encouraged above all by debates about the CAP taking place at the same time in Washington. In effect, the environmental impacts of the project were increasingly being called into question, and the existence of the project itself was threatened by the Carter administration on the grounds of costs. To ensure that it was not deprived of all federal funding, the government posed a precondition, relayed by the secretary of the interior of the time, namely that the

State of Arizona had to introduce, as speedily as possible, a new legal framework for regulating the management of groundwater. Faced with an impasse in negotiations at the local level, the Democrat governor of the time, Bruce Babbitt, who was from the West, assisted by the Republican senator, Stan Turley, introduced a new dynamic by serving as a mediator between the cities, the mining companies, and the farmers, a commitment that was doubtless linked to his university career (he had graduated from Harvard Law School) and professional itinerary (as a former attorney general), combining law and politics, both of which were useful in reconciling a respect for the law while at the same time taking local issues into account.

These negotiations legitimated a new belief in the need to legislate seriously on groundwater in order to guarantee that the CAP was implemented. They culminated in the promulgation, in 1980, of the Groundwater Management Act, which limited rights regarding the use of groundwater in four areas (Phoenix, Tucson, Prescott, and Pinal County), referred to as "Active Management Areas" (Arizona Water Resources, News Bulletin, January–March 1980). In the end, the CAP did not lose its federal funding. It should be noted that realty promoters, the Chamber of Commerce, and private water companies were not invited to the negotiating table (Connall 1982), even though the urban development of the region – particularly the sale of properties – appeared to be a decisive factor.

Consensus was actively sought at the local level: FICO provided its support (Reisner 1985); decision makers in Tucson attempted to maintain a belief in the necessity of the project – City Hall voted on funding for the CAP Association on several occasions – and the Chamber of Commerce lobbied in favor of the CAP (source: Dames & Moore 1995 *Cap Use Study for Quality Water*). However, at the same time, two agrarian economists from the University of Arizona broke ranks by rendering public the fact that farmers in Arizona were financially unable to buy CAP water. While they were later forced to leave their university positions, their actions nevertheless marked the emergence of local protest against the CAP project.

A realignment of coalitions

The arrival of the CAP in Tucson illustrates the fact that if a city in the American West wanted water, it had to buy it from water transport infrastructure projects – for Arizona, the CAP. In 1989, construction work started on a CAP processing plant in Tucson, as well as on the Clearwell Reservoir, designed to stock water treated with a mixture of ozone and chloramines, a process considered by some as at best experimental, but by its supporters as "progressive" (Kupel 2003: 193). CAP water was finally officially first delivered on October 5, 1992, but numerous problems came to light over the next few years. In the first few months, leaks were detected in the pipes, and the press reported complaints against the "water mafias" and corrupt bureaucrats who swamped their fellow citizens with "toxic substances" from the Colorado River. Among the opponents of the CAP water delivered by Tucson Water throughout the 1990s, Richard Wiersma was the spokesman of the Citizens Voice to Restore and Replenish Quality Water.

66 *Supporting the economic order*

> In 1992, disaster struck Tucson. The water utility began serving chemically treated CAP water to half its customers, and the switchboards lit up with complaints almost immediately. This brown, foul tasting, highly corrosive water destroyed plumbing and appliances. It killed pets and plants, and caused rashes and allergic reactions in people.
>
> (Wiersma 1995: 1)

When CAP water arrived in Tucson, it destroyed pipes and flooded private homes. In 1995, 20,500 complaints were made against Tucson Water due to leaks (Dames & Moore 1995: xvii). Popular trust in the city's leaders was rapidly eroded and strong opposition emerged. For example, Bob Beaudry became one of the most vehement activists and critics of the use Tucson Water made of CAP water. Moreover, the water's brown color, which was due to a slightly acid PH and corroded pipes (Dames & Moore 1995: vii) added to the malcontent of the local people in regard to political leaders. It should be noted that, at the time, Tucson's infrastructure system was one of the oldest in the state (Dames & Moore 1995; Kupel 2006; Colby & Jacobs 2007). The lack of maintenance of this infrastructure was at the root of most of the damage caused by CAP water and had triggered a high degree of mistrust in local people in regard to the state and the federal government, a mistrust that informed their oppositional strategies.

Between October 1992 and October 1993, Tucson City Council was led by the Democrat, Molly McKasson, of Ward 6. It was in City Hall that a number of coalitions promoting water quality in Tucson emerged, among them Citizens for Water Protection, headed by Molly McKasson; Citizens Voice to Restore and Replenish Quality Water, whose president was Richard Wiersma; as well as lobbies headed by Ed Moore, the Republican Supervisor of Pima County, Bob Beaudry, the Tucson entrepreneur and car salesman, and Gerald "Jerry" Juliani, who promoted the idea of holding a referendum on water quality. These coalitions aiming for better quality water acted against the Pro-Development Coalition, centered on the local car salesman, Jim Click, Chuck Freitas, director of the Safe and Sensible Water Committee, and the Southern Arizona Leadership Council. These campaigns in favor of water quality in Tucson resulted in a number of decisions being taken by City Hall in October 1993, including the withdrawal of CAP water from the city's pipes, and limiting CAP water to the west of the city, since the majority of complaints had been made by residents of the east (Kupel 2003), who were excluded from the supply zone. In this context, Mike Tubbs, the head of Tucson Water, resigned.

By 1994, most of the administrative agencies had become aware of the situation in Tucson. Reports indicate that most difficulties caused by CAP water derived from obsolete infrastructure, mostly in the east of the city. CAP water was entirely dissolving the solid material (Kupel 2003) produced by corrosion in the pipes, thus causing major damage. Anxious to keep the federal government out of the dispute by respecting provisions of the Safe Drinking Water Act (SDWA) and other legislation in the field, the Arizona Department of Environmental Quality (ADEQ), an administrative agency authorized by the Environmental Protection

Supporting the economic order 67

Agency to apply the SDWA, levied a fine of 400,000 dollars against Tucson Water in November 1994 on the grounds of having failed to respect drinking water quality regulations by testing wells inadequately. In a declaration made after the fine was announced, the ADEQ attempted to reassure those concerned, claiming that the CAP situation was under control (Newman 1994). Furthermore, Tucson Water adjusted its prices in an attempt to compensate for the fact that the water was brown and contaminated (Kupel 2003: 194). Tucson Water, then directed by John S. Jones, was forced to stop using CAP water due to maintenance issues associated with draining the canal (Newman 1994: I; Kupel 2003: 194). Then, still in 1994, Tucson Water appointed a new president and vice president.

The temporary closure of the CAP enabled the coalitions headed by Molly McKasson and Richard Wiersma to lobby the city government on behalf of the Citizens Water Protection Initiative (Proposition 200). The proposition, which achieved a 57% majority among the city's voters (Chesnick 1999: 4; Kupel 2003: 194), was voted through the legislative system in the form of the Water Consumer Protection Act (WCPA). The Act outlawed chloramines and ozone, which Tucson Water had previously added to the supply. Mention was made of the fact that, unless the company could ensure that the quality of its water was as high as that of groundwater, the law would be subjected to another vote in five years (Valdez Diaz 1996). In the end, Tucson City Hall proved to be the main link between local people and government bureaucracy. From the outset, Michael Brown, mayor of Tucson, Molly McKasson, city councilor, and Michael Tubbs, head of Tucson Water, organized task forces to study the CAP and examine social responses to it (Dames and Moore Inc. 1995: 10). In fact, in 1994, the City of Tucson hired a consulting firm (Dames and Moore) to find solutions to the city's water problems.

Molly McKasson and the Water Consumer Protection Coalition
In Molly McKasson's family, an interest in local politics was cultivated from one generation to the next. In an interview with the Pima County Oral History Project, Molly recalled that her mother had become politically active as a protester of the Vietnam War. She encouraged her daughter to remain faithful to her values, but always to be willing to change her opinions in line with any new knowledge she acquired. In the 1990s, Molly McKasson focused on improving the quality of life of Tucson's citizens by promoting initiatives like the WCPA. Furthermore, thanks to the political and social satires she delivered in Tucson theaters, and by attending political rallies in Phoenix, she was able to better define her beliefs and make important political contacts. In 1991, five different associations in the city supported Molly McKasson in her campaign to become councilor for Ward 6. At the time, she was in the process of emerging as a public figure in the theater and writing articles for the local papers. The fact that she was not a career politician was one of the factors that enabled her to gain support. As McKasson recalled in her interview with the Pima County Oral History Project, "in 1993, the pipes broke and a firestorm of anger was created and people felt ignored. Growth was on the

68   *Supporting the economic order*

front burner and quality of life on the back" (McKasson 2011). She claimed that development and planning initiatives did not take long-term concerns into account. In Tucson, greater emphasis was placed on growth and urban development than on increasing living standards.

In 1994, McKasson and Wiersma began to collect signatures supporting the Water Consumer Protection Act initiative in view of the 1995 vote in City Hall. Among the opponents of the CAP, Gerald "Jerry" Juliani can be considered as "the Pro-Prop 200 Group's researcher." From 1993 to 1999, he wrote a number of articles for local papers arguing that protective measures should be introduced on behalf of water consumers, as did other members of the Water Consumer Protection Coalition. Between 1997 and 1999, he was spokesman for the Pure Water Coalition. On the other side of the fence, a pro-development/pro-CAP coalition began to take shape in 1997. It included the Southern Arizona Leadership Council (SALC), a group criticized by some for being largely Republican and lacking in racial and ethnic diversity (the group has been white historically), but that represented local business leaders anxious to defend strong values and contribute to the development of urban areas. The SALC made substantial contributions to causes that they believed would aid economic growth and urban development, including 1997's Proposition 200, which advocated a return to CAP water for Tucson. Thus, Bob Beaudry and Jim Click, rival car salesmen, clashed throughout the 1990s over water quality and CAP-based legislation, using their financial resources to support their initiatives until a decision was finally taken in late 1999 to reinstate CAP water. From the beginning, Jim Click played a central role in the Tucson dispute. He started out his career in Los Angeles, working at a car dealership before buying his own in Tucson. He was a generous donor to numerous political organizations, citizen movements, the University of Arizona, and various causes involving health and welfare.

In 1997, Proposition 200 was approved by a 59% majority. The SALC then became actively involved in supporting Proposition 201 (1999). Jim Click came out against the Coalition for Adequate Water Supply, making a contribution of 30,000 dollars. Another local entrepreneur, Karl Eller, owner of the Circle K supermarket chain, made total contributions of $25,000 to the 1997 and 1999 campaigns (Beaudry 1999). Closely involved in the world of business and politics in the state for decades, he played a pivotal role in encouraging the Phoenix Suns NBA franchise to come to Arizona. Meanwhile, the University of Arizona recognized his efforts by appending his name to the School of Management and the name of his wife to the campus-based dance studio (Wang 2012). It is reported that the Pro-Development Coalition spent over one million dollars bringing CAP water to Tucson (Davis 2001: 3). In 1999, Tucson Water's "Ambassador Program" was designed to instill new faith in the CAP. A number of homes on East Fourth Street, between Craycroft Road and Wilmot Road, were supplied with a mixture of groundwater and CAP water (Chesnick 1999). The Pro-Development Coalition distributed bottles of this mixture at football games and in shopping malls to enable the people of Tucson to form their own opinions.

Supporting the economic order 69

According to the SALC, the 1999 vote proved a great success with the election of Bob Walkup, who beat Molly McKasson, as mayor of Tucson. This was one of the "clear signs" that strong leadership was emerging in Tucson's business community (Southern Arizona Leadership Council 2014). The SALC stated that this did not represent "a business community that seeks unfettered growth and development (…) but a business community that, for once, saw that it needed to be involved in creating Tucson's future." The new mayor, Bob Walkup, a retired aerospace executive, declared that "water is our No. 1 problem … the vitality of our community demands a solid, long-term water policy and everybody knows this" (Davis 2001: 3). In 1999, Mitch Basefsky, now a public relations manager for the CAP, but previously spokesman for Tucson Water, added that "the majority in this community were willing to accept CAP water. They understood this was an alternate resource that we had to make use of in order to sustain our environment" (Chesnick 1999: 2). The CAP was supposed to solve the problem of the overexploitation of groundwater and the risk of shortages that it involved. Instead, it seems to have generated additional tensions between economic leaders, citizen organizations, local politicians, and Tucson Water. The relative absence of the CAWCD, the company responsible for managing water quality, and federal institutions, in the struggle for water quality can be partially explained by the fact that their responsibility ended with the delivery of the resource to the city company, which was responsible for treating it.

The logic of the struggle within Tucson regarding the delivery and subsequent fight over the CAP is a historical case study that is indicative of larger structural dynamics operating in the field. Just as the main protagonist, Molly McKasson, explained of the struggle against the CAP in the 1990s, the debate over water ultimately was decided by economic interests and for the short-term well-being of the community, not the long term, and, furthermore, the sustainable agenda that would rely more fully on the local. Thus, the core of the economic pole remained intact. The reintroduction of the CAP would free up many new opportunities for housing developers especially. In this regard their foresight was striking, and their money on new candidates for office, to make sure that water was synonymous with growth and eventually sustainability, was well spent. Throughout the 1990s and 2000s and until the economic crash of 2008, peri-urban expansion and suburban development would be among the key industries for places like Tucson, outlying cities such as Marana, not to mention Phoenix. Using the theoretical tool of social field thus allows us to understand the linkage between the water sector and the housing market; it is therefore necessary to analyze these dimensions together. The notion of "urban sprawl" is usually used to understand the spatial effects of economic development on Western United States cities and, in this next section, we approach this topic more directly, having established some of the linkages between urban growth, water, and struggles for political power.

Water and urban sprawl

Beyond its spatial connotations, the term "urban sprawl" refers to residential units beyond the immediate outskirts of the metropolitan city center, associated with an

70 *Supporting the economic order*

individualized lifestyle, including such commodities as privately owned homes and one or more privately owned vehicles (Graham & Marvin 2001). Indeed, the process of growth described as "urban sprawl" is generally tied to the generic term "suburbanization."[2] Inspired by a country-in-the-city philosophy and the idea of an urban society based on suburban communities (Abbott 1993), urban sprawl is not exclusively the result of a demand for suburban living. In fact, in the aftermath of the Second World War, it was encouraged by two factors: the cheapness and availability of land and a lack of obstacles to economic development and consumerism. The leitmotif of this trend was focused on the advantages of urban growth and access to individual property ownership (Archer 2005). Far from being the expression of a spontaneous demographic explosion, the urban sprawl is embedded in economic, political, and cultural dynamics encompassing structural transformations in the United States (the industrial process), institutional initiatives, federal programs (new legislation encouraging the building of homes), and the founding myths of the country's history (the frontier, individualism) (Jackson 1985; Wiewel & Persky 2002).

More than the cities of the East Coast, the "Desert Cities" of the American West, located in huge, arid, and frankly hostile spaces, represent a desire to create "oases" that provide a pleasant lifestyle, using commodities such as air-conditioning and private vehicles. Such "Desert Cities" enable us to study the social logics underpinning suburban sprawl in a region in which urban expansion is much more rapid than in the rest of the country. For the last 15 years or so, the region has been experiencing the worst period of drought in its history, not only threatening ecological systems but also the "hydric security" of its resident populations (Scott & Pasqualetti 2010). In the second half of the 20th century, Phoenix and Tucson, the two biggest cities in the Sun Corridor, experienced urban expansion triggered by a quest for natural resources that were not available on site. They benefited from water policies historically implemented by the states of the American West with a view to boosting economic growth (Cortinas et al. 2015). Taking the form of infrastructural mega-projects (dams, canals), these policies presented local leaders with an opportunity to exploit federal funding originally made available by the 1902 Reclamation Act. In the following year, the Salt River Project (SRP), an irrigation system dependent on the Roosevelt Dam, was launched. Intended to provide water to the Phoenix region (Keane 1991; Smith 1972; Zarbin & McCabe 1986), it was the first of a long series of infrastructure projects that culminated in the Central Arizona Project, a 500-km-plus canal completed in 1968 designed to channel water from the Colorado River to southern Arizona (Coeurdray, Cortinas, & Poupeau 2014).

---

2 Suburban approaches focusing mainly on the emergence of residential communities on the outskirts of towns emphasize a "private" way of life that is "close to nature" implied by urban sprawl. The term "urban sprawl" is retained here because our objective is not to analyze the lifestyles of the residents, but to concentrate on urban growth dynamics generated by various alliances and the formation of social groups in the land and water market.

Supporting the economic order   71

After the Second World War, the expansion of Phoenix and Tucson accelerated. Between 1945 and 1960, the population of Phoenix grew from 65,000 to 439,000, while Tucson's leaped from 38,000 to 212,000. Besides the local promotion of the defense industry and new technologies, growth focused on tourism and services, whose comparative advantages – a sunny climate and a cactus-filled desert – were part of the "Western Ranching Lifestyle" of the cities of the American West (Gober 2006; Logan 2006). In the 1950s, real estate became a prime component of the Sun Corridor's economy. Land purchases (investment) and exploitation (construction) – farmland was frequently used for the purposes of urban development – generated a substantial economic windfall: "Fortunes in post-war Arizona were not made in gold or silver mining but in real estate. The State became a vast monopoly of new lands waiting to be developed" (Sheridan 2012: 353).

Entrepreneurs and heads of companies affiliated to the Chamber of Commerce and supported by numerous local councils also influenced urban and environmental policy through tax rates and regulations introduced to encourage major infrastructure projects (Gober 2006). Business leaders knowingly used local government to encourage economic growth in order to benefit from the financial manna provided by the residential and commercial construction industry (Shermer 2011: 6). The increasing number of "shadow governments" – agricultural corporations, interest-based associations, committees, districts, homeowner and resident associations – in all sectors of social life (Garreau 1991; Guttman & Willner 1976), under cover of an alleged plurality of power centers, reinforced the pro-growth coalition's decision-making capacity and influenced city governments and the state legislature. The pro-growth coalition, which received little criticism, promoted the urban expansion of Phoenix and Tucson through a proactive policy designed to encourage economic development. Suburban expansion in the Sun Corridor based on "unfettered growth" has gradually been called into question due to the emergence of new environmental constraints imposed by the federal government.

Projects for the future

If in the 1970s, major projects (like the CAP) were subject to criticism from environmentalists and politicians due to their impact on the environment and their prohibitive cost, the continued expansion of cities (like Phoenix and Tucson) caused ever greater competition for water, involving farmers, mining companies, and municipalities that did not operate in the same hydrological configuration. The ideology of growth, on behalf of which leaders in Arizona (senators, representatives of farming, and urban interests) had been lobbying Washington for over 30 years to guarantee the economic development of the region, was adjusted to a new environmental situation. A new coalition, largely made up of politicians (and without real estate developers) then began to encourage a change in policy with a view to encompassing the protection of aquifers, a *sine qua non* for the CAP to provide water to "Desert Cities." As seen before, the Groundwater

72   *Supporting the economic order*

Management Act, promulgated in 1980, was designed to address the need for groundwater regulation for companies and municipalities. Federal funding for the CAP was dependent on the Act being passed (Coeurday, Cortinas, & Poupeau 2014). The Act limited the use of groundwater to the perimeter of four water management areas (AWR 1980). Before this legal framework was introduced, the construction of new housing developments and golf courses, in addition to already existing farming and mining activities, had contributed to the overexploitation of available groundwater.

The Groundwater Management Act imposed strong environmental constraints on real estate developers as has already been mentioned, although these ended up being sidestepped in some ways. They were now obliged to demonstrate their capacity to provide water for a period of 100 years in specific and authorized zones (Assured Water Supply, or AWS) without using groundwater resources. Development, although still possible, was limited to land that had access to water via major infrastructure like the CAP, or, in other words, to towns located in the counties of Maricopa, Pima, and Pinal. This legislation forced developers to use already existing surface water provision systems and forbade them from drilling unmonitored wells outside authorized areas. This approach was designed to limit urban fragmentation, which, all things considered, did not help to protect water resources. Developers had to obtain a certificate from the Arizona Department of Water Resources, an obligation that represented an important regulation tool for the Department (Vincent 2006). By controlling AWS, the Department could control urban growth and limit the peripheral development of existing metropolitan areas, since promoters had no choice but to buy water and pay to have it treated and transported. This procedure was met by opposition from real estate developers, particularly those who wanted to develop isolated areas that were not under the administrative control of the major cities.

In the early 1990s, when the CAP became increasingly indispensable to the implementation of urban policy, powerful real estate developers expressed a desire for the environmental constraints now weighing on their activities to be made more flexible. Among these developers were to be found industry professionals and the designers and representatives of residential retirement communities (Robson Communities, Sun City, etc.) who kept an eye on new opportunities outside the city limits, or, in other words, in the heart of the desert. These individuals took their concerns to the board of the CAP and argued that although it was impossible for developments located in the desert to link up to the CAP due to the onerous costs of building a pipeline, they could nevertheless, thanks to groundwater supplies, offer their clients the guarantee of 100 years of water supply. They agreed to make their future clients pay a tax to purchase water from the CAP, that water being used to restock the aquifer. From their perspective, this was a balanced approach, in that housing developments would not consume as much water as urban and agricultural activities, and that the water thus saved would contribute substantially to replenishing the aquifer. Along with their lawyers, these developers helped to draw up the law on the CAGRD prior to expressing their views in a series of parliamentary sessions. By employing legal

Supporting the economic order 73

means and organizing lobbying campaigns to ensure that their arguments were legitimately heard, these developers managed to retain control over the future expansion of their communities. In other words, they found a way of preserving their autonomy in regard to the cities while at the same time publicly displaying their contribution to the so-called "national" campaign to protect natural resources.

While the voices of private interests were heard and supported by senators, and approved by the CAP and the administration responsible for water supply, the CAGRD's approach soon started to cause problems. Initially, restocking aquifers had been proposed to help create and maintain desert communities that did not have direct access to the CAP. However, the area attracted a greater number of investors than anticipated. According to a former board member of the CAP, the CAGRD was, at that point, "a ticking time bomb" (G.G. interview, April 2015). Instead of encouraging regular growth, this institutional innovation opened the doors to the development of a growing number of construction sites. Investing in the desert became, by default, an option authorized by the law while potential sources for restocking the aquifer were diminishing rapidly. Thus, the CAGRD also contributed to a decentralization of power centers by increasing the number zones of political influence beyond city government; developers eventually imposed a fragmented vision of the urban landscape at the expense of a controlled use of resources. The CAGRD also made it possible to develop a number of small rural communities. By developing intermediary strategies, these communities attempted to operate autonomously in order to retain control not only of their water resources and the way in which they were able to diversify them, but also of their expansion policies. Farmers and local politicians joined forces to protect their towns' and villages' natural resources, which were threatened by the cities. In order to support their suburban expansion, the strategy of these small municipalities was to buy up agricultural land and, consequently, acquire the right to exploit groundwater sources. In sum, major cities were experiencing an economic slowdown and suburban sprawl, these rural communities gradually started to experiment with new forms of urbanism thanks to coalitions composed of city administrators, politicians, and developers' intent on creating a form of urbanism that was more than gradual urbanization, but also more concentrated than traditional notions of sprawl.

The growth of small rural municipalities

Since the beginning of the 1970s, neighboring rural communities had faced the suburban expansion of Phoenix and Tucson. The cities had to go together in an attempt to keep control of their water supplies. In order to maintain their role in decision-making in the face of the threat from the cities, farming families and rural communities developed strategies designed to create a new form of suburban development. Land-use conversion strategies rapidly took into account both the crisis in agriculture and the issue of urban development: families of migrant farmers became investors and waited for the right moment to sell their land to

74 *Supporting the economic order*

developers. A coalition articulated around a new alliance was gradually formed. Social logics leading to the transformation of farming areas into suburban zones thus called into question the approach of groups of local entrepreneurs – real estate developers, farmer-investors, and city administrators – who were intent on speculating on land prices and capturing natural resources.

The history of Marana, located on the outskirts of Tucson in the heart of the Sun Corridor, gives us an insight into the dynamics of small cities that, situated on the periphery of larger conurbations, defend their autonomy by developing a specific form of suburban expansion different from the urban sprawl of the cities of the American West. The farming community situated on the site currently occupied by the city of Marana was transformed in the late 1970s by an approach to economic development that contrasted sharply with the Tucson authorities' official aim of regulating the ecological impact of their activities. This important period in the history of Marana's development predated the introduction of the GMA. Expanding cities such as Phoenix and Tucson were accused of buying up farmland in small municipalities in order to guarantee access to groundwater sources. These municipalities took the view that they had been dispossessed and that, furthermore, due to their lack of administrative clout, they were unable to defend themselves effectively. The decision to incorporate Marana was taken in order to counter Tucson's expansionist policy. In the 1970s, the city's farmers had no way of exercising any rights over their water. Consequently, they believed that Marana's autonomy was a precondition for securing the resource, as witnessed by the mayor, whose family were farmers:

> The reason the town incorporated in 1977 primarily is because of water, and the reason for that is the City of Tucson was coming down from over in Tucson, they were coming up and buying farmland, and they were taking the water from the farmland, and it was taking it back over into the Tucson area, so the farmers were obviously very concerned that the city was doing that, and that they would basically leave the farmland and they didn't like their water being taken from their aquifer, the only way to stop them from doing that was for the people of the area to incorporate so that Tucson couldn't come in and take the water, so the driving reason for why this town exists is because of water.
>
> (R.D., farmer, interview, May 2015)

Two managers of the Marana Irrigation Trust, both of whom were farmers, stated that they went to Phoenix to hold discussions about the Central Arizona Project. In the end, they realized that what Tucson was really interested in was their water:

> I was sitting right in front of Bill H., Tucson assistant city manager and Frank B., the water director and they were both talking about what their next plans were for water supply. They were planning on drilling in the Cortaro Farms Company area. I immediately thought: we have to stop them! They were talking about coming out in this area, and drilling wells because of the strong

Supporting the economic order 75

aquifer we have here. It made us nervous. We knew we needed to do something. Mainly farmers because the water was probably the biggest issue with most of them, they were concerned about a big city close by, buying out farms around and breaking the water, bringing it so low so there were not gonna be enough water, you know, for some like myself. My granddad was a farmer, and my dad was when he was young but we decided, my dad subdivided his land, and then my brother and I got some land as well, it was part of the family trust but once we incorporated, we had control. Because you cannot go into another city and buy land water up. It's your own land you can pump the water.

> (B.P., farmer and manager of the Marana
> Irrigation District, interview, April 2015)

Upon their return, they hired a lawyer to restrict Tucson's access to water in Marana. Supported by the farming families provided that they do not ever introduce property taxes, the campaign to set up an administratively autonomous city was launched in March 1977 with a petition containing 1,250 signatures collected from farming families and local residents. The farming community was not fully aware of the issues associated with access to their water: "I don't think at the time they had (…) a vision for a dynamic thriving city, I think they wanted to save their water and keep their farms, (…) they wanted to stop Tucson from doing that, they wanted to protect what they had" (J.D., Marana town manager, interview, May 2015).

In the late 19th century, Marana was a rural community with a population of a few thousand people located on the outskirts of Tucson. While Marana was essentially oriented toward ranching, the Silverbell Copper Mine also played a fundamental role in the local economy. In the 1880s, the Southern Pacific Railway came to town, thus considerably expanding business opportunities. The new rail link also gave rise to a wave of migration, particularly from China, with most of the newcomers employed in the agricultural sector. The cotton industry really became established in the area in 1937, while other fields of activity, including wheat, barley, and pecan nut production also began to develop. The Pacific State Loan Association funded Cortaro Farms' acquisition of a plot of land to the north of where Marana is currently located. These agricultural activities meant that access to water supplies had to be secured. In the 1940s, Cortaro Farms set up a cooperative, the Cortaro Water District. Concurrently, work was begun on the construction of water infrastructure and the digging of wells. A financial crisis and a lack of available labor in the late 1940s forced the owners to sell their land (divided into plots of 370 acres) to farming families, thereby increasing the number of water rights. Up until the 1970s, most of the residents of the area in which Marana is now situated were farmers who, naturally, consumed a great deal of water. P.G., a farmer, president of the Arizona Municipal Water User Association, and manager of the Marana Irrigation District, which started to supply water to Marana in 1956, was thought of as the "Water Man." He guaranteed access to CAP water for the city of Marana in 1992 (Marriott 2012).

76 *Supporting the economic order*

Converting farmers into growth entrepreneurs

By the end of the 1970s, problems concerning access to water were exacerbated by an economic crisis in the agricultural sector. A number of farming families talked about how they left agriculture for the suburban sector, gradually winding down their activities and selling their land and water rights to real estate developers. Those interviewed depicted certain families as "visionary." One migrant family, the Kais, was described as having built their fortune on land investments. Thanks to a bank loan, they were able to purchase farmland, which they cultivated for a short time before selling it to developers. Moving into the sphere of real estate speculation, they sought out land that they could sell on in the short or medium term. At the time, the Kais were seen as leaders in the field of real estate development in Marana, acquiring plots in the most out-of-the-way corners of the township, assessing their potential and either selling them on to developers or selling them directly to construction companies: "With an intuition about when to sign a deal and a fearless approach to acquiring property, the Kai turned that first plot into real-estate holdings across the country – and a sizable fortune" (White 2006).

After the state of Arizona introduced laws against drilling wells for irrigation purposes, the father of the Kai family encouraged his sons to get involved in politics and, more particularly, in municipal water management. Indeed, one of his sons, Herb, was elected to the city council. Furthermore, the family maintained relations with local politicians including Senator Morris K. Udall and Governor Bruce Babbitt. The family's contacts, allied with their burgeoning reputation, made it possible for Herb Kai to exert a degree of influence over how water was managed in Arizona:

> As Marana has exploded, Herb has guided his hometown as the council's water guru and vice mayor. He recently set off a conflict with Tucson by getting the inside scoop about extra water in the Flowing Wells district and nearly beating the Old Pueblo to the purchasing punch.
>
> (White 2006)

Another of the family's sons, John, lobbied the legislature in Phoenix to use wastewater and help to conserve fresh water. The Kais, in turn farmers, developers, and real estate speculators, were one of the Arizona families who made their money by buying and selling land, a process described in the local Tucson media:

> [The Kais] turned humble Chinese roots into millions of dollars, simultaneously playing roles of unassuming farmers and no-nonsense CEOs. The Kais made smart, aggressive deals. The family bought land, farmed it, bought more land and increased its wealth. Today, there remains little land in the Northwest untouched by the Kais. Pick a parcel in Marana – at some point, the Kais probably owned it, leased it or had an interest in the property next to it.
>
> (Unsigned article in *The Explorer*, 2002)

Supporting the economic order   77

Urban development thus became a new source of profit. As farms started to lose value, they were replaced by homes, and farmers began abandoning their properties. By 2004, most of Marana's ranchers and farmers had sold their land. In the same year, the local construction industry generated a turnover of over a billion dollars. Agriculture, by contrast, generated a mere 26.4 million. Furthermore, in terms of employment, for every farmer, there were ten construction workers (bricklayers, carpenters, architects, etc.).[3]

While some farming families abandoned their activities, others decided to make a number of adaptations and persevere. Having made its fortune in the cotton industry in the 1950s, the Wong family gradually diversified and, in the 1990s, started to grow cereals (wheat). They did not need to use the town's groundwater sources because, by then, irrigation in the area was based on CAP water. The family was able to benefit from a critical moment in the history of the CAP. While the water supplied by the CAP was primarily intended to stop farmers using groundwater supplies for irrigation purposes, they were unwilling to pay for that water. Indeed, they were particularly keen to avoid additional expenditure at a time when agriculture, most of which was based on cotton farming, was struggling against fierce foreign competition. CAP leaders, in conjunction with the City of Tucson, offered financial incentives to farmers on condition that they retroceded water to the city and stopped using groundwater sources. Echoing increasing demands from consumers in regard to the quality of agricultural products, the Wongs began producing organic cereals. In so doing, they helped give more credit to a sector often criticized for its lack of environmental responsibility. Their ability to negotiate with the local authorities was well known to the region's politicians and water sector professionals (D.R., CAGRD manager, interview, June 2015). The Wongs, in spite of the fact that they lived in Marana, presided over Tucson's Citizens' Water Advisory Committee, which included, notably, engineers from the Water Department as well as representatives of the CAP and of various consumer associations. The committee met on a monthly basis in the presence of the mayor to discuss the financial and technical resources used by the City to manage water. Thanks to an agreement between the City of Tucson and the CAP, the Wongs have been able to maintain Marana's agricultural heritage, a point that administrators were eager to emphasize throughout the interviews, while simultaneously playing down any tensions between the small town and the neighboring metropolis of Tucson.

Meanwhile, Marana continued to generate profits outside the agricultural sector. In 2000, developers made offers for land that was not for sale. The north of the city was a particular point of focus in this regard. Indeed, the major national construction companies present in Phoenix and Tucson were also active in Marana. This expansion strategy was part of a new factor

---

3   Although agriculture was, historically speaking, of fundamental importance in the development of the state, its role has become increasingly less central. In the 20th century, Arizona's economy was based on the "5 Cs": cotton, cattle, copper, citrus, and climate.

78 *Supporting the economic order*

impacting urban policy: the town had joined the CAGRD, the body set up as a result of lobbying carried out by developers in the wake of the Groundwater Management Act to support homebuilding on Marana's outskirts. It also served as an example of the desire of city administrators to assert their autonomy of action (recently won in various legal battles) in regard to Pima County, which had long denied them a responsibility of major importance – directing the use of wastewater – for a small municipality seeking an ever-increasing number of investors.

The history of farming families in Marana illustrates how suburban development in the Tucson metropolitan region has been conducted since the 1970s. This kind of suburban expansion should be distinguished from the urban sprawl characteristics of city outskirts around the world on a specific point: it is integrated into the agricultural heritage of a small, neighboring town, whose rights to groundwater were sold to Tucson for residential purposes. This style of development takes advantage of the gradual disappearance of agriculture. Agricultural land can be left fallow in times of aggravated drought, thus helping to preserve groundwater reserves while at the same time safeguarding it at the margins in order to protect the myth of a "pioneering" past. This approach to development, in which farmers strike alliances with local politicians or themselves become investors, is part of a wider struggle to defend the ownership of a territory and the water rights associated with it, in order to retain autonomy and control over future development.

From growth to green sprawl

Motivated by ensuring economic growth locally, environmental concerns caused coalitions to evolve in the 1980s. While the initial phase of suburban development was characterized by a relative lack of administrative control, the introduction of environmental and town planning norms mandated by federal laws legitimized growth. The Groundwater Management Act and town planning laws that respected the environment were examples of a framework seen as a form of compromise. Public administrators emerged as new professional players (town managers, urban planners, water administrators, etc.), acting as guarantors of a new regulatory framework intended to promote a form of sustainable growth. New coalitions made up of developers and administrators contributed to the emergence of an original kind of real estate development.

Developers and city administrators, particularly in the Phoenix region, but also in Marana and Oro Valley in the Tucson metropolitan area, expressed strong ideological positions concerning the benefits of economic growth, which they perceived as necessary in terms of maintaining the economic and urban potential of the West, a region in which the model of suburban development was not generally called into question. However, the administrators interviewed voiced their concerns about the potentially adverse effects of any slowdown in urban growth. Competition between cities to attract new investment and new residents is apparent at a number of levels. On paper, new developments are not only calm and

Supporting the economic order 79

secure places located in natural settings and enjoying high standards of living, but also dynamic communities including shops, companies, and jobs. While the Marana town manager expressed a palpable fear of economic stagnation, he did, at the same time, evoke a proactive policy designed to attract new stores and support new residential communities:

> We want to make sure we have a dynamic thriving community. To do that, you've got to have companies that are employing people, you've got have jobs, neighborhoods (...) I think we see it as we want to be a place where people come and live, and they want to come and invest here, and they want to be a part of the community, we want diversity, (...) and I think when you see a community that gets the reputation that they are not pro-growth, if you were to ask them, if you aren't pro-growth, you want to ask them: "Are you for death?" because if you're not growing ..., it's not that you need to keep adding more population in a sense you do, because if you have people leaving your community is gonna get smaller (...) there are less people to pay into the systems, the infrastructure gets older and it's not able to be replaced, so, it's not that you have to keep growing out either, you don't have to keep growing big in terms of size but if you're not trying to attract new people that want to be a part of something.
>
> (J.D., Marana town manager,
> interview, May 2015)

Developers also see growth as a necessity, especially in that a lack of economic expansion is associated with a suppressed job market. It would seem that the environment is subordinate to job creation and a dynamic view of the homebuilding industry. In this regard, state and city governments need to provide support:

> Unless we don't want any growth or any community and we say we go live somewhere else, a solution that I'm not willing to take, then we got to have people that work here, and work with conservation and alternate source of water (desalinization, underground water that is not used ...) at the same time (...) The builders' biggest challenge is the slowdown of the economy, and the lack of job creation. The government is preoccupied with what the future workforce want, but it's like the chicken and the egg story, we need to bring the jobs here in Tucson.
>
> (Paul G., Arizona Homebuilders Association,
> interview, April 2015)

While developers always, at least initially, described the issue of the environment as "important," interviews made during the survey revealed that ecological concerns were quickly given second place whenever profits were threatened. In such circumstances, they employed a different rhetorical approach, this one focusing on the benefits of growth for the community and for job creation, and the potential for cohabitation between human activities and nature:

80 *Supporting the economic order*

If you have environmental conditions that are very sensitive and obviously, development could be impacted, and then maybe the development doesn't happen because it's trade-off between destroying something people really love and development (…) I do think that there are things that you can do that balance the need of the environment, and the wildlife and the animals and the plants and the need to also house people, and help their community, I think there's the design of the community that can play into that, you know we talk about wildlife corridor or clustering homes in one area living as much space as possible so there are things that you can do, you can achieve both, and sometimes I find that the animal species that we're concerned about actually benefit by having people nearby, people feed them, they put water out, they do other things, people do that, or the wild animals jump into the backyard and takes the little dogs, I hear that all the time, people's pets become food for coyotes and bobcats (laugh), that's good for the bobcat.

(J.D., Marana town manager, May 2015)

Developers and city employees frequently mentioned the efficiency of water management in Arizona, especially compared to California, which is experiencing one of the longest droughts in its history (Mount et al. 2015). In their view, the healthy situation pertaining in their state is largely attributable to conservationist measures taken since 2005, notably by Pima County. These measures have, among other things, increased the use of recycled wastewater and transformed farmland into residential real estate, a sector that consumes less water. Arizonan municipalities promote regulated but strong growth based on a consensus about environmental norms in regard to the construction of new homes. Developers thus used new water recycling and conservation techniques as authoritative arguments in favor of their approach:

I see water management as a success story. As of 2015, we have the same average consumption than in 1987. Even with CAP water, in Tucson, we can have 140,000 acre feet a year, we use only 100,000 acre feet a year, 40,000 just back into the ground, so we are good! We have declining water consumption, and even on a conservative trend, we still have till 2040–2050 and then we can use the water stored. Water is an important commodity, so we need to be efficient in water uses, and we are.

(Paul G., Arizona Homebuilders Association,
interview, April 2015)

Optimistic about the state of water resources, a number of developers and local politicians have joined pro-growth lobby groups, such as Growth Nation, the Greater Phoenix Leadership Council, the Arizona Homebuilders Association, and the Water Coalition, and local chambers of commerce. These organizations help to obscure environmental problems. For example, brochures on Phoenix focus on the advantages offered by a region in which opportunities are plentiful and water does not present any kind of problem:

Supporting the economic order   81

Phoenix has an abundant supply of water, both from the local rivers and from a canal that transports water from the Colorado River. (...) Water supplies to Phoenix are enough for home builders to comply with the state law which requires a 100 years water supply. About 70% of water use in Arizona still goes to agriculture.

> (Growth Nation, a pro-growth organization based
> in Scottsdale on the outskirts of Phoenix)

Similarly, the local academic community (Arizona State University in Phoenix, University of Arizona in Tucson), most of whose local shareholders are semi-private organizations, tends not to call this vision into question. Many public events focus on solutions allegedly within reach, while problems inherent in the growth-based model and the overexploitation of water receive very little attention. One of the developers interviewed recalled a discussion about water issues he had with a well-known scientist who claimed that he was confident about water management in the medium term. Concerns about the viability of development were voiced by local figures active in environmental groups and by residents opposed to the destruction of their community. However, they were unable to raise sufficient awareness among members of the public to trigger a popular movement capable of calling the suburban development model into question.

In the early 2000s, growing concerns over problems linked to the exponential growth of the early 1970s associated with access to CAP water, coupled with a desire to preserve the desert as a protected natural habitat, led to the introduction of new legislative norms designed to meet the demands of sustainable development. Town planning approaches incorporating a "smart growth" policy were elaborated with a view to regulating land use, conserving natural resources, and protecting air quality. In the Sun Corridor, the exponential growth of the 1990s (from which both developers and the cities benefited enormously), allied to burgeoning ecological concerns, led to a resurgence in the popularity of conservationist ideas focusing on ways of guaranteeing growth while simultaneously respecting the environment. Examples of this trend include a substantial number of reports, committees, and town plans integrating approaches to protecting the environment and developing environmentally themed design projects, including communal gardens and wildlife corridors in residential communities.

As Chuck Huckleberry, administrative director of Pima County observes, the political solution applied by the cities and Pima County to water supply problems in the mid-2000s, was presented as being compatible with local economic growth. In spite of the emergence of environmental groups who campaigned against various commercial and residential projects, alliances between advocates of growth, most frequently made up of representatives of city governments and local economic leaders (real estate promoters, investors, entrepreneurs, etc.) focused on zoning laws and adopted an ensemble of measures designed to draw attention to the importance given to the environment. According to developers, most amendments made to their projects were marginal in nature; indeed, most of their

82   *Supporting the economic order*

complaints focused on how slow the bureaucratic process was and how many different bodies they had to cope with:

> You deal with Marana Development Services, you have one acre and they complain that you don't have enough roads for all the lots, so they're going to argue and not approve it, so you'll have to come back and argue with them that it's not an issue. Then, you go to Marana Fire District, if they don't think that you have proper fire access, so same process. You also have Tucson Water, they will say that you're in a bad zone, lift station, and you have to pump, and put more pressure in your pumps.
>
> (M.L., developer in Marana, interview, April 2015)

Developers did not complain about municipal opposition to specific projects but, rather, about bureaucratic problems that slowed down construction. Meanwhile, municipal administrators highlighted the political nature of the process. For the developers, the first contact was with the town planning departments:

> They contact the planner first and see the possibilities for properties. It's not the mom and pop type of guys, it's more sophisticated developers, they know us, use us regularly, they sit down here with us, it's like they have an idea of what they want to do it, a schematic of the property, the basic uses (residential, commercial), it's like an informal meeting to discuss ... It's a political and administrative process. You look at it, the policy is never that black and white, and what we do is we make sure they include landscaping, trails, parks.
>
> (P.C., director of town planning in Marana,
> interview, May 2015)

Consulting firms, whose members essentially include town planners and engineers, operated as intermediaries between municipalities and developers. Working alternately for different clients, they insist on the importance of the reputation of developers, which derives, at least partially, from their capacity to negotiate projects directly with the director of urban planning or with development services. Most developers in the Sun Corridor are known to city departments and have ongoing relations with them, a fact that facilitates the advancement of various projects. A consultant described the importance of discussions held before the formal submission of projects to gauge how likely they were to be approved. Such discussions made it possible to develop a more effective negotiating approach:

> Usually, you start with the planning director. Then, after that you go to the city engineer. It's all about relationships. Well you know, it's networking, I've been here for 20+ years, business it's all networking, it's all about the people that you know. Some developers will even go to talk to the council members, mayors and town managers included, and the elected for the districts.
>
> (B.P., director of a consulting company in Tucson,
> interview, May 2015)

Supporting the economic order 83

Furthermore, developers collaborate with engineers and town planners who deal with the various bodies that intervene when problems arise: "Well, actually, my job is to intervene on screw ups or on deals that do not work and talk to the government jurisdiction and figure out how to make that work" (Max L., developer in Marana, interview, April 2015). Administrators support development projects because, by creating the infrastructure required to supply water and by finding more consumers for the city, those projects indirectly cover the costs of operating and maintaining water services. In spite of the downward trend of consumption, a water manager from Oro Valley – a small, expanding town near Marana – expressed concerns about the viability of the financial model suggested by the conservationist approach:

> So we have to look how we gonna blend that, make it potable for the customers, how we can do with our education programs, and have them understand, how we gonna pay for this, where do we collect the money from. You know we have impact fees to collect it to new growth, we have a groundwater preservation fees, and to try to collect from the existing customers, and that is growing and the cost to build infrastructures is going up to up. So we're in a process now analyzing all our options, do we want to pipe everything or pump it from Oro Valley, or do we want to put it in a recharge base, and pull out, and pump and out, and drink it.
> – Q: So, it's great for you if there isn't so much demand?
> – Sure, it's great for us, but you can see that the demand is declined, and so, what we are faced, it's what that is doing to our revenue then? I do the revenue part, what kind of rate and budget. And I'm saying ok gentlemen, we're not selling so much water, but what we gonna do. I mean it's good that we're not selling water in a way, but what we gonna do to bring the revenue, because we have a lot of debts.
>
> (S.B., manager of the Water Service in Oro Valley, interview, October 2010)

This new attitude to growth as the only possible horizon of measured expansion did not, therefore, call into question the model of suburban development. Indeed, that model has been amended and legitimized by new regulations encouraging a "green sprawl" approach (Cadieux & Taylor 2013), which mirrors, in the specific context of suburban development in the American West, the "green cities" of the East Coast and Europe. Environmental issues are generally employed to promote and get projects approved, rather than to call urban growth into question. While developers work alongside public administrators to implement a "green sprawl" approach focusing on growth regulated by environmental norms, they face another challenge, namely the dwindling stock of land available for sale (only 20% of land in the West is in private hands, as against 95% of land in the East). Developers hope that this land can be claimed for urban development in the region, pointing to the lobbying campaigns conducted since 2005 by developers and other business leaders at the Arizona state legislature in Phoenix.

84 *Supporting the economic order*

This survey on the Sun Corridor highlights the emergence of an urban form, the specificity of which resides in a tangle of local and federal policies implemented by professionals working as parts of alliances that have shifted over time, depending on the degree of pressure exerted on their approaches by environmental constraints. It is difficult, therefore, due to the region's hydrological situation, to separate the emergence of the suburban forms we observed from the management of natural resources. Without water, the Sun Corridor's economic development would not have been possible. On the one hand, water is an environmental constraint that must be overcome by the development of federal projects – in the form of irrigation systems for farmland and expanding urban areas – designed to underpin the expansion of the local economy. On the other hand, water has become the focal point of a struggle between coalitions that, rather than exploit the resource for profit, attempt to transform it into a long-term source of revenue either by taking advantage of access rights, or by legally getting around institutional constraints in order to anticipate future growth. It is, therefore, not by chance that the ongoing drought in the west of the United States has led to a compromise between sustainable growth and the management of increasing water scarcity. Finally, environmental constraints, which, in the past, tended to be ignored, circumvented, or sidelined, seem to have become a more central concern in terms of the participation of public and private sector decision makers in the learning process. These decision makers have taken this new factor on board by adopting a relatively consensual, conservationist approach, and by promoting, without giving up on their ambitions for growth, an original form of "green sprawl."

3 Reinventing water conservation
Institutions for sustainability

Coalitions for water policy

The State of Arizona is of particular interest in terms of understanding policies designed to deal with drought and the effects of climate change. In this state, the protagonists of the water sector (engineers, public administrators, politicians, consultants, certain academics, etc.) often present themselves as the guarantors, if not of the ecological cause, then at least of "sustainable" and "responsible" development – an approach that marks them out from the elites of neighboring California, whose stance is characterized by anxiety, or even consternation. It has been argued that, thanks to its specific situation, Arizona has accumulated decades of experience and elaborated a politico-administrative framework oriented toward a form of balanced water management in which various institutions implement ecosystem protection programs and water recycling projects, referred to here as "water conservation." Thus, conservation involves public policies designed to "protect species, ecosystems and their processes, and support their contribution to human wellbeing" (Lopez-Hoffman et al. 2009) as well as to develop more specific water conservation measures (Sheridan 2014). In a state like Arizona, with its deep-rooted Republican values and affection for individual entrepreneurship, such an approach to environmental issues may be surprising.

This chapter shows that the adoption of water conservation policies originates in a realignment of the dominant coalitions active within Arizona's political institutions. Consequently, the reasons for adopting such policies have more to do with the production of an institutional consensus between the various protagonists in the economy and management of water in the region than they do with the putative victory of an ecological discourse that is finally getting a proper hearing. The task before us is, then, to show how water conservation reactivates ecological ideas within a new political configuration, and therefore, to analyze the links between coalitions and the implementation of water policies; or, more precisely, to explain how a "minority coalition" has succeeded in promoting measures that have gradually gained the upper hand among the state's water managers.

Water conservation policies have a long history in the American West, and they can be considered consubstantial with the development of major technological systems since the early 19th century (Taylor 2016). In effect, since they

86 Reinventing water conservation

first emerged, mega-projects have raised concerns about land use (Walton 1993; Espeland 1998). However, the aim of the "conservationist crusade" (Hays 1969), supported by major engineering companies (civil engineering, mining, etc.) and by federal agencies (Geological Survey, Forest Service, Reclamation Service, etc.) was *not* to preserve biodiversity, but, rather, to provide protection from the harmful effects of unfettered industrialization, which had the potential to destroy the natural environment exploited by corporations and, in the end, to cause a slow-down of economic growth (Gottlieb & FitzSimmons 1991). A few decades later, in the late 1960s, under pressure from the environmentalist movement, ecological ideas were incorporated into institutional policies by means of the Environmental Protection Act (1970) and the Clean Water Act (1972) (Van Tatenhove & Leroy 2003; Colby & Jacobs 2007; Kraft 2015). Today, conservationism is no longer a monopoly of engineering companies operating in the name of science for the good of the community as a whole; rather it has become one among many partici-patory initiatives taken in residential communities in the region by environmen-talist organizations and municipal and county administrations (Sheridan 2014). Beyond the local level, ideas associated with water conservation, ideas no longer considered hostile to the ideals of economic growth, are now accepted and pro-moted by actors in the sector, for example the Los Angeles Water District and the Yuma Irrigation District. Protecting natural resources is entirely compatible with the entrepreneurial spirit, which has traditionally structured water policies in the American West (Gottlieb 1988). In order to understand the transformation wrought by conservationism, it is useful to consult the works on environmental history and the conflicts characterizing the construction of the American West.

The empirical survey on water professionals (2014–2017) began its focus in Southern Arizona, but it also involved most of Arizona's institutions related to water. Indeed, the City of Tucson is particularly dependent on the Central Arizona Project (CAP) in that the various rivers in this semi-arid region dried up several decades ago due to the impact of humans (Serrat-Capdevila 2016); the manage-ment of the CAP depends on the Arizona Department of Water Resources, a state institution mandated by the governor but representing most of the water users and organizations of the state. As a consequence, the Tucson region contains a net-work of institutions involved in the fight against drought (Mott Lacroix & Megdal 2016). By attending public meetings on the subject (thematic workshops, district assemblies, consumer meetings, commissions, etc.), it was possible to identify the degree of influence wielded by various protagonists. As the participants them-selves admit, the issues discussed at those meetings go beyond the immediate concerns of the City of Tucson and even the State of Arizona. A localized study of the fight against drought necessarily not only implies an analysis of the system of institutions involved in water management, the parameters of which are not limited to the initial scope of the survey, but also requires that neighboring states confronted with a similar situation in regard to the distribution of water from the Colorado River should be encompassed.

In this way, the methodological approach is classical in that one could begin to build the structure of social relations by beginning with a "small" object. In the end, the choice of methodology for the survey was based on two approaches. The first consisted in contacting the directors of institutions considered to wield influence on drought management in Southern Arizona (local administrations, municipal companies, state and federal agencies, etc.). Insofar as the private sector is concerned, real estate promoters were targeted as a priority due to pressure on natural resources exerted by urban growth in Tucson and, more generally, in the Sun Corridor between Phoenix and the Mexican border (Benites 2016). Lawyers involved in water disputes were also contacted. By constructing a sample from the very diverse assemblage of individuals and institutions present in the field, the Advocacy Coalition Framework (ACF) was used to identify the social units beneath the level of what is traditionally considered a "field," considering them as coalitions. It is in this sense that the research could begin with "small" objects, and yet simultaneously keep in mind the "large object" of the field of water policy, of which coalitions are constitutive.

A second strategy consisted of asking interviewees for contacts with people who worked with/for them, or who in their view played a role in the implementation of water policies. The survey was, therefore, based on the principle of snowball sampling (Strauss & Corbin 1990), an approach that enlarges the circle of interviewees in order to analyze relations between the various protagonists involved and shed light on pertinent coalitions. The survey was complemented by an ethnographical approach realized during one year spent inside and working with the administration of Pima County. This was then supplemented by shorter stays of three months and various other visits for meetings, conferences, and interviewing to follow up on the initial observations. This provided the opportunity to understand the reason for the differing, but not incompatible, visions of how to handle such a large problem as drought, and how the institutions that manage water and those in positions to solve these problems, related to one another. Therefore, how they seemed to be a part of coherent system of social relations, indeed part of a group of self-described "professionals," raised certain sociological questions.

To be a water manager in Arizona

Although it might appear ostensibly as a desk job, the work day in the water business is routinely described as exciting and engaging to the point where every day holds something new to learn and discover. The day will likely begin with the regular arrival at the workstation, the checking of emails, and reference to various newsletters, etc. These can arrive by mail as well as electronically and may be from non-governmental organizations (NGOs), water think tanks, such as the Pacific Institute in California, or research centers, such as Arizona State's Morrison Institute for Public Policy or the University of Arizona Water Resources Research Center. Such a "checking up" helps to keep different people in touch easily and helps water professionals keep up to date on the latest events and reports that they may need to consult for later grant writing or projects, not to mention for general interest and knowledge.

88 *Reinventing water conservation*

These of course are very general activities that might as well begin the day as well as taking place at any other time. The more important work occurs in the field, that is, making phone calls, meeting with partners on various projects to discuss future plans, or perhaps visiting other regional or state offices for meetings. For example, as Pima County holds a Local Drought Impact Group to monitor the drought,[1] it has to check in with larger players, such as the Arizona Department of Water Resources (ADWR), the Central Arizona Project, the National Oceanographic and Atmospheric Association (NOAA), the United States Geological Survey (USGS), and others, all of whom can contribute different forms of information about water flows, hydrologic predictions, and the possible paths of ongoing legislation, or even information about new hiring in the variety of administrations that impact water use and management in general. These meetings are held more regularly and are a kind of subsidiary to the larger meetings held at ADWR headquarters in Phoenix, which are attended by most of the water institutions of the state. Notes of the meetings and the reports that were approved at such meetings are often sent back to the home offices. These are in fact important because they decide the recommendations that will be given to the governor and will be funneled to the lower regional stakeholders. Other business is done in these types of settings, although sometimes in more regional offices, and often in public meetings where information can be exchanged and questions can be asked. In such venues it is important for representatives from the southern part of the state (e.g. Tucson and Pima County) that their perspective is considered by the central part of the state (e.g. Phoenix), which can be seen as an over-represented group of professionals on whom large institutions such as the ADWR and CAP call regularly, and so there is a constant awareness of how to maintain the concerns of the southern region on the larger agenda.

Although there are some of these larger events, there may also be local meetings and working groups that regularly take place, which are important for the maintenance of relations as well as the production of professional knowledge in the subfield and various advocacy coalitions. In some senses, one observes various processes of agenda setting, here happening between and among local and regional coalitions, as opposed to Kingdon's classic example of Capitol Hill (Kingdon & Thurber 1984). For example, meetings might be held with local NGOs to determine their interest in moving forward on a joint project for rain-barrel installments, or with a university to view presentations and discuss how the school might assist the agency with internships or data analysis, and vice versa. With these kinds of activities of a typical schedule sketched, it is also helpful to take into account a brief mapping of the relevant institutions and their characteristics that can facilitate clearer understanding of water management in this region.

---

1 See the memorandum describing the functioning of this group in more detail at this link: https ://webcms.pima.gov/UserFiles/Servers/Server_6/File/Government/Drought%20Management/St age_1_Declaration.pdf.

A network of professionals

The relationships between the network of water professionals can be complex, especially if considering very small allocations of water, wastewater, water rights, etc. However, many institutions for the purposes of this qualitative sketch are too tangential to mention and so the focus is maintained on the major players. For example, Phoenix water deliveries come to about 275,000 acre foot (af)/year.[2] In contrast, the City of Tucson, with its water department, Tucson Water, has roughly a 145,000 acre foot (af) allocation, of which about 45,000 af are "banked" every year in the ground in case of a shortage declaration. In fact, because of the conservation measures taken in Southern Arizona especially, the actual water demand has also decreased, allowing for more water to be stored.[3] Pima County and its counterpart, the Pima Association of Governments, also in close geographic proximity in Southern Arizona, each have differing functions from one another and from the more traditional water providers described above. The Pima Association of Governments (PAG) is a unique entity: that serves as the "region's federally designated metropolitan planning organization, PAG oversees long-range transportation planning and serves as the region's water quality management planning agency, lead air quality planning agency and solid waste planning agency."[4] In terms of water management, this means that it serves the function of a kind of meeting ground of professionals invested in managing water, often providing venues for collaboration, but also providing some technical resources and expertise when multiple agencies become involved in a project. The administration of Pima County holds a different function as well. Although not a water provider as traditionally defined, because they do not have a federal contract for water, they have a small cadre of people who work as water policy analysts specifically and who hold many coordinating responsibilities on drought. Outside of this, the administration relies heavily on a team of engineers and technicians in a variety of departments related to sustainability and planning, not to mention pure engineering and "public works." It has eight water reclamation facilities in total.[5] The building of several treatment plants to produce highly treated effluent, and additionally their plants, handle all of the city's wastewater, some of which, through innovative engineering techniques, is used in the conservation of ecological habitats. The map below (Figure 3.1) shows the impressive number of all the environmental projects that are running currently.[6]

---

2   More can be found on the City of Phoenix water plan at:https://www.phoenix.gov/waterservic essite/Documents/wsd2011wrp.pdf, pp.14-40

3   More information can be found at https://www.tucsonaz.gov/water/waterplan

4   More information can be found at https://www.pagnet.org/Default.aspx?tabid=56.

5   More of such information for Pima County can be found at: https://webcms.pima.gov/UserFiles/ Servers/Server_6/File/Government/Wastewater%20Reclamation/Publibations/FacilityPlan_20 16.pdf

6   Figure taken from http://webcms.pima.gov/UserFiles/Servers/server_6/File/Government/Floo d%20Control/Reports/water-environment91109.pdf on page 17 of the City/County Water and Wastewater Study

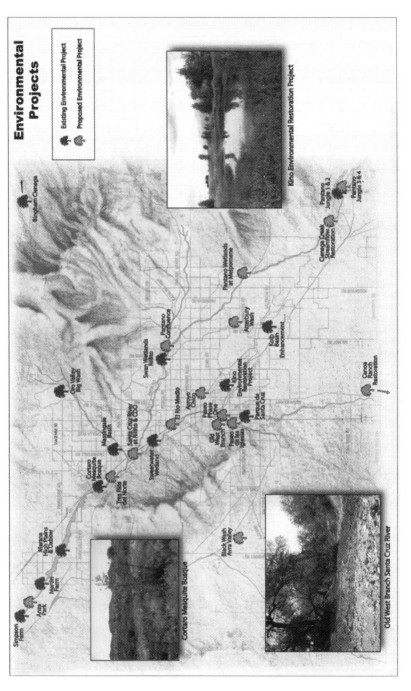

Figure 3.1 Map of Pima County Environmental Projects sourced from the 2009 City of Tucson/Pima County Water and Wastewater Study".

Reinventing water conservation   91

Finally, there is the ADWR, the state governor's representatives in federal and interstate water negotiations. The function of the ADWR is to coordinate with all the state entities and produce technical reports, projections, and recommendations of its own. Therefore, the ADWR must actively engage with city and county groups to ensure that the plans are adequate and that the necessary measures are implemented. The ADWR also established the Arizona Monitoring Technical Committee (AMTC), to create long-term planning maps and tools. This system of social relations is held together by many meetings, reports, phone calls, emails, and correspondence, all aimed at guaranteeing the "water future" of this western community. Drought is an interesting context in which to study such a system because in its absence such a high degree of coordination may not be made clear. Indeed, state, and sometimes federal, officials need to be present even at very low-level meetings within this hierarchy.

This hierarchy began to take its current shape when, in 1980, after years of over-drawing the aquifer, the state of Arizona mandated new laws and norms to replenish the most vulnerable areas in Arizona, calling them AMAs or Active Management Areas. A new bureaucracy was developed for these roles, and with it there began to emerge a new category of water professionals who were committed to this new agenda and this tradition. In light of the deepest drought in more than 1,300 years in the Colorado River Basin and with the reservoirs of Lake Mead and Lake Powell at dangerously low levels, these meetings have become important hubs of information from the state to the regional and local levels. Furthermore, regional governments like Pima County, in the process of all this and seeing the potentially dire nature of the situation of drought, have formed small planning groups and local drought impact groups to monitor and collaborate with stake-holders as to what to do next and when to declare new drought stages. All of this has an impact on how much water will be used in the area. In the following sections, we describe in much more detail the characteristics, social trajectories, and dispositions of this varied milieu.

Water professionals: a varied milieu

If the milieu of water managers seems, at first sight, to be relatively complex and fragmented, and characterized by the involvement of a large number of institutions, the systematic, relational study of their perceptions of and preferences in regard to water policies reveals four distinct groups (Table 3.1).

> The classes are defined by means of a hybrid clustering technique, combining the two methods of traditional iterative classification: on the one hand, Hierarchical Ascendant Classification or HAC (at every iteration, what is sought is the distribution maximizing inter-class variance and, therefore, minimizing intra-class variance using Ward criteria); and, on the other, Mobile Center Classification, or CCM (which, based on initial centers, iteratively affects an individual in the center closest to them, employing classical Euclidean distance). Mixed classification is divided into three stages:

Table 3.1 Classes of water professionals in Arizona

Group	Local professionals	Local conservationists	State administrators	Expert managers
Perception of the situation	No conflict Irrigation problems	Risks concerning ecosystems and human water use	No conflicts and avoidable risks	Technical resolution of problems
Priority of water policies	Economic development	Water conservation and ecosystems	Sustainable development	Planning and management
Level of action	Municipal	County, municipal, and federal	State-level	State-level
Water policy instruments	Mobilization of local authorities	Planning participation	Legal and incentive measures	Lobby
Type of expertise	Good management practices	Hydrology administrator	Political decision-making	Good management practices
Type of action	Management and local coalitions	Management and political implementation	Coalitions and regulations	Coalitions and lobbying

1. Defining stable groups by combining two sections derived from the CCM;
2. Selecting optimal distribution derived from an HAC of stable groups;
3. Consolidating optimal distribution via a second CCM. These operations were carried out by Lala Razafimahefa, Design Engineer CNRS (ART-Dev – UMR 5281).

Two classes operate at the local level, which includes municipalities and counties. The first of these classes includes individuals who mostly belong to municipal institutions (Tucson, Phoenix), municipal water distribution companies, or consumer associations that play a role in water management institutions in Arizona. In terms of the positions they take, the members of this class focus on irrigation problems and the funds available to solve them. They present their expertise as a management approach characterized by "good practices" in terms of the implementation of water policies. The policy instruments they emphasize are situated as much at the level of administrative measures as at that of lobbying and the private sector. Members of this class are referred to as "local professionals." The second class, or categorization, encompasses individuals, most of whom are from Pima County, who express a clear preference for water conservation policies and initiatives taken by/for local communities. According to the members of this class, the situation is characterized by uncertainties concerning the protection of local ecosystems and the provision of drinking water for the poorest sections of the population. In close contact with ecological groups, but without joining them in their opposition to economic development, they represent a specific form of expertise in which institutional management consists of the implementation of conservation measures, either by elaborating alliances on the ground or by promoting measures

Reinventing water conservation 93

for the protection of natural milieus and the recycling of stormwater. We can discuss the members of this category as "local conservationists."

The actions of the other two classes, unlike those of the two described above, are situated at the state level as well as at the local level. The third class mainly encompasses individuals belonging to state institutions such as the Arizona Department of Water Resources and the Central Arizona Project. It includes public administrators who emphasize the importance of legal instruments (see Box below: The new face of water management in Arizona); they have a more global view of problems of water supply, which they often situate at an interstate level without, however, neglecting the importance of local initiatives, for example the use of wastewater and stormwater. The members of this class of "state administrators" are characterized by their contacts with all protagonists in the water sector. Tasked with applying environmental norms and laws, they encompass various organizations responsible for running major technological infrastructure projects such as the CAP. The fourth class is closer to private organizations than to state institutions. It is characterized by positions that are less centralized and institution-based, and more favorable to the private sector, for example pressure groups, state-level consumer associations, and law and consultancy firms. Some of their action tools are situated in the legal sphere, but the class's members have, like the local professionals, a propensity to promote rules based on private interests, particularly those of real estate developers. Due to their characteristics, members of this class are referred to as "expert managers."

The new face of water management in Arizona

In 2014, T.B. was, thanks to his recognized expertise in the field of water management, appointed director of the Arizona Department of Water Resources by Republican governor, Doug Ducey. Although he is not from the region (he graduated with a BSc in geology from the State University of New York at Cortland in 1977), his first post in water management was an internship in 1982 in the Phoenix AMA, an administrative body set up following the introduction of the Groundwater Management Act. There, he continued his career, occupying various legal and administrative functions. He became a programs administrator in the Adjudications Division before being recruited in 1988 by the city of Phoenix as a hydrologist in the Law Department where he provided assistance to city management and attorneys on issues relating to the city's water rights, water use, and water supply. He was swiftly given responsibility for the management of water from the Colorado River, notably as chairman of the Arizona Water Banking Authority and co-chair of the Drought Interagency Coordinating Group. He also represents the State of Arizona in negotiations concerning the rights of Indian Nations. As an ADWR administrator, he held positions of responsibility in most official state institutions, including the statewide Water Resources Development Commission, the Regulatory and Permitting Group of the governor on sustainable water, the statewide Water Advisory Group, and the governor's Drought Task Force.

94   *Reinventing water conservation*

Furthermore, his work with academic institutions (the Julie Ann Wrigley Institute for Sustainability at Arizona State University, the Water Resources Research Center at the University of Arizona) put him in contact with most of the expert managers, whose scientific competencies are recognized at the state level. Unsurprisingly, his position as director of the ADWR, politically the most important institution from a hierarchical point of view, makes him a central protagonist in the elaboration of water policy. He is an essential broker in the introduction of associated norms and rules.

The problem here is to examine how the classes described above interact to form coalitions and how these coalitions influence water policies. First, on the level of social interaction, it should be noted that the members of these groups are protagonists in the water sector who "bump into" each other on a frequent basis at meetings, on commissions, and in boardrooms. The importance of Arizona's state institutions (particularly the ADWR) is easy to understand. In the context of the drought, they must apply the norms issued by the state governor and the federal government and advise on those norms. As staging posts for measures issued by local institutions, they are also consulted by municipal officials. This was confirmed by observations made at several meetings held in Pima County between 2014 and 2017 in which representatives of state agencies were involved in discussions with local professionals. The director of the ADWR also plays a role as a "producer of consensus," not only due to his role as an administrator, but also thanks to the fact that he personally attends a substantial number of public meetings. But this kind of influence and the predominant role played in the development of collective responses to the drought are relatively new phenomena. At the turn of the century, the ADWR seems to have been something of an "empty box," as some water professionals recalled (G. G., interview, July 2015), underlining the new influence wielded by the agency in times of crisis, and the possibilities in that organization for new leadership. As an institution that depends on the ADWR, and as the main distributor of water in the south of the state, the CAP also plays a key role with regard to the risks of water outages and possible declarations of shortage. Not only is it supplied with forecasts by federal agencies, but it also serves as an interlocutor vis-à-vis the municipalities, and its representatives often attend public meetings with the director of the ADWR. Last but not least, there is Pima County, whose role in the promotion of water conservation measures has already been discussed. This research focuses then on how local and state administrations, whose role could be imagined as exclusively local, have in fact been able to promote conservationist themes among managers in the water sector successfully.

Based on interviewees' attitudes to drought management, one of the most influential coalitions in the sphere of water policies is composed of local conservationists and state administrators (Classes 2 and 3), incorporating not only a significant fraction of the members of Class 4 (expert managers), but also, and above all, of Class 1 (local professionals). The conservation measures applied to water seem now, in the context of the drought, to be the only ones capable of guaranteeing ongoing regional development. The policy, given impetus in the Tucson area by Pima County, is recognized de facto as representing a pioneering approach that has since spread statewide. Indeed, it has enabled some water managers, whose functions are situated between the local and state levels, to further their careers by promoting solidly conservationist ideas while occupying in increasingly influential positions.

The social foundations for the realignment of water policy coalitions

Through the process of interviewing, we were able to then collate our collected data and input it into a unique relational database of actors based on their characteristics, perceptions of drought, what policy to pursue, etc. Through this, we determined four classes of water protagonists, but this differentiation did not always deliver clear differences between them. In effect, due to the consensual nature of the discourse of the main protagonists on water policy in Arizona, attitudes about drought management were not that different from each other, at least at first sight. On the other hand, notable differences, and potential convergences, do emerge in perceptions of the kinds of initiatives that should be taken.

If the objective of the ACF paradigm is to determine how systems of belief underpin the development of cooperative links and coalitions (Thatcher 1998), answers relating to perceptions about the local water situation show that local conservationists (Class 2) emphasize the deterioration of ecosystems, inequalities in access to the service, and risks linked to drinking water, most of them due to irrigation and subsidy issues. Local professionals (Class 1) and expert managers (Class 4) both highlight irrigation problems, paying little attention to environmental issues. However, they differ on several points: the first deny the existence of conflict, while the second emphasize the interstate dimension of the issues at hand (notably, the upstream-downstream dynamic characterizing past agreements concerning the Colorado River). Meanwhile, the views of state administrators (Class 3) are widely shared. Like local professionals and expert managers, they place no emphasis on conflict or deep-lying problems; however, they do recognize the issue of biodiversity. Their sanguine outlook can probably best be explained by reference to the fact that, due to their position, they tend to seek consensus. From this point of view, we should note the relative proximity of state administrators and expert managers in terms of perceptions and analyses. The consensual vision of collective expertise about drought management is shared by all water managers in Arizona. When all is said and done, if we focus exclusively on the beliefs and values expressed in regard to political objectives and assessments of the general situation, it is difficult to understand the emergence of a conservationist coalition – unless we foreground the relative consensus about the need to adapt to the impact of drought (the "external factor").

However, replies to questions about instruments of action provided a more precise description of potential rapprochements between the different classes of protagonists studied, as well as of certain "skillful capacities" that could be applied to the context. Of all the classes, only the local professionals are to some extent opposed to ecological measures and community initiatives. On the other hand, members of this class agree with local conservationists and state administrators in

96 *Reinventing water conservation*

recognizing the importance of anti-drought action plans, a first indication that the "external factor" capable of realigning coalitions is only operative to the degree that it encourages the adoption of shared management tools. But while local professionals focus on the institutions of the state of Arizona and on the private sector, local conservationists call upon the federal government to take initiatives, thereby agreeing with the state administrators, whose approach is based on the application of environmental norms introduced at the federal level. In the meantime, while expert managers' attitudes to initiatives taken in the private sector are similar to those of local professionals, they are more favorable to taking on board environmental ideas, a trait that places them in the conservationist coalition. This is probably due to their more global perception of the issues within Arizona itself and at the interstate level.

From engineer to consultant, an expert manager in water policy

B.P. grew up on a small farm in Vermont where he was active in "Young Farmer" associations at a very young age. He graduated with a BSc in hydraulic engineering, after which he was recruited in the late 1980s by the Bureau of Reclamation in Boulder City, Nevada. From there he was transferred to Yuma, Arizona. While in Yuma, he worked on dam and canal projects for the Wellton-Mohawk Irrigation District and on water supply to Mexico. His skills quickly attracted the attention of people in high places and he was appointed to a post in a new government program in Washington, DC, the Planning, Programming, and Budgeting System (PPBS), which, applied to the water sector, led to more water managers being trained. At the time, just under 90 engineers were appointed to seven elite universities (Harvard, Princeton, etc.). In his 2004 interview, given in the context of the Oral History of the CAP, he reported that:

We had a lot of people start engineering. I don't remember the exact numbers but there was like 85 or 90 Civil Engineers. Four years later, six of us graduated. Most of them ended up in the Business School and became known at our college as "The School for Flunk Out Engineers." But there are a lot fewer people, I believe, entering engineering now.

After graduating with a Master's in engineering economic systems from the University of Stanford, he was recruited by the secretary of the interior in Washington as a water policy budget examiner, focusing on the CAP water canal project. He was also involved in the elaboration of a substantial number of environmental impact statements, the first of which was on the Auburn Dam in California, which was never built. In 1985, the needs of water administrations in the State of Arizona, along with the introduction of the GMA, encouraged him to join the ADWR in Phoenix. He spent three years there as senior analyst and manager for water and power systems, before being appointed director of the agency. Later, in 1991, thanks to his contacts and expertise, he was able to set up his own consultancy firm. His main area of interest is drought management, and he acknowledges, not without reserves, the strategic action of the State of Arizona, to which he himself has contributed:

I really believe we ought to be able to do some cloud seeding up in the Colorado Rockies. I really do because no matter what we do, drought or no drought, were in a perpetual drought in Arizona. When I was director of ADWR, I set up a team to try to define what a drought is. We couldn't do it. Now the governor has a task force on drought and they've come up with about 15 definitions they've lifted from a lot of different places, but they really don't really apply here. We're in a perpetual drought. The question and what I told the Drought Task Force is that at least on the river to a certain extent in Central Arizona, we don't care what the weather is here.

(Archival Interview - 2004)

However, compared to California, the State of Arizona can, in his view, be confident of overcoming the crisis, with the proviso that water conservation policies are applied over the long term.[7]

The rapprochement between expert managers and the coalition of local conservationists and state administrators is characterized by the adoption of shared instruments (Baudot 2011), rather than shared policy objectives. These instruments consist of skills in the field of technical information and in an understanding of the kind of policies that play an essential role. Many expert managers have an engineering background, having occupied important posts in public water agencies before becoming consultants in the private sector (see Box on p. 96 in the same chapter). Attentive to state and interstate issues, they are capable of intervening in very localized issues, providing more general expertise about the Colorado River Basin.

This convergence of interests has also encouraged a number of local professionals to join the coalition. In this regard, the director of the City of Phoenix Water Services represents the reconciliation between the promotion of conservationism and the constraints of management. During an interview, it was mentioned that the support provided by the city to measures limiting water consumption and water recycling are due, not to accepted ecological values underpinning those policies per se, but rather to the assessment of the interests of the institution to which she belongs. The trade-off is between guaranteeing a water supply to Phoenix and the desire for the continuous expansion of small, neighboring cities that may attempt to circumvent the Groundwater Management Act by exploiting aquifers in order to demonstrate the existence of sufficient water resources for new construction projects. Moreover, there is a recognition that the municipality does not, for obvious reasons linked to economic profitability, want to see a fall in consumption of water; therefore, its rapprochement with the water conservation coalition is, once again, based on a shared use of a number of approaches to water management.

---

7   In addition to the information here that was gathered from archives and an interview, the quotations are taken from archived interviews from the Central Arizona Project Oral History project.

98 *Reinventing water conservation*

The conditions of social success in the "water business": technical skills and their variations

To understand what a water department director does on an ordinary day, that is, what are the institutional abilities required and how does one have to adapt to it, we can study a nationwide job search for a new director at the municipality of Tucson, which manages a share of the Colorado River. It reads as follows:

> Reporting to an Assistant City Manager and serving as a key member of the City's Executive Leadership Team, the Director manages the City's largest enterprise department with an operating budget of $120 million, a capital budget of $65 million, and 580 employees. Ideal candidates are progressive leaders with a strong background in regional collaboration, possess outstanding interpersonal skills, display a proven background in financial and utility management, with the demonstrated ability to work in a team environment with city management and staff. Ten (10) years of progressive management experience in directing, planning, and administering the operation of a water utility required, as is a Bachelor's degree in Business or Public Administration, Public Management, Engineering, or a related scientific field; Master's degree in business or related field desired.

This is a description of a "manager," of a professional with a specific skill set. What is desired in terms of educational trajectory is not necessarily a technical degree though. Knowledge of hydrologic models and formulas, for instance, may be helpful, but not the most important factor when taken together with a series of other traits. There is a limit to such "professional," technical qualities. Being able to work with a diverse group of people and navigate different institutional and therefore bureaucratic hierarchies is also key. All this is clear from the first lines, which do not so much emphasize managing flows of water, but flows of finances and people, millions of dollars, and hundreds of employees. Such a description could go for nearly any water agency. Such are the calls for a manager of people, or in the words of the outline above, a "leader" who is not only that, but "progressive" (a word used twice in the space of four lines), thinking and anticipating what the future might hold. This is but one generalized portrait of what someone who "makes their living in water" might look like and an account of the concerns that someone in this position must navigate. Thus, these individuals have to navigate much more than water and there are several dimensions to this habitus that can be discussed. The question here is what type of person might be predisposed to, or perhaps it is better to say, be "a natural" in, water management. What this examination reveals is the specific disposition of "water professionals."

The first case presented here[8] is of interest because it represents the specificity of the *ecological habitus* that becomes cultivated, and indeed is rewarded; that is,

---

8   In this part of the book, different from previous sections presenting public functions, the names of the interviewees will be anonymized. Additionally, much of what is included in these sections is based on interviews and archival materials gathered from May to September of 2017 in Arizona.

it can be seen that one finds oneself *naturally* in a position to be a part of certain institutions and the collective conservation ethic that they espouse. Such a trajectory is not atypical and might be considered part of a kind of "new guard." This is part of a historical process within the field of water professionals that (as it was seen that the technical habitus alone was not all that was needed) – with its final realization in the building of dams and other infrastructures aimed at taming the West – we see that the project of expansion had to become one of conservation and ecological concern. Such a concern is only becoming more ubiquitous in the field as the Bureau of Reclamation (BOR) itself has recognized some of its faults and, as was explained on many occasions during the fieldwork, the BOR needed to create a kind of "new brand" for itself, emphasizing its ability to provide and assist lower-level administrations, for example, Pima County with financial and technical skills (often by providing the expertise of PhDs with experience in advanced statistical climate, groundwater, and other kinds of models), as well as the ability to collaborate. The federal role then is often to unite strategic interests that would benefit the ethic of forward-thinking (conservation-minded) agencies in specific regions where they face severe problems, such as ongoing drought.

Genesis of an ecological habitus

M.A.'s career is an example of the variability that can encompass the trajectories of the new guard of water professionals, but also of the inculcation of the ecologically minded habitus that comes to be engendered in the Pima County region as one comes into contact with more traditional agencies of water management, but also NGOs, universities, and community groups. It is these types of institutional relations that codify the specific ecological orientation aimed at the reintegration of man and nature and a opposing against the old technocratic model of pure engineering. Although M.A. would begin their university career with an interest in languages, these interests quickly altered and, by building partnerships with professors, they were able to earn credentials in conservation ecology during graduate study. Their interests then came to be in an array of related watershed management best practices based on ecological research into vegetation, erosion, and species conservation. But, it was more than just an academic interest that furthered M.A.'s career. During time spent as a research assistant after graduation, M.A. would gain skills that, combined with a strong background in ecological and sustainable management principles, would translate well into later roles working toward almost identical ends in Pima County, where work on watershed management, etc. could easily be coupled with drought planning and conservation. Through work at the university, research was coupled with the coordination of various projects, budget tracking, writing grants, and also designing web tools and conservation films. These qualities were coupled with some technical skills, however, such as the ability to use geographic computer modeling, as well as work with databases and the dissemination of the best practices in using such tools for sustainability planning. These skills are useful of course within the dimensions of formal positions with governments in achieving water management

100 *Reinventing water conservation*

plans, etc. However, they are also useful for other activities such as education and outreach, for which there have been a growing number of programs like those at the University of Arizona, Arizona State, and Northern Arizona, each of which have specific applied water research centers. Along with the work that is involved with these centers, a strong linkage is often made with stakeholders such as the Watershed Management Group in Pima County, whose mission is to use and promote sustainable water practices in their community.

The second case presented here is of interest for understanding the movement from general and perhaps more tangible technical skills toward more intangible abilities like project management, drafting policy, etc., which is what really is at stake in upper-level water management positions. It also shows a homologous variant of some aspects of both the old and new guards. C.K's trajectory, begun in the early 1970s was at the juncture of this structural transformation. The trajectory also presents a very clear interest from an early age in engineering, finally realized later at the university, and then more or less jettisoned by the time "professionalization" in the water sector occurs.

From engineering to building a career in water policy

C.K. grew up in a semi-rural town near Phoenix, Arizona. Although it was difficult finding the right fit with a major at the university, eventually civil engineering felt like a vocation that could provide a good career. In fact, becoming an engineer began to present itself early on in unexpected ways. A good student in high school, C.K. made the National Honor Society. As a reward for the upper classman in this association, the members were taken on a school field trip to the Hoover Dam. It was an enthralling experience. "It was so cool!" The impression that this massive structure left inspired the rest of C.K.'s career, and left an indelible impression, being referenced many years later as an influence and motivation. Shortly after graduating, a job was secured with a private engineering company in an entry-level civil engineering position, which was certainly interesting because it entailed working on the CAP canal in the early 1980s. It was a time of "paying dues," leading to work that would later garner much greater passion. This was a time before the widespread use of computers as well, and all the calculations and drawings had to be done totally by hand. And so, working on a large project, the CAP, even though it was just one section of it, was an education in technical know-how, that still seems marvelous by today's standards. Yet, technical skills were not what would remain of ultimate value over the long duration of C.K.'s career.

Those early years were formative in C.K.'s thinking, moving forward, and perhaps the most important skills learned there, working long days in the desert and living out of a hotel for long periods of time, were about project management, coordination, and communication. It was these non-technical skills that became important, which at that time were not explicitly a focus of engineering programs, although now they have become much more a focus of the curriculum. It was only once C.K. got out into the field and got their hands dirty that they could really develop these abilities. Needing a little more stability in life, and always loving the town where they went to college, C.K. was eventually able to find long-term employment working as an engineer for a regional government, looking to work up through the ranks. Later C.K. would come back to water policy and management specifically, though after spending time doing further pure engineering work in the early days. Elaborating projects with different government agencies, working for species conservation with Pima County, and tying that work to the federal Bureau of Reclamation to study water use and conservation became long-term projects that required a sustained effort. All of these traits are clear examples of the need and importance of the abilities achieved in different institutions and realized only through the implementation of water policies and organizational practices beyond traditional engineering.

What is surprising here is that such early exposure to the realities of major engineering projects is often recalled as being the keystone of a successful career, but not for the technical skills that are gained. Such competence is often only used indirectly. It is used in reference, as something transformed into a *symbolic capital* giving authority to the work. Especially in the cases of those professionals with engineering backgrounds, there would be a lack of legitimacy to their careers without it, as this is the main source of knowledge on which they rely. This is one of the forms of capital that are often at stake in this field in the process of being called upon to do more advanced work. Indeed, some water professionals hold "PE" designations, the abbreviation for professional engineer. They put this on their business cards and at the bottom of emails. And yet, this is about as far as this distinction goes, because, as several professionals explained, they "have it [the PE certification], but I wouldn't feel comfortable signing off on plans or anything like that ... not *really* qualified." At least this is how it functions for water professionals who must deal in water policy more often than in the construction of dams, canals, pipelines, and wastewater treatment facilities. Not really being qualified means that although they had passed the difficult exams and took the years to complete the process, the reality of making and approving plans for bridges that people walk on and dams that hold back the floods is not a part of the job anymore, and such things require consistent practice. But, the symbolic profits of this have already been reaped. Once these skills fall out of use, it would take a lot for someone to get back up to speed with them.

It has an important symbolic quality though and, interestingly, it is not at all the same for others who hold PhDs or Master's degrees. Especially in relation to more "scholastic" endeavors, like a PhD, this diploma is not very useful unless it is of an applied nature to the point that they will be resistant to mentioning such an achievement among water professional peers. However, a Master's in Business Administration (MBA), just like the job outline described above, is a very desirable advanced degree, as it has some practical application. Although a PhD in statistical modeling, for instance, might be at the top of a resume (such a trajectory is not uncommon in management positions even in the federal BOR), it

102   *Reinventing water conservation*

is the *practical skills* that a water agency or government can *use* that are desired. However, advanced degree holders generally are considered to be "unemployable, because they spend so much time on one thing for five years." This is not to mention the fact that a PhD can be unattractive to a smaller government body that may not want to pay top dollar for such competence. The degree of technical specialization then is a fine line to walk between what is too much and what may be too little.

The case described above of C.K. goes to show the utility of a technical background and how this may be engendered from an early age, but transform later in a career. It also shows the necessary transition into "soft skills" of collaboration and management expertise that often refer back to engineering expertise, and yet it represents, beyond that, a more collective and interpretive model of thinking that forms the backbone of everyday practice. Such practices often consist of daily meetings, briefings on drought, writing memos to other agencies about a common issue they wish to work on together, etc. As is seen in the next example, a fondness for technical and formulaic ways of doing things can be seen early on in some careers, but the ability to move up in the hierarchy of this field is totally dependent on reorienting oneself toward the mobilization of interpersonal skills and social properties.

Moving up the hierarchy in the field of water professionals

F.B. explained his trajectory in similar terms to C.K, but also emphasized that he could not have predicted that he would be "working in water." This is a common sentiment. Introduction to the field is often portrayed as serendipitous, but once socialized, one is unable to abandon it. F.B. had the skills to work in water engineering based on his university training and so it was an easy fit for him once he got into the work. It would eventually become a lifelong passion and interest. It was mentioned that some characteristics that relate back to a more general habitus informed his career from very early on, even to his childhood. He explained that he has always liked a complex challenge. As a kid he loved to solve puzzles and to tinker with toys and machines.

Surely, engineers might generally say that this kind of general inquisitiveness is a necessary component to the type of mind that will be useful at solving differential equations and designing bridges and other structures as might be required in a college engineering curriculum. However, F.B. was quick to point out that one can have these skills, technical abilities, and a mind that likes to solve problems, and give a clear answer to an equation, but in order to "move up a level," something else is needed, a kind of "X-factor" of interpersonal skills and management abilities that allow one to function in areas less focused on making a nice blueprint and more on how to bring diverse agents together and to articulate goals for the collective benefit. This was a common point of agreement among many of these professionals. F.B. described it in reference to some of his staff and in reference to upward mobility within the water community. He explained these skills and the

Reinventing water conservation   103

concerns that occur at the level of water policy as something occurring beyond the technical, and as opposed to water management, in the following way:

> [I]f you just want to be a water system engineer or wastewater engineer, just get your engineering degree and those are the skills you need, you don't need public speaking and good written skills necessarily, I mean it does help, but … something I see with my highly technical staff is that they are great at design, at building things, but aren't great at communicating what they're doing, and why they are doing it, because so much of what we do in the water business is collaborative, policy, you know we've got to get our water rates through mayor and council, which we do every year. You have to get up and explain what you're doing and why you're doing it and you have to understand all the technical aspects so you can explain what we need to do and you have to understand the technical and a lot of times the policy and regulations are driving the things as well.

Where the technical staff are competent in building and designing infrastructure, and making decisions that will affect the physical functioning of water delivery in its material dimension, the ability to deal with water policy issues exists on a different plane. There is a kind of intangible competence that is often not learned in engineering programs, and it is what can be gained with perhaps a Master's degree in civil engineering with a specialization in environmental policy, or an MBA, or of course with direct experience. This involves knowing how to deal with city councils and the public for instance. This helps to explain some of the diversity that was observed in the field. For example, when the state agency ADWR sends representatives to speak on water policy issues of the state, these people especially were found to hold degrees in interdisciplinary programs or management, or at least have a career built in legal departments where they have had to argue for specific policies or interpretations of law. It is also important to know how to communicate well in a way that lets people know that you are technically competent, and also to realize that you have to keep projects running on time and allow the system and staff to function effectively, often while keeping an eye on what the larger administration wants. You must keep people satisfied that the economy and potential of the city or town is not being neglected.

As mentioned before, some levels of diploma are more attractive than others and offer different skills and can help or hinder the trajectory of a career based on the experiences gained. What has yet to be questioned though, especially in light of the common narratives of technical mastery of the Western landscape by engineers, is how someone can function in this field without a technical background at all.

The non-technical water professional

One surprising finding of this research has been that some of the most successful water professionals have had humanities and social science backgrounds. When

104 *Reinventing water conservation*

they lacked in technical competence, they were able to learn on the job. The aptitude to deploy other skills, for example of negotiation or often nuanced knowledge of laws and water agreements, has allowed them to manage water more effectively as well as the staff that surrounded them. In this way, with such a trajectory, one has to tap directly into the more intangible abilities that are often gained later in a more typical professional's career. Such people are often described quite vaguely as being "really smart,"[9] and have critical thinking skills that could allow them to "think differently," in ways that a purely technical mind, apparently, does not allow. One professional, who holds degrees in the humanities, explained that some people can say the right things, but it's an ability to innovate and "be different" that sets the more successful ones apart.

> ... a lot of people are saying the right things, but it's just a matter of watching and making sure the action is there. A lot of folks talk about large projects like desalination or moving water is around. I think it's important to look at those, but I also think it's important to look outside the box.
>
> (Interview, 2016)

This statement identifies that projects often thought of as being technical, like desalination plants, are not always the answer, nor are they quite as "technical" in the way one might suppose. The so-called "box" is a technical one. What lies outside that is the job of those in water agencies and districts who must negotiate new delivery deals while staying within existing infrastructural constraints. The "action" has to be there to collaborate, to sit through long meetings that try to hammer out new deals, instead of just "talk." While some are able to cite a career development that moves from the technical to the more policy-oriented side of this line of work, once inside water management and the semi-autonomous professional sphere, some are able to cultivate certain qualities to allow them to move up the ladder of this hierarchical field, which is often based on taking advantage of opportune moments along the way. At these moments, one can find a "back door" into water policy and therefore the more "professionalized" work. They draw from legitimacy gained in the area of technical engineering practice that is fostered by the institution and rewarded by it. Below is one example of such a career development.

From engineering skills to managerial functions

I.B is an environmental engineer by training with a Master's degree from a university with strong ties to local water agencies in the area. Many people are often hired through this university because of their expertise and the school's commitment to applied sciences. His background as a foreigner is

---

9   This kind of notion is especially espoused by those with long exposure in the field. See the transcript of Kathy Ferris, who was at the genesis of Arizona's innovative Groundwater Management Act in the late 1970s. See Interview from 2005 at http://www.cap-az.com/about-us/oral-hist ory-transcripts.

quite interesting as well, and unique among the managers and professionals of this microcosmos. But in fact, the same processes and dispositions are at work in him that have already been shown in some of the others.

For example, I.B. explained in great detail that the organization that hired him liked that he had some business experience. As a young man, before coming to America, he was able to work for his father's business where he learned how to deal with people over the counter, keeping track of funds, and generally being responsible. For some, they must wait until they actually get into the job as a water systems engineer, for example, to start gaining these interpersonal skills, but for I.B., this came easy due to his previous exposure to the necessity of these characteristics. This ability to be responsible and to find a way for people to trust him with work would prove highly useful as he made the transition into the field of water management. He has technical beginnings similar to the others described, but such commitments eventually transform into different responsibilities and practices.

I.B.'s career started to take off because, when working in a temporary position doing advanced testing on a new wastewater treatment facility, he was willing to do the hard work of trying out new chemicals and compounds, of balancing equations, of carefully measuring the quality of water – all things that he was learning on the fly, in conjunction with his classwork, that no one else was apparently willing to do. From the perspective of the agency, why would they pay thousands of dollars for a full-time consultant when it would be possible to have a student do it for free? Over time though, this commitment paid off. He was able to make a lengthy report that was widely circulated to staff and also upper-level management who were very impressed by the work to the extent that they offered him a longer appointment with regular pay. After a couple of years, and consistently receiving high scores on his evaluations, he was able to move up to project manager. It was at this moment that his skills and competence would be rewarded in the form of a challenge. Could he move outside of his technical competencies and handle policy? Could he go outside the box? He explained the situation this way in three phases toward work on a water treatment plant:

I learned a lot and especially from the legal committee, every month we would meet twice, the legal committee was all lawyers, I am the only non-lawyer … I wrote the contract from the second phase of the project. I wrote the contract and took it to the city contract specialist, he read it and he said, come back tomorrow and we will go over it. I came back the next day and he said, what law college did you graduate from? I said, come on, I am a technical person, I have no idea about law. He said, are you kidding? I said no. I just learned from these guys who make the contracts.

With the legal and policy teams impressed, this experience was a kind of "rite of passage" from the technical universe into the policy universe. In the policy universe, the expectation is to deal with laws and regulations, writing contracts, etc.

106 *Reinventing water conservation*

Technical competence was present, because the feasibility of this or that project, of this or that plan, has to be understood and communicated at a general level. But then the project has to be negotiated, to be mediated by certain criteria that are often beyond the scope of the technician. This type of experience was often reported – to have a moment in a career that seems to suddenly make everything clearer, that is, to open up the *space of the possible,* to use Bourdieu's terminology. A career that may have been somewhat limited, after exhibiting certain qualities, can be transformed into something that was previously unimaginable. As this habitus begins to cement itself with its tools of law and norms of institutional behavior though, it is not enough to cement oneself in this field. For that, a vast network of interpersonal contacts must be made and maintained.

T.T. is another engineer by training, but, as he himself described, he has often not functioned in an engineering capacity. As he has built his career, he mentioned that the ability to build human connections has been a vital dimension of his development, to the extent that the jobs he had been hired to do, both in the public and the private sectors, hinged on this. In addition, potential employers look for this component of a resume in someone who will function at the level of municipal water policy director, for instance. Having a strong network within the water community in Arizona, or even internationally, was a characteristic that his employer was looking for in a manager. This also has very practical implications on the job toward building consensus, a principle of the field, which is essential to effective, efficient management and policy. This is realized in opposition to a sense of competitiveness. "Local water providers are not our competitors," as T.T. explained, "but they are our partners ... these are all things to the extent that we can interconnect from a planning perspective, but also from a physical infrastructure perspective ... it helps us all." The ability to have a strong network of people who have a common vision is a central component of this process of water management, where people are not thought of as competitors as in a market-based approach to water delivery, but as collaborators and cohabitants in this field of "water professionals." When something needs to be achieved, the whole agency needs to be able to stand behind it, and it should ideally be in accordance with the rest of the field's interests.

The example of how networking is approached as well as how a common vision comes to embed itself at all levels of water management toward a consensual approach shows the necessity of adherence to this frame of thinking and acting, but also it shows how powerful the legal and political dimensions have become for water management, in a way that could not possibly be seen if only understanding it from its technical dimension. In order for one to participate in the debates at the highest levels of water governance, one has to carry a habitus that has shown the dual ability to exist in a political and legal world, that of water policy, which is nearly always learned in a practical way, by spending years working on plans for the state or a water agency, of writing contracts for a new water plant, of negotiating deals to exchange groundwater for surface water and the associated rights. All of these processes are intensely complicated and require years of institutional commitment.

Institutional architecture and the production of consensus

If water conservation might seem to be the expression of a local realignment of coalitions, the Groundwater Management Act provides an example of the persistence of state and federal levels of action, which serve as resources in the struggles and processes that characterize the construction of coalitions. The way in which various levels of water policy are articulated must be taken into account, in that, in relation to the drought, water management in Arizona involves, for both historical and conjunctural reasons, a vast array of different institutions. Since the introduction of the Groundwater Management Act, water managers have gradually formed a fully-fledged professional milieu that, although encompassing a multiplicity of different points of view, is nevertheless characterized by an ensemble of shared beliefs.

On the one hand, it is generally accepted that the Arizona authorities know how to manage drought and that, since the state was founded in 1912, they have had to deal with problems associated with boosting economic development in an arid context.[10] This idea was mentioned both by directors of state agencies and experts working in various public and private institutions.[11] According to the director of the City of Phoenix Water Services Department, "in Arizona, we have learned to manage drought for more than one century, we know how to handle it" (interview, June 2015). On the other hand, the view was expressed that Arizona's accumulated expertise makes it possible if not to resolve, then at least to avoid, disputes, and that the quest for a consensus constitutes at once the goal, the means, and the precondition of effective "water governance." This is the main difference between Arizona and California, a state whose role in the regional economy is based on an overexploitation not only of its own natural resources, but also those of neighboring states.[12] California refuses point blank to renegotiate agreements that, on the basis of largely overoptimistic predictions about available water supply, guarantee it the lion's share of Colorado River water.[13] In comparison to their profligate neighbor, water managers interviewed in Arizona presented their initiatives as sober, prudent, and based on realistic forecasts about the future of the resource.

This consensus about the "sustainable" objectives of water policy and their compatibility with the economic development of the region involves not only the directors of state agencies, but also city administrators and leaders of local environmental organizations. J.T., statewide AMA director at the Arizona Department of Water Resources, who set out on his career as an engineer in the Pima County

---

10 Sheridan T. (2012) *Arizona: A History*, Tucson, The University of Arizona Press.

11 ADWR (2014), "Arizona's Next Century: A Strategic Vision on Water for Water Sustainability."

12 Reisner M. (1985) *Cadillac Desert. The American West and its Disappearing Water*, New York, Penguin; Worster D. (1986) *Rivers of Empire. Water, Aridity, and the Growth of the American West*, New York and Oxford: Oxford University Press.

13 Summit A. R. (2013). *Contested Waters. An Environmental History of the Colorado River*. Boulder: University Press of Colorado.

108 *Reinventing water conservation*

Wastewater Reclamation Department, before holding positions in a variety of regional water agencies, affirms that "finding an equilibrium between the economic development of Arizona and ecosystem conservation is one of the goals of ADWR, meanwhile we stay in the frame of the environmental norms of the state code" (interview, July 2015). This reflects the position taken, albeit in a different register, by one of the heads of the ecologically minded NGO, Watershed Management Group, when promoting initiatives to safeguard the watershed around Tucson. Citizen action makes it possible to protect water that "renews your spirit, recharges our land, and so much more. With water, we give you shade, food, beauty, community, and hope." But this points out that this conservationist approach must be financed, notably, to establish a "water balance model," a tool shared "with area residents, policy makers, and land managers.[14]

It would, therefore, seem unthinkable to promote water conservation policies that fail to pay heed to economic interests, even in the minds of the most progressive of this milieu. The risks associated with drought mean that it is imperative to develop "good practices" and "good governance," guaranteeing water supply. While environmental concerns are taken into account, they are not treated as ends in themselves. Instead, they are subordinated to the needs of collective well-being, with an emphasis placed on economic development. Rather than focusing on the protection of ecosystems and biodiversity, water managers emphasize the importance of conserving the resources required to underpin the state's continued development. Their discourse establishes a consensus, at once broad and flexible, that covers a variety of approaches to balance economic and ecological needs. It is in this context that water conservation in Pima County has succeeded in realigning water policy coalitions and promoting new beliefs based on local initiatives.

Local conservationism and federal norms: the specificity of Pima County, Arizona

For a long time now, Southern Arizona and Pima County in particular have been considered as unique within the *water community*. Indeed, the citizens are highly aware of the need to maintain a strong *conservation ethic* and push government officials and water professionals to stay true to these ideals, which are often viewed in opposition to that of Phoenix and larger metropoles. Below is an excerpt from a newsletter to local citizens that is debating the representation of a new "Governor's Council" in Arizona that aims to handle water augmentation and drought.

> This is an important one to follow [the new council]. As noted, it's an odd mix of local control versus identifying an issue of statewide concern and giving the state the ability to set policy that preempts local decision-making. In this

---

14 Water Management Group, "We are water people," July 13, 2015.

Reinventing water conservation 109

case, I'd concede the state's preeminence in this issue as long as that defer-
ence results in protecting our long-term groundwater supply – but that leads
to yet another example of an unhealthy direction we're seeing in Phoenix on
the issue of water and setting policy for our water future.

(February 16, 2016, Tucson City Council
newsletter. Excerpt from S.K.,
city council member)

Ensuring the autonomy of Southern Arizona and its leaders is a key concern for
many. It is these and other concerns that have a long and storied history that must
be handled on a daily basis for water professionals as they aim to not go back to
the early 1990s when, with the introduction of the CAP to the region, *"Growth
was on the front burner and quality of life on the back"*, as Molly McKasson said
in her interview with the Pima County Oral History project. Therefore, there has
been a consistent and strong need to reconcile such differences, realized in the
ecological habitus of its water professionals. This has become manifest in specific
policies that demand further scrutiny here, which will help to illustrate the leadership of Southern Arizona for the state.

The 1998 Sonoran Desert Conservation Plan (SDCP), which, while not specifically targeting water, focuses on ranch conservation and the protection of natural
habitats and biological corridors, as well as on the restoration of riparian areas and
historical and cultural heritage, can be seen as the birth certificate of conservation
policies. Now considered in the United States as a trailblazing program, the SDCP
concentrates on protecting 44 species threatened by urban expansion, conserving working ranch lands, and protecting vast areas of open space. A scientific
committee mainly comprised of biologists and ecologists from the University of
Arizona, but also from the consultancy firm, Recon Environmental Inc. of San
Diego, decides which initiatives on threatened species of fauna and flora should
be taken and when. On this basis, the Land Use Plan was adopted in 2001, setting
up the Conservation Land System, which imposes restrictions and genuine planning schedules on new construction, and protects at least 80% of natural spaces
around Tucson. The SDCP thus represents an attempt to regulate the real estate
market. In 2004, the county's voters approved a credit of $174.3 million (in the
form of a bond fund) so that the county administration could acquire privately
owned parcels of land located in sensitive areas of the Conservation Land System.
Although the fund was discontinued in 2015, the initiative has since acquired
other sources of financial support at both the local and state levels (C.H., Pima
County administrator, interview, July 2015). Initially articulated around territories surrounding Tucson, conservationist policy was gradually developed in the
first decade of the 21st century, via a whole series of water conservation measures
applied across Pima County, encompassing domestic water reuse, collective uses
of stormwater, restoration, etc.[15]

---

15 See the following reports: *Plan 208. Areawide Water Quality Management Plan. Prepared in*

110 *Reinventing water conservation*

In ecological terms, there is nothing radical about the measures promoted by Pima County. They are part of a strategy focusing on compatibility with local development. Indeed, conservationist rhetoric is employed by entrepreneurs and political decision makers whenever the issue of drought – considered both as a natural phenomenon and as the object of public initiatives designed to counter its effects – cannot be avoided. While one can point to an "instrumentalization" of environmental ideas to legitimize the pursuit of growth – "business environmentalism" to use Dorceta Taylor's phrase[16] – it is also possible to view this approach as offering a platform for green ideas, putting them into the public domain and helping them acquire "social acceptability."[17] And, to an even greater degree, because water conservation is not, at first sight, incompatible with economic objectives, it contributes to the emergence of a consensus about how the resource should be managed and – to apply the paradigm of the ACF – imposes itself on the terrain of beliefs and ideas. The pragmatic position of the Pima County administrator (a sort of managing director of services) helps to spread those ideas.

C.H.: squaring the circle

Pima County administrator since 1993, C.H. is a native of Tucson, where he went to university. Holder of a Master of Science in civil engineering from the University of Arizona, he is a professional engineer. After starting out on his career as an engineer in Pima County in 1974, he was appointed head of the new Department of Transportation and Flood Control in 1979 (frequent flooding during the monsoon months of July and August create numerous problems on the roads). He then served as the assistant county manager of public works from 1986 to 1993, before being elected to the post of county administrator. Honored by the University of Arizona, he received national recognition for guiding the county to several "national awards in public works, disaster assistance and recovery, and environmental conservation." He is recognized as the "primary author of the nationally recognized Sonoran Desert Conservation Plan, which received the National Outstanding Plan Award from the American Planning Association" (*Annual Pima County Local Drought Impact Group Report* 2015).

In an interview from July 2015, he was modest in describing his career at the head of a county administration that employs over 7,300 people and has a budget of 1.3 billion dollars. First, he emphasized riverside and park development projects, and improving approaches to water recycling and the use of stormwater (some of these projects received financial aid from the

---

fulfillment of section 208 of the Clean Water Act, Pima Association of Governments, 2006; Pima County Drought Management Plan, 2006.

16 Taylor, D. (2016): 391.

17 Mayaux, P.-L. (2015) « La production de l'acceptabilité sociale », in *Revue française de science politique*, 65 (2): 237–259.

Reinventing water conservation   111

Army Corps of Engineers). He insisted on the importance of stormwater in the fight against drought, both in terms of the production of recycled water and the conservation of the watershed's ecosystems. Stormwater is used to replenish groundwater sources in areas in which Pima County is attempting to regulate urban expansion, notably by purchasing land on which to develop ranches and protected zones. This approach to the sustainable management of water resources is, according to him, a precondition of sustainable economic development. Even when he talked about Pima County's opposition to opening a mine on its territory, he pointed out that he was not against the project per se, but that he was, instead, critical of the technical approach by which it was underpinned and its impact on ecosystems. In his view, mining companies should focus on the use of recycled water rather than pumping aquifers or purchasing water from the CAP.

On the subject of the effects of climate change on resources, Arizona water managers regard water conservation in Pima County as the most appropriate "sustainable" solution to the crisis in the distribution system and to potential shortages for the region as a whole. Since 2010, the approach has been taken up, in a broad and flexible way, by directors of state agencies. In order to understand how various interests have been subsumed by this consensual discourse on water conservation, it is necessary to examine how the ideas coming out of Pima County have taken hold among water managers, thus realigning the coalitions exerting an influence over water policies. In that perspective, the academic trajectory of water professionals gives explicit correlations. Most of the local conservationists of this survey have studied engineering – especially civil engineering, but also environmental engineering. This is also the case for state administrators. In general then, it is possible to make the following hypothesis: coalitions for water conservation are based on specific technical skills linked to engineering studies. Relations between Pima County administrators are based on this common background even though they occupy different functions in state institutions, such as ADWR and CAP (Cf. Table 3.2 and Figure 3.2).

Furthermore, membership of the coalition is not restricted to the local conservationists of Pima County and Arizona state administrators. Indeed, water sector protagonists from other groups in the water sector have gravitated toward it. The rapprochement between expert managers and local conservationists is articulated around shared instruments (drought planning, water reuse measures, etc.),[18] rather than around shared political objectives. Such instruments require technical knowledge and an understanding of the policies being implemented. Like the local conservationists and state administrators, the expert managers who joined the conservationist coalition also had a background in engineering and occupied important functions in public water agencies before turning toward consultancy work in the private sector and developing their approaches in decision-making

---

18   On the role of instruments as agents of change in the field of water policy, see Baudot 2011.

112 Reinventing water conservation

Table 3.2 Repartition of water policy orientations (lines) in function of academic training (columns). The Khi-2 test between the two variables is very significant: they are strongly related, especially for the following modalities: Ecological Conservation – Formation: Engineering/Hydrology. Economic Development – Formation: Business/Management (for more statistical details, see Muñoz, Poupeau, & Razafimahefa 2019)

Formation Orientations	Business/ Management	Law	Administration	Engineering/ Hydrology	Natural sciences	Social sciences	Total
Ecological conservation	0	2	0	5	2	3	12
Institutional conservation	1	3	2	5	5	8	24
Management and planning	0	4	2	1	1	2	10
Economic development	4	3	2	0	0	1	10
Total	5	12	6	11	8	14	56

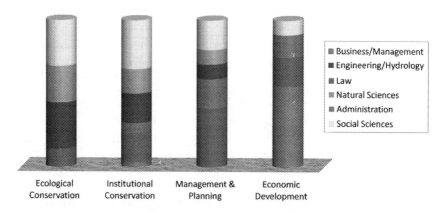

Figure 3.2 The academic trajectory of Arizona water professionals.

milieus close to state institutions. Attentive to state and interstate issues, they are capable of intervening in highly localized problems and providing expertise that takes into account broader arbitrages at the level of the Colorado River.

It was also due to this shared use of instruments and to the technical skills associated with them that a number of local professionals have joined the conservationist coalition. The director of the Water Department of the city of Phoenix described additional mechanisms for the acquisition of shared skills underlying the adoption of water conservation instruments within the constraints of urban management. During our interview, she talked about the support provided by the city for measures designed to limit consumption and encourage water reuse.

Reinventing water conservation 113

These measures do not reflect solid ecological beliefs underpinning the values of the city of Phoenix, but, instead, are the result of her assessment of the interests of the institution to which she belongs, which are largely defined by a concern with guaranteeing water supply for Phoenix and placing limits on the ambitions for the continual expansion of the surrounding towns and cities. Her organization's rapprochement with the water conservation coalition is, here again, based on the idea of sharing a certain number of water management instruments that respect state norms on groundwater resources and water recycling.

An ecological economy

Holder of a PhD in resource economics, K.S. is director of one of the biggest municipal water distribution companies in the country. Phoenix Water Services serves 1.5 million consumers on a territory of 540 square miles (approximately 1,400 square kilometers), with an annual operations budget of $280 million. She is also responsible for the processing of wastewater in the Valley of the Sun, the area in which Phoenix is located. The very size of the concession doubtless explains why so many initiatives are being pursued there. As her departmental biography states:

Phoenix's water supply is sound and sustainable as a result of multiple water sources and a logical, methodical approach to supply planning, infrastructure management, conservation, and drought preparation. All of the city's highly treated wastewater is recycled and reused for crops, ecosystem restoration, aquifer recharge, and energy production at the Palo Verde Nuclear Generating Station. Phoenix's water and sewer rates are among the lowest of large cities nationwide.

While keeping this in mind though, she remains realistic about the situation that her city and the Colorado River Basin face. On March 22, 2018, she testified before the US Senate Committee on Energy and Natural Resources stating in her opening remarks that:

The 2018 Water Supply Outlook for the Colorado River Basin is terrible. Basin-wide, snowpack stands at a paltry 72% of normal and on the Salt & Verde River system, which supplies 60% of the water used in Phoenix, it stands at only 22%. The last time we faced these conditions was in 2002 – but back then, we faced them with a Colorado River reservoir system that was nearly full. Today, we face those conditions with a system that is only half full. After nearly two decades of drought on the Colorado River System, we have no way of knowing whether this is year eighteen of an eighteen-year drought or year eighteen of a 100-year mega-drought. Perhaps the word drought no longer applies. It appears that diminished snowpack and precipitation, along with record-breaking heat, is the new normal.

In this new normal, we must plan methodically for worst-case scenarios, because the consequences of failing to deliver safe, clean, reliable water

114 *Reinventing water conservation*

supplies are unthinkable. A recent Reuters article noted that three years ago the chance of a three-year drought in Cape Town, South Africa was less than 1%. Cape Town is now learning, in the most tragic way, that any scenario that results in a loss of water supply to a major city – however unlikely – is unacceptable and must be proactively avoided. The kicker is that planning for water supply resiliency, and the infrastructure necessary to achieve it, is a long-term, continual effort. By the time Cape Town knew it was in serious trouble, it was too late to build the necessary infrastructure to prevent worse-case outcomes. When it comes to water supply availability, Phoenix is held to a higher standard than any other city in the country. That's as it should be. We are after all located in the middle of the Sonoran Desert and therefore our standard must be absolute certainty. Public health mandates it. Economic investment is contingent upon it. Quality of life depends on it.[19]

While she is, due to her institutional allegiance and the preferences that she declares, a "local professional," her position at Phoenix Water Services means that she is nevertheless able to bridge the gap between academic experts and consultants employed by the state. She is a member of the Scientific Committee at Arizona State University's Decision Center for a Desert City, of the Water Resources Research Center at the University of Arizona, of the Kyl Center for Water Policy at Morrison Institute, and of the Focus Area Council of the Water Research Foundation. She is also a member of the Rates and Charges Subcommittee of the American Water Works Association, a powerful professional association based in Denver, Colorado. The convergence of her interests with those of the conservationist coalition is expressed more in terms of the connections established at the level of state action in favor of collective equilibria than in terms of local concerns about ecosystems. Highly revealing of the instruments shared by the conservationist coalition is "Drought, Drought Everywhere: Arizona's Planning," the paper she delivered at the National Conference of the American Planning Association, held in Phoenix in April 2016.

The emergence of a conservationist coalition led to focus the attention on the practices and instruments applied by water managers in the fight against drought.[20] The results suggest that a shared agreement about what instruments should be applied encourages the emergence of a consensus and the formation of a new coalition in which a formerly marginal entity (Pima County) is able to promote its tools and ideas in a manner convincing enough to be appropriated by most of the protagonists of drought management. This is why it would doubtless be preferable to

---

19 This and other testimonies are available to the public through the US Senate Committee's website. See for example: https://www.energy.senate.gov/public/index.cfm/files/serve?File_id=F8D 0EBDB-A7F5-49BC-A142-36B5A30538B6.

20 Le Bourhis, J.-P. (2003) « Complexité et trajectoires d'apprentissage dans l'action publique. Les instruments de gestion durable des ressources en eau en France et au Royaume-Uni », *Revue internationale de politique comparée*, 10 (2): 161–175.

Reinventing water conservation 115

consider these instruments not as simple tools of governability,[21] but, instead, as "second rank institutions," in the sense defined by Dominique Lorrain:[22] markers of differences associated not only with beliefs, but also with institutional positions and the interests of organizations in administrations whose power is based on a strict management of natural resources.[23] However, through this and other chapters we have not tried to chart a causal chain of events, but rather a contingent historical lineage in which the diffusion of the ideas of conservation and ecological management may seem accelerated only because of the reconstruction of events that our project necessitates. However, what we have done, through the empirical work and the analysis of networks of water professionals is provide evidence for how the cross-fertilization of these ideas occurs, which gives credence to the claim that, when considering water policy as a field, homologous, that is, structurally similar, the positions taken over time can develop in quite geographically distant locales. In the end, two avenues of research, both with a strong methodological dimension, emerge from this approach.

First, the analysis of the realignment of coalitions articulated around water conservation – an environmental theme largely neglected in such research – leads to revisiting the debate about the invisibility and fragmentation of the institution of the state in the United States (Béland & Vergniolle 2014). Consequently, to understand the realignment of drought management policies, we need to take into account the articulation of different levels of action and the way in which the institutional architecture impacts on the development of water policies. In such a complex sphere, the more central institutions need minor institutions to ensure that their policies are implemented, appropriating what are, a priori, the most improbable ideas (water conservation in Arizona). This perspective is capable of filling certain lacunae in the coalition analysis of the process of production of public policies by demonstrating that a subsystem of institutions in which interdependence and the absence of a regulatory monopoly exerted by any one of them produces such a degree of uncertainty about the results (Teisman 2000) that conflicts are, in practice, either marginalized or ignored in order to produce consensus and agreement, which is all the more vague and flexible in that it is based on "second rank institutions" that can be used by everyone (drought action plans, for example).

On the other hand, the introduction of new variables, for example academic backgrounds and career paths, which have mainly been addressed from a qualitative point of view in this chapter, suggests a potential for an analysis of the social determinants of systems of action – particularly the role of engineers and strategies designed to convert engineers' technical skills to the sphere of water

21 Sterner, T. (2016) *Les instruments de la politique environnementale*, Paris, Collège de France/ Fayard; Tirole, J. (2016) *Economie du bien commun*, Paris, Presses Universitaires de France.
22 Lorrain, D. (2008) Les institutions de second rang, *Entreprises et histoire*, 50 (1): 6–18.
23 Molle, F., Mollinga, P. P., & Wester, P. (2009) Hydraulic bureaucracies and the hydraulic mission: Flows of water, flows of power, *Water Alternatives*, 2 (3): 328–345.

116 *Reinventing water conservation*

management. What is required is an analytical framework adapted to the study of the multilevel dimension of water policy that goes beyond visible interactions between protagonists in the water sector in Arizona and takes into account all the variables affecting the emergence of conservation and the consensus about its implementation (Cortinas et al. 2019). Such a multilevel field could reveal links between a number of networks that function as so many empirical points of entry for research (Boyer et al. 2007). Coalitions in Arizona provide an insight into water distribution issues in the Colorado River Basin and enable an understanding of the state's – over-determining – relationship with California. Therefore, the objective of a multilevel sociology of water policies will be to integrate, via a relational, systemic approach (Dubois 2014) the emergence of various theoretical frameworks used here in order to understand links between positions in networks of relations, policies adopted, convergences between second rank institutions, and the production of consensus. In this perspective, the ACF will have served a very valuable role by encouraging the application of new theoretical and methodological approaches to empirical surveys, which constitutes the first step of a field analysis. The scope of the analysis needs to be extended now in order to complete the understanding of the structuring principles of the implementation of water policy.

4 Sharing flows

New professionals with old methods

From Arizona to California: the paradox of technical instruments

In the ongoing context of climate change in the US, as well as abroad, scholars are now considering how and why there seems to be a shift, or return to "mega-projects" (Crow-Miller et al. 2017; Cortinas 2018), those infrastructures that provide huge volumes of water representing a general supply side management strategy, which was common in the mid 20th century. It is a puzzling problem to understand, for, as seen before, the era of big infrastructures seems to have ended some years ago, when the pro-growth coalitions allowed them to be achieved. Moreover, the Southern Arizona case revealed how specific forms of conservation have been emerging, mainly as a result of very high levels of institutional integration, brought about by influential protagonists seeking to protect the environment without questioning the economic order. This has led to a large, but flexible, consensus on water conservation policy – perhaps a more precise way of describing this phenomenon would be conservation tempered by institutional public necessity. At the same time, these protagonists of the water sector have consistently found ways to conserve land and water and to provide what they see as responsible sustainability. The choice of the Arizona case though does not have to do with its "representativeness," but because it is part of a field whose structures contribute to structure all the subregions of it (Bourdieu 1996).

For all these reasons, it becomes of interest to supplement the analysis of the Arizona case in the broader space of the production of water policy in the West. In that perspective, the study of California can reveal different logics. The debates about the return of mega-projects provide an intriguing angle on this. If Southern Arizona is indeed governed by a conservation ethic that is mainly promoted by university-affiliated engineers and technicians who seek to reconcile the economic order with the needs of ecology by small-scale conservation, then the paradox of the technical instruments of water policy is that they are used to combat issues that the first era of big infrastructures helped to bring about. However, in California, what could be considered apparently as the same technical fixes do not seem to be the direct result of conservation, as the practices of water professionals, politicians, and public administrators are based on double-edged logic.

118 *Sharing flows*

In some instances, they are making a return to the same basic strategy that was present so many years ago – build to get more water supply – but for the most part, in the higher echelons of the water field, the engineers have been, or are being, replaced by social agents with new expertise and social profiles. On the other hand, though, the role of engineers is mainly in the realm of operators and technicians, and in the logic of this group, conservation takes on a completely different form from Arizona because it is mandated from the state.

With this in mind, some recapitulation on Arizona/California relations and California's specific situation are in order. The historical legacy is that Arizona's and California's water supplies are linked in a way that is unlike any other two states in the country. Indeed, the *Arizona v. California* Supreme Court case is still taught as the great epic of American water legal battles in specialized water law courses in the American West. However, in recent years, and despite the often poor relations existing between the representatives of these states, today's water professionals are much more likely to reach consensus and achieve shared goals.

However, in spite of a degree of quelling the tensions between state representatives, the hydrological situation in Arizona and California remains unequal and therefore the socio-ecological stakes remain high. California continues to have priority on the Colorado River and Arizona remains the state whose supply would be cut first in the case of a "declared shortage" (declared by the secretary of the interior [SOI]) on the river. However, California has faced a "deeper" and perhaps more unequally spread drought than in Arizona insofar as there are intensely dry "patches" of land in California, such as in the Central Valley where rainfall is uncommon, only exacerbated by the less than average rainfall. Indeed, the history of drought remains within the historical legacy of the state. Notably from 1987 to 1992, a "state-wide drought emergency" was declared, as well as in 2007–2010 and 2012–2017. To be sure, droughts are part of life in the American desert West. But what has changed in the most recent droughts, is that below-average rainfall is now being increasingly associated with above-average temperatures. Such observations are consistent with what the numerous recent reports documenting climate change in arid regions have noted as well. In what follows, we map the institutions of water management in California as way to grasp the finer points of the response to the situation of life with less water.

The fragmented and unbalanced space of water institutions in California

The institutional and regulatory water framework in California seems totally fragmented at first glance to the point of it being a popular pronouncement. As one commentator noted,

> We have very dumb governance here in America on our water. Well, if I told you in the state of Texas 4,600 separate water districts and water utilities and the state of California 3,000 such areas – every state has multiple, multiple,

Sharing flows 119

multiple irrigation districts and utilities which means that you have a gridlock on policy and you cannot come together.

(Fieldnotes, March 2016)

If the statement that the California water system is fragmented is nothing new (Pincetl et al. 2016), the logic and outcomes of this fragmentation provide a socio-logical interest. California is composed of a great number of agencies and suppliers, each with their own powers over different water areas (livestock, water quality, water distribution, permissions for use, etc.). This heterogeneity already appears at the level of the water sources used in California, although the waters of the Colorado River serving Southern California fall under the ultimate authority of the Department of the Interior. Some users are direct contractors of the latter, and, in that capacity, they negotiate the Colorado River water issues directly with the federal department through their representative organ, the Colorado River Board of California. In this sense, the state government agencies are in a weak position with regard to the Colorado River's water, while contractors such as the Metropolitan Water District of Southern California (best known as the MET) enjoy significant political power. Two authors have made extensive investment in the study of the MET, easily the most written about agency in the West. Erie (2006) and Gottlieb (2007) maintain that this agency is the "product and agent of California's 150 years experiment in water resources planning" (Erie 2006: 241). The MET is important for its links to all major Colorado River water users by means of physical infrastructures (26 agencies and 38 board members), but, per-haps even more importantly, it's general manager will always be a key negotiator not only within the state, but also with the federal and state government and on any interstate agreements.

But, although the MET might appear to centralize authority, one cannot for-get that the MET does not act alone. Not only is the relationship between some of the larger members, such as the Imperial Irrigation District (IID) or the San Diego County Water Authority (SDCWA), contentious, there are many other water interests to satisfy. In Los Angeles alone there are more than 100 responsi-ble agencies (Pincetl et al. 2016). Furthermore, California state institutions have power over the management of water circulating within the state, but these pow-ers are limited to certain areas of water management: quality, wildlife, planning, etc. The power over water management in terms of prices, distribution systems, development of projects such as the construction of recycling plants, reservoirs, etc., remains in the hands of water suppliers who are controlled by municipal or county governments or by farm producers. In addition, these suppliers are finan-cially autonomous, as they produce their own resources through the sale of water or receive them from local governments. Indeed, as the need for new projects has been realized, these local entities have increasingly sold their new schemes as a form of local autonomy to their constituents.

This same structural logic takes place at the level of the state. There are dif-ferent agencies having powers over water issues (Gottlieb 1988): the Department of Water Resources (planning division), the Department of Fish and Wildlife,

120 *Sharing flows*

the Environmental Protection Agency, etc. Altogether, 29 agencies with powers over water issues, which act in a relatively autonomous and not necessarily coordinated way. All these groups establish standards that have an impact on water management, but they are not integrated into a centralized water management framework. Compared to Arizona, a long-time rival for the use of the Colorado River, California's regulations on environmental issues have been consistently on the political agenda at least since the days of a fairly progressive republican governor in Arnold Schwarzenegger and today with Democrat Jerry Brown who has made water issues a key area of concern.

There is also a great difference in the rights that govern the use of water in California. There are basically two kinds of water rights: riparian rights and appropriative rights. The former is linked to the ownership of land and the latter to a system of prior appropriation of amounts of water in which whoever uses a particular water first acquires a priority over others. In parallel to these two systems, in 1914 the first state water code was created, which established that a state agency, the Water Resources Control Board, was to be held responsible for the management of water usage to maintain a certain control over the resource. However, users with appropriative rights prior to 1914 are left out of this control. These "pre-fourteen rights" basically concern some irrigation districts, among which are Imperial Valley, Palo Verde Irrigation District, and Coachella Valley. Again, state powers can be exercised in a limited way over water suppliers. Despite this apparent disequilibrium, the protagonists of this subfield have over time been able to adapt themselves, even sometimes creating new institutions (e.g. Colorado River Board of California) to provide a common vision for the many disparate institutions and interests. In order to understand this in practical sense and the power issues at stake in the struggles for water, an overall view on water institutions and their main characteristics is necessary.

Positions and skills of the water protagonists

Beyond the ascribed fragmentation, an overall view of California's water institutions allows us to determine several distinct principles of organization (Cortinas 2018). It reveals several kinds of practices related not only to the institutions themselves, but also to the socio-professional characteristics of their managers. More precisely, water institutions in California can be differentiated between operating institutions that manage water flows (canals, pipelines, prices, etc.), and regulating institutions that develop environmental standards, which is tantamount to referring to the water suppliers, whose main function is to sell water, and to institutions that are in charge of establishing the use of these waters.[1]

---

1 In this text, the term *regulators* refers to institutions from government and administration having political jurisdictions on water issues. *Operators* are water agencies supplying water to smaller water agencies or to the final consumer (water districts and irrigation districts) and not having

On the operating side, the water suppliers manage different water resource allocations, giving each of them a certain presence and influence. These suppliers can act as negotiators in matters relating to the Colorado River being contractors (MET, Palo Verde Irrigation District, Coachella Valley, Los Angeles, and San Diego), and can also bargain indirectly as they belong to the boards of directors of the negotiating agencies (Colorado River Board of California). The opposition between those who essentially sell water (cities) and those who not only sell it, but also negotiate in some way the use that will be given to this water (MET or IDD), is also based on the level of education of their managers. In most cases, municipal water district managers have a lower level of education than those in charge of larger agencies, but a higher civil engineer workforce operates at the head of small municipal districts, where "diplomatic" dispositions are not such a necessity. On the regulating side, institutions have to be considered in connection with NGOs, think tanks, and academic institutions. Such groups are able to exercise legal influence on the responses that address the hydrologic transition: state or federal agencies or state or federal regulators.

Management skills are important in any institution. For example, holding an MBA or a Master's in public administration is not an indicator allowing the differentiation of operators and regulators, as many of the managers of regulating institutions or water suppliers possess an MBA or public administration diploma. Hydro-engineering skills (e.g. managing water resources through aquifer recharging, recycling water, and any other technique different than building mega-projects such as dams, canals, etc.) play the same role that management skills do. Civil engineering skills can be found in many city water agencies. Managers of big water suppliers present characteristics closer to the regulators than the smaller suppliers. Big suppliers are essentially differentiated from the regulators by the type of professional career they hold – in water agencies and not in state or federal institutions – which supports the hypothesis that local agencies are working to differentiate and set themselves apart from the big players. As many agencies note in their public relations campaigns for new water reuse and desalination projects, these are promoted for "local and reliable water for the future."

The institutional regulators (State Water Resources Control Board, Planning Division of Department of Water Resources) are chaired by people whose technical and environmental expertise has been recognized in public institutions that deal with extremely strong economic organizations in California. Some common profiles include education at prestigious, but also progressive, universities such as Harvard University, New York University, University of California, at Berkeley, etc. Such an education enables them to achieve prestigious professional positions that allow them to focus their interests and aspirations to participate in the public

---

any seat in any political institution related to water (e.g. West Basin Water District, etc.). Finally, *contractors* are all the water and irrigation districts having a contract signed with the SOI allowing them to use a certain amount of Colorado River water (e.g. MET, Imperial Irrigation District, Palo Verde Irrigation District. etc.).

122 *Sharing flows*

interest. From the 1970s to the 1980s (that is, when environmental standards were established in California), these professionals were called on to offer their service in the public sector. These people, who have been referred to as those "Fighting for the environment from inside the Establishment,"[2] have slowly helped to turn the state's focus onto specific environmental activities.

A good example is the chair of the State Water Resources Control Board. The mission of this agency is to manage water use in California and implement water quality standards. F.M. was appointed to this agency and designated chair by the governor of California in 2013. She was born in Los Angeles into a middle-class family with both her parents working as civil servants. She graduated from Harvard University with a degree in East Asian studies due to her interest in politics. She then received her juris doctorate focusing on environmental law from New York University and at the same time was a founder of Heal the Bay – an environmental organization in Los Angeles fighting to reduce pollution in the Santa Monica Bay. From this position and with the political network she was able to develop when the political climate of the city was favorable, she was appointed by the mayor of the City of Los Angeles for the development of environmental regulation. From there she served on the board of many non-governmental organizations (NGOs) and public agencies. It is worth mentioning that she was hired as director for an important environmental group, the Natural Resources Defense Council, and in the public sector she served as regional administrator of the US Environmental Protection Agency.

As far as the directors of large water agencies are concerned, they are lawyers, managers, or hydro-engineering specialists, as they are on the regulator's side, but often without formal training in environmental matters. Due to the water supply they manage, they are intermediaries and they are also recognized as contractors for the Colorado River, therefore, official negotiators (representatives or contractors) able to negotiate on Colorado issues with the SOI. The professionals with access to high level positions often develop within the same water supply agency or in any case, in water supply agencies in the same geographical area. In the first group (state regulators), there could be job variation from NGOs to the public sector, but in this other group where there is horizontal movement, it occurs between the private sector and the water supply agency. The chair positions are maintained thanks to the capacity to furnish water supply to the clients, juggling the multiple interests at play. As these large agencies usually group together on their board, different municipalities with different interests or farmers with different features – farms of differing sizes, products and characteristics must be handled diplomatically. This interest-based bargaining within boards of directors goes along with the need to deal with the set of existing environmental and regulatory standards while continuing to generate the necessary economic benefit for its

---

2   Los Angeles Times, 1990. Fighting for the Environment from Inside the Establishment, *Los Angeles Times,* September 2, 1990. Available from: http://articles.latimes.com/1990-09-02/opinion/op-1718_1_felicia-marcus/3

Sharing flows 123

activities. The path of J.K., the general manager of one of these large agencies, is a prime example of such a trajectory.

Management and legal skills become valuable in the water world
J.K. was born in Los Angeles into a middle-class and educated family – his father is a criminal court judge. He received his bachelor's degree in history from the prestigious University of California at Berkeley. After a legal career, he received his JD from Santa Clara University Law School in California, also near San Francisco. He began his career as a criminal defense attorney following in the footsteps of his father and grandfather, but after a year he moved into the sector of transportation, dealing in the purchase and sale of land. He worked as an urban planning consultant for municipalities, having legal insight into the regulations governing these issues. From this experience, J.K. was hired by the major water supply agency of the Los Angeles metropolitan area to work on the development and negotiation of contracts regarding the agency's land purchase and infrastructure construction activities. His ability to deal with the California Code of Regulations and obtain permits to build large water reservoirs planned by the agency or new canals to bring more water to the south of the state, earned him the appointment of MET general manager. This nomination is a milestone in the water management field, all the more since assigning the chair position to a lawyer rather than a civil engineer in one of the most important water supply agency in the country, had never been done before.

In municipal water agencies that are not Bureau of Reclamation (BOR) contractors and that manage small amounts of water, the directors have developed their professional careers at the municipal level, in the same or different cities. They are likely to have a bachelor's degree and may have experience in the field of municipal management as managers or in private companies in the water sector or municipal water agencies. In these cases, it is important to point out their local context of working experience. The professional career of K.L., director of a water agency mapped in this position, is a good example of this kind of path. K.L. was born in New York in 1949 in a working-class family. He was able to study at university, and, after receiving his bachelor's degree in industrial engineering, he worked in the Los Angeles County Sanitation District. Then he worked in the private sector as a water resource management consultant. After the birth of his first child, he started his management career in a number of local water supply agencies in Southern California.

But there is still one more category of positions that should be explicated. It corresponds to those people working for non-governmental and academic institutions, grouped together under the category of "think tanks." The case of the director of the Water Program of the Pacific Institute is a good example of such a profile. H.C. was born near San Francisco in 1975 in a middle-class family. Her father was an environmental engineer with a highly technical profile, specializing in technologies for cleaning up contaminated groundwater, and her mother

124 *Sharing flows*

was a nurse. She received a degree in molecular environmental biology from the University of California at Berkeley. More precisely, she specialized in molecular biochemistry. This choice stemmed from her desire to engage in technical study related to nature. At Berkeley, she came into contact with the issue of climate change, leading her to enroll in an MA course in energy and resources, which combined scientific knowledge and public policy with the intention of becoming a more engaged civil actor. Using this knowledge, H.C. began to work at a Berkeley research center for climate change and energy efficiency for about five years until a lab director told her about the opportunity to work at the Pacific Institute (PI), which was founded by the person who had created the Master's program previously attended by her and the lab director. H.C. has been working for the PI for eleven years. She believes that public policy questions must be informed by scientific knowledge and that the water transition in California lacked data production and research, something that she hopes to provide to improve decision-making.

Controlling water and gaining political power

To go further in the analysis, it's possible to see that the implementation of water policy instruments is determined by institutional power, the instruments available to each position, and the professional and academic profiles of each water manager. As far as regulators are concerned, the guidelines focus on socio-environmental issues (ecosystem restoration). They are also about planning a water policy able to meet the industrial/agricultural and human demand, taking into account the need to protect the environment. To reach this objective, specific policies need to be developed (e.g. to reduce water demand). Bearing in mind the professional and academic profiles of the regulators in question, this goal can be achieved by changing the institutional architecture in order to improve the role of the state. As far as the professionals in this space are concerned, those with a more technical profile in water resource management have the goal of creating new organizational structures, promoting integrated water management. As to those with expertise in legal issues, they need to create control and inspection instruments leading progressively toward the implementation of public control (better control and centrality of ecosystems) over the economically oriented approach of the water suppliers.

The regulatory and control instruments of this space have been applied to promote one of the directions shared by all the agents of the regulatory space: conservation. The point is to reduce water consumption by conserving more water: replacing garden lawns with gravel or other materials that do not need water, such as artificial turf, using more water-efficient irrigation technologies, building reservoirs to capture and hold rainwater, etc. Thanks to the force of law and its regulatory capacity, this position has crystallized in California where a compulsory reduction in water consumption has been promulgated by Governor Jerry Brown and for the Colorado River by the SOI.

Within suppliers there is homogeneity with respect to the priority guidelines to be followed to address the water crisis. They continue to provide water supply

Sharing flows 125

meeting the present and future demand of the industrial, urban, and agricultural sectors. The difference as to the guidelines used to meet this demand appears between BOR contractors with Colorado River water rights that allow them enough supply to meet their water demand (Imperial Irrigation District, Palo Verde Irrigation District) and the suppliers with adjudicated water rights, that instead can only meet their water demand using more water than the share allocated by law up until the water crisis: that is, the MET and all the municipal agencies depending on it. The water crisis and the conservation position of the SOI led them to lose the water supplement they were using, forcing them to seek other sources. The member agencies to whom the MET delivers water also need to look for alternatives to the no longer available water supplement.

The result is that the irrigation districts that hold Colorado River water rights that correspond to the level of demand they have need, above all, to protect their water rights (Presented Perfect Rights). Apparently, the regulators could modify these rights, as the share allocated to these irrigation districts is considered disproportionate to that of the urban sector. This threat leads the irrigation districts to develop defensive strategies with a strong conservative connotation. The key is to comply with the regulators' demands in order to maintain the status quo, revealed one manager of the Imperial Irrigation District, responsible for the Colorado issues; as this civil engineer from California State Polytechnic University has followed a Master's degree in public administration at San Diego State University, he takes into account all the technical and institutional dimensions of the issue:

> We have the single largest entitlement of any other Colorado River water user, we have 70% of California's share. Metropolitan water built an aqueduct that was twice as big as their water rights and they have been using entitlements from other states. In the early 90s the other states decided to bank this water and it wasn't available anymore [for MET] so that supply got cut in half and everything was in the context on how can we keep their pipeline full [...] so we had to go in that program [water transfers] in the 90s [...] where they pay for improvements [e.g. more efficient technologies in irrigation] and they receive the benefits of that conserved water, so IID is the solution for everybody's water problem. We only do it as a defensive mechanism [...] the hope was that we became so efficient that they [water urban agencies] couldn't twist on our water anymore.
>
> (Interview with T.S., manager at IID, 2016)

The strategy and the instruments of water districts like the MET and smaller agencies, are defined according to the institutional properties and the academic and professional profiles of their managers. Thus, faced with the decision of the federal and state regulators, MET is no longer entitled to supplement its allocation from the potential excess of the Colorado River, but holds a large financial capacity due to the large amount of water that it sells and its managers' profiles, who portray both policy and management competences above technical skills.

126 *Sharing flows*

MET will base its policy on addressing the crisis on both typical measures, such as building reservoirs to store water, recycling plants, and other hydro-technical solutions of water management, as well as a whole set of instruments to tackle the situation from a management and social sciences point of view.

A new water market?

One of the instruments developed by the MET to address the water crisis is the creation of a kind of water market in California where agencies can make transactions within an established legal framework. Water markets refer thus to "the transfer, lease, or sale of water or water rights from one user to another" (Erie 2006: 170). For example, the MET signed agreements with irrigation districts within the state to receive water in return for payments that MET issues to farmers that decide to fallow their fields for a period of time so as not to use water. The MET also contracted Colorado River water users from other states to store water in their aquifers. These operations need to be based on management and policy competences; they represent a cost of millions of dollars that can only be afforded by agencies that manage a lot of water. As mentioned, the presence of water managers whose academic profile is in hydro-engineering, such as in the case of the Los Angeles Water and Power department, facilitates the appearance of these supplier strategies of water management techniques (water recycling, aquifer recharge, etc.). Some of these techniques are also promoted by the regulators and this has resulted in several hydro-engineering leaders. For the managers of these big water agencies, the choice between implementing water markets and building new reservoirs to store rainwater is not based on conservation values, but a management strategy that takes into account economic costs and efficiency to address problems such as the "structural deficit" in the Colorado River system. For example, these managers know that to build a desalination plant will increase the water rates dramatically. So, if building a new reservoir is a cheaper solution, they will choose this second option in many cases. Therefore, a desalination plant is not the favorite solution promoted by the regulators and NGOs. Additionally, it is something that would be very costly to build as well as take a very long time to obtain the permits to build it.

Some of the small agencies that buy water from the MET do not usually opt for water interchange operations among water suppliers, preferring the technical solutions of tapping water from local resources: pumping groundwater. This choice emerges in the agencies, whose managers have technical profiles (civil engineers) and bachelor's degrees. These agencies buy small amounts of water, which is tantamount to saying they have a reduced political and often financial capacity, so they cannot afford the kind of solutions developed by MET. The fact of becoming independent from MET and the uncertainty linked to the Colorado River flow, represents a strong incentive for the development of local resources. This preference is also linked to the fact that these agents lack influence in California's water issues. They can only participate in the MET's board together with dozens of other agencies with varying interests.

Concerning the protagonists from "civil society," they seem to strike back against the status quo. There is a readiness to go beyond the positions of the regulatory agents claiming that socio-environmental issues are a priority, even to the detriment of economic profitability. For this reason, they stand outside the formal institutional architecture of water policies; their influence is related to their competencies and professional careers, based on the technical skills applied in the field of natural resource management rather than the "hard" sciences. In this respect, the tools developed are very technical (better control and planning), consisting of reports on the costs and benefits of water policies that include innovative and sophisticated mathematical methods to allow the calculation of economic costs caused by environmental degradation in the production of water for the urban or agricultural sector. The director of the Pacific Institute Water Program (PIWP) elucidates the situation well saying that:

> Here we work in this science-policy interface, so doing this more technical analysis, but then I inform policy [...] unfortunately, we have so many policies without any good science and good policy has to be based on good science, but there's nobody crunching the numbers, so that's what we like to do here [at the PI].
>
> (Interview with H.C., PIWP, 2016)

Some civil society organizations do not focus on defending a specific water policy, per se, but are oriented to defend a specific natural space. Their mode of action is promoting media attention that casts more light on the problem, such as beach cleaning campaigns carried out by NGOs (e.g. the Surfrider Foundation). However, these water professionals are more clearly separated from the positions and stances of regulators. They promote a "radical" position, which consists of advocating for a paradigm of change in land-use policy in California in order to control urban growth. They also advocate for a change in the economic model of California's agricultural sector. The story of the Carlsbad Desalination Plant in San Diego is an example to examine the logics described until now in California (see Box below).

Desalination as a new instrument?

The most recent and most important desalination project to date is a plant located in San Diego County, CA, at the Encina power station. The Claude "Bud" Lewis Carlsbad Desalination Plant is "the *largest salt water desalination plant in the western hemisphere* and provides 50 million gallons of desalinated seawater per day" (Poseidonwater, emphasis in original). However, desalination is an expensive effort, and also requires legal and political resources out of reach for most agencies (Swyngedouw 2015). Of course, the right connections in the social network of people making their living in the "water business," have to be made, and the support of the private sector and large government actors is key. But, is it also possible to take into consideration the social variables that lead to the legitimization of a desalination

128   *Sharing flows*

project? This means that the basic arguments for and against desalination as a *technical practice,* are not enough to explain how and why a project is adopted or not, nor is it purely a calculation of the "hydraulic bureaucracy" conspiring against citizens out of a pure will to build new and impressive projects.

If it was true that desalination and other large mega-projects, costing millions of dollars to build in order to turn billions of gallons of sea water into a drinkable resource, was as simple as a cost-benefit analysis, or the ability to suppress environmentalists, or for politicians to rally support, then we could say that there really is a return of big infrastructure. However, our empirical research suggests that only the most skilled experts, using knowledge and technology that has advanced dramatically in the last 50 years, take on these projects with careful planning and consideration, even though it remains controversial. In 2012, the final legal agreements for water delivery were signed that said the SDCWA must purchase a minimum of 48,000 acre feet (af)/year over the course of the next 30 years from Poseidon Water. There is also an option to increase to 56,000 af/year. The water is intended to create long-term security for cities and towns within the San Diego County service area, an area that is expected to continue to grow in population and water demand. Although the idea for the project started in 1998, the drought of the last 16 years on the Colorado River was certainly an influence for decision makers to realize the need to create water security for the future, as the situation with the Colorado River continues to be uncertain. By 2020, it is anticipated that the desalination plant will be able to provide roughly 8% of San Diego's regional supply and 30% of the water created for use within San Diego County. The influence of the success of the project has yet to be fully understood, but already desalination projects are being proposed in California in places like Huntington Beach, and across the border in Rosarito, Mexico, and Puerto Penasco. It has also been reported that some defunct desalination plants may be brought back online.

The Carlsbad desalination plant is also interesting due to the fact that it is the result of transnational collaboration. Indeed, this phenomenon seems to be the only way by which to realize these massive projects. The day-to-day operations of 36 full-time employees in Carlsbad, for instance, are handled by IDE Technologies, an Israeli company that has worked on over 400 desalination plants in the past 40 years. IDE is owned jointly by Israel Chemical Ltd., a specialty mineral and chemical manufacturer, and the Delek Group, which buys and processes the shares of many major infrastructural companies throughout the world – most of the holding company's efforts have turned to natural gas lately with the discovery of significant gas fields in Israel. Many negotiations were made between Poseidon Water and the SDCWA over the course of the development of the plant. Poseidon Water, a company based out of Boston, Massachusetts (the parent company is the Canadian firm Brookfield Infrastructure Partners LP), with regional offices now in Carlsbad and Huntington Beach in California, is the main owner and developer. "Poseidon," as it is called, worked with the San Diego County Water

Sharing flows   129

Authority to create a "drought-proof" supply, something that had become a point of emphasis in the past decade and formalized in the SDCWA water plans. At the commemoration of the plant on December 14, 2015, California politician Toni Atkins hailed this public-private partnership.

Since the last major drought here a little over 20 years ago, the San Diego region has worked to conserve water as well as identify new water sources... the Poseidon project not only provides San Diego County with a drought-proof water supply, it also demonstrates how California can meet the water needs of future generations.[3]

With this background to the Carlsbad plant in mind, it is also important to consider the role of specific individuals who make their careers as water professionals in these projects. By taking their trajectories into consideration, it is possible to see how it might complicate some of the previously bifurcated visions of water policies and the many water agencies involved, where engineers have traditionally ruled supreme. Two influential figures that were intimately involved in the almost two decades of effort that it took to produce the Carlsbad plant are prime examples of this. In their profiles, we can see how their political and legal capital, their expertise beyond the technical, has made them that much more valuable for such projects.

Fighting for autonomy: a "new guard" of water professionals

In her book, Espeland (1998) describes a "new guard" of water managers. Although it is limited largely to the BOR, she explains them in the context of their work on Environmental Impact Statements (EISs), where biologists, social scientists, and others were gathered together due to new rules calling for greater environmental awareness. With the examples given here, it might be said that this phenomenon has expanded to many other facets of water management, at least since the 1990s, to show that political and legal experience have come to prominence. The trajectories of two "new guard" water professionals (P.M. and M.S.) provide insight into the valuable capital for which water professionals must compete in their work.

First, P.M. is a senior vice president of California project development with Poseidon Water. He has a variety of expertise, but his focus professionally has continued to be in the realm of desalination, which led him from a career as an engineer to law to the private sector, helping with projects in California and in other water-scarce regions. As a certified professional engineer (PE),[4] he

---

3   The Carlsbad Desalination Plant press release can be found at: http://www.poseidonwater.com/u ploads/7/6/3/6/76361825/newsrelease_12-14-2015_desalplantdedication.pdf.

4   This designation is significant in that it requires one to pass some examinations and undergo extra training over and above that for a bachelor's degree. The main function of the certification is to allow the engineer to sign off on public plans that would make him or her legally liable for any

130 *Sharing flows*

received his BS in civil engineering from in 1979 and is on the Advisory Board for the College of Engineering at San Diego State University. He began his career with a 1978 internship and then, shortly after graduating, he began as an engineer with Fluid Systems (owned by desalination membrane pioneer General Atomics[5]), the San Diego-based manufacturer of desalination membranes. When he was working there, Fluid Systems held contracts in Mexico, Saudi Arabia, and Israel. In reports, he describes being "hooked" on water, even though he was unsure about which field of engineering he wanted to follow.[6] By the 1990s though he had moved on from the private sector, maintaining his ties to water by holding several positions in the San Diego County Water Authority. It was his experience there in the public sector that made him realize the need for legal expertise. He then went on to receive his JD from the University of San Diego Law School. He described this as a professional necessity and a growing passion in one report:

> We were pushing aggressively to implement water recycling projects, and the laws and regulations in California hadn't been designed to accommodate that [...] They were really designed to get rid of sewage. We were spending a lot of our time in Sacramento, advocating for legislation and regulatory reform to allow us to recycle water.

The ability to litigate and to understand the specific laws that pertained to the technology that he was interested in, all came together around this time and, and by 1997, he left the water authority and became a consultant. His legal training became an important component of his career and provided the necessary link with Poseidon Water, who, in 1999, hired him to review and work on a permit for one of their plants. By 2000, he had joined the company full time. His trajectory is evidence of the changing nature of the multifaceted dimensions of water management in the 21st century. Furthermore, when it came to building the plant in Carlsbad, he would be a natural fit for heading up the project and partnering with a company that helped alter his career. One of the individuals with whom Poseidon aneeded to collaborate effectively was the general manager of the San Diego County Water Authority since 1996, M.S.

M.S. has been one of the more successful general managers since the inception of the SDCWA in 1945. She holds a bachelor's degree from California Polytechnic University in Pomona and a Master's in public administration from California State Consortium at Long Beach. Water was not always on her agenda as a career, although she was able to gather highly useful skills of negotiation and

---

future issues with them in the design. However, after someone like MacLaggen moves up the ranks, as another water professional explained, they often "don't feel comfortable" signing off on plans as they become out of practice and separated from pure engineering.

5   General Atomics was also San Diego-based and patented reverse osmosis in 1964.

6   He describes this experience with some detail here as well: http://www.sandiegouniontribun e.com/news/drought/sdut-desalination-carlsbad-poseidon-opening-2015dec14-htmlstory.html.

Sharing flows 131

political know-how as the assistant city manager in her hometown and then for San Diego from 1991 to 1996, before coming to the water authority. The authority serves 2.8 million people with 23 member agencies in the San Diego area. M.S. managed 250 employees and a $450 million annual budget. One of her main goals was to diversify the supply of the water authority, which was done mainly through effective negotiations on the Colorado River and by bringing desalination to Carlsbad. Outside of the desalination plant, she was influential in the 2003 Quantification Settlement Agreement (QSA) that allowed for more water to be brought from the rural farming area of Imperial Valley and a decreasing dependence on the MET in Los Angeles.

Both individuals show how desalination can reveal the social relations surrounding water management. They show that, although perhaps some technical background is needed to be an effective participant in this field, having the more intangible skills of negotiation, deal-making, and knowledge of law and politics, can coalesce into an effective career. Without the public/private alignment and without sufficient international connections, it seems that the project could not have been completed. Over the course of planning the project, the budget continued to rise and some thought it would never be built. Take this into account alongside several legal cases that were brought against the project by activist groups, like the Surfrider Foundation and San Diego Coastkeeper, and we can see that there was a real battle over this project. The lawyer for the Surfrider Foundation said in a Wall Street Journal article, "We're going to be opposing this project for the next 20 years."[7] This sentiment is indicative of some of the struggles that can be observed around these projects and how the logic of increasing a municipality's autonomy is an important factor in these struggles. But, from the perspective of the water providers, without this new plant, it would not be possible to continue to diversify supply, satisfy the growing economy of the region, and become more independent in the face of future environmental changes like climate change and water scarcity – a situation that would likely cause the citizens to pay for more expensive water from MET.

To understand the background for the issues between the SDCWA and the MET, a quick recounting of history is necessary. A significant drought struck Southern California from 1987 to 1992, which was the spark that has eventually led to the two agencies being on rather unfavorable terms. By the fourth year of drought, the MET board was contemplating how much to cut back deliveries to its member agencies. In fact, there are 36 member agencies of the MET. In particular, the SDCWA, due to the fact that it had a large and growing population, felt very threatened and vulnerable. Major rains came in 1991, but SDCWA was already beginning to think outside of their usual approach and looking at desalination as an alternative. By the late 1990s there were more serious and formal discussions about the possibility of a plant. At the turn of the century, things began to

---

7   Adapted from a piece in the *Wall Street Journal* about this project. It can be found at: http://www .wsj.com/articles/SB10001424127887324049504578545661598973132.

132 *Sharing flows*

change more dramatically. Journalist Bradley Fikes[8] has covered the evolution of the desalination plant in Carlsbad and described the situation in the early days of the idea for the plant in a recent newspaper article:

"The Poseidon plant arose out of two events at the turn of the century. First, Poseidon began a feasibility study in 2000 about building a desalination plant in Carlsbad close to the Encina power plant, the location that was ultimately chosen. Second, the San Diego County Water Authority voted in 2001 to spend $50,000 to search for good locations for a desalination plant."

The Carlsbad site had the significant advantage of being able to piggyback on an existing seawater intake-and-return system that was used to cool the power plant. It meant that the desalination plant should have less of an environmental impact than at other coastal locations. Moreover, the city of Carlsbad was interested in securing the water. By the time the feasibility study was complete in 2001, the cost for desalination per af had dropped to about $2,400. However, today the price is still lower than it would have been in 1991, but much higher than analysts were predicting.

Summary of SDCWA Cost and Conveyance Reporting - Carlsbad Desalination Plant[9]

WATER DELIVERIES			
YEAR	**2017**	**2018**	**2019**
Projected delivery (af-acre feet<?>)	49,615 af	51,772 af	50,109 af
delivered	40,419 af	40,892 af	45,038 af
Shortage	***−9,196 af***	***−10,880 af***	***−5,071 af***
WATER COST PER ACRE FOOT			
YEAR	**2017**	**2018**	**2019**
projected	$2,368	$2,439	$2,559
actual	$2,412	$2,511	$2,685
difference	***+$44***	***+$72***	***+$126***
%	***+$2%***	***+$2.87%***	***+$4.69%***
VIOLATIONS			
YEAR	**2017**	**2018**	**2019**
#	4	4	5
POSEIDON PENALTIES			
YEAR	**2017**	**2018**	**2019**
$	$3,584,478	$5,359,070	$1,965,989
TOTAL PURCHASE COST AND CONVEYANCE			
YEAR	**2017**	**2018**	**2019**
$	$101,117,803	$108,028,982	$122,889,148

---

8   See article describing part of this evolution and from which the below quote is taken at http:// www.sandiegouniontribune.com/news/2015/dec/13/poseidon-water-desalination-carlsbad-openi ng/.

9   All based upon the San Diego County Water Authority's Fiscal Year 2017-2019 Reporting for the Carlsbad plant

Sharing flows 133

As the customary planning reviews, public hearings, and reports followed, with more formal planning in the mid-2000s, several lawsuits from environmental NGOs came too. Namely, the Surfrider Foundation filed several suits, whose main lawyer filed several cases alongside the San Diego Coastkeeper and their legal team.

Environmentalism – an extreme position being brought to the center

M.G.'s involvement in the siting of the desalination plant was mainly the product of his affiliation with the San Diego Chapter of the Surfrider Foundation. He is well known for his environmental activism and counsel, but he is truly a legal polymath, having handled development projects and represented professional athletes, including surfers. He also frequently speaks at universities on environmental issues and public policy. Today, he works through the Coastal Law Group as a partner.

His commitment to environmental issues and progressive politics stems from his days at the University of California at Santa Cruz from which he graduated with a BA in biology and environmental studies in 1992. By the next year, he had received a Master's degree in conservation biology from San Francisco State University, before moving onto Lewis and Clark College in Portland, Oregon, which is highly ranked for environmental law. He would graduate with a JD in 1997.

Today, he lives very close to the site of the desalination plant in Carlsbad in Encinitas and enjoys surfing and mountain biking near there. It seems that he has found a way to pursue his passions while also becoming a major advocate for them. Including his filings, at least six unsuccessful challenges were brought against the desalination plant, mainly ones that challenged the environmental assessment and the coastal management plan that was approved, on the grounds that during the different permitting processes, the best available technologies were not being considered and the project was not in accordance with the California Water Code. In 2009, Poseidon's vice president had this to say about such legal tactics: "If not for obstructionist tactics, the Carlsbad Desalination Project could have been operational today, in which case San Diego County and its economy would have been completely inoculated against the cuts to imported water."[10]

These failed cases do not seem to have fazed this interdisciplinary lawyer though, as he was named a San Diego "super lawyer" in 2008 and 2009. Without significant experience in environmental law and policy, it would prove difficult for environmentalists to be able to legitimately act in opposition to projects such as this. The layers of regulation and law can be overwhelming for anyone not well versed in the appropriate literature in this field.

---

10 Quotation taken from http://www.waterworld.com/articles/2009/05/court-rejects-surfriders-lawsuit-over-carlsbad-desalination-project.html.

134 *Sharing flows*

But it is not so simple as to say that environmentalists are strictly opposed to desalination. In fact, desalination could be an appropriate option, but it has thus far been inappropriately explored and implemented, according to many in the region. It needs to be "done right" is their general message. The best technology needs to be used and regulations must be strictly followed. They also recognize that things have changed in environmentalism and that the situation around these plants is obviously political. In order to be up to the task of fighting for proper coastal management, they have to reconcile the challenges they face with their ecological concerns. But, in the end, the game is bigger than their local communities and these desalination plants bring in not only regional and state authorities and political powers, but also international interests who continue to build a market for desalination technology.

A different kind of water management

The challenges that are faced by the investment in reliable sources of supply such as desalination have repercussions that extend beyond the building of the plant. The MET and the SDCWA were locked in a legal battle as a result.[11] In 2016, a San Francisco Superior Court heard a second part of San Diego County Water Authority's rate case versus MET, but no ruling was made. In 2015 though, it was ruled that the rates charged by MET in 2011–2014 were illegal. This means that they were seen as violating multiple provisions of California's law and state constitution. The second ruling determined the amount of damages that the SDCWA should be awarded as a result of MET's breach of its contractual obligation to set rates for water and its delivery. The water authority has calculated that MET has overcharged San Diego County ratepayers tens of millions of dollars each year since 2011, and it is possible that SDCWA could receive greater than $180 million in damages. The SDCWA board of directors decided that they will deduct litigation expenses from whatever damages it receives and return the remaining money to its 24 member agencies in proportion to their payment of MET's overcharges over the course of the four years involved in this dispute. In addition, the SDCWA has a legal entitlement to water from the MWD system, what is known as a "preferential right." SDCWA believes that the MET has underestimated the amount of water that SDCWA has an entitlement to, which they feel should be more than the annual production of the Carlsbad Desalination Project. So, far then, these projects can be some of the most arduous logistical, legal, political, bureaucratic, and managerial endeavors to embark upon. Where, at the turn of the century, mega-projects could be built and people and landscapes devastated, this cannot happen today. So, desalination is not just a feat of engineering anymore, or at least we can justify that there needs to be a closer examination of some of these struggles – something that perhaps has not fully been taken into account before.

---

11 See http://sdcwa.org/annualreport/2015/sites/default/files/sdcwa_2015_ar.pdf (p. 24).

Sharing flows 135

One environmentalist explained that because his organization was so involved in the regulations surrounding the Carlsbad plant, even though that plant was finally permitted, it will not be possible for another like it to get through the legal system. The legal landscape has undergone a transformation in just a matter of years. Today such projects are very carefully investigated, sometimes decades in advance; and if time is not taken to build the right relationships locally as well as abroad, it would seem impossible that they can go forward. Certainly, a much more diversified approach is frequently seen in water management and planning in the West today, and desalination may be only beginning to be a part of that equation. Smaller agencies, municipalities, and districts of different kinds *have the will* to develop local supplies, which for them means, *reliable and controllable supplies*, whereas wholesale agencies, such as the Central Arizona Project (CAP) or the Salt River Project (SRP) in Arizona, or the MET in California, can only provide certain amounts of funds depending on the type of project and the political situation in the state or region. These smaller agencies sometimes would like to have greater autonomy and independence. Their boards are made up of people elected by the public and so they want to have a reliable water supply and also some stability. They want to show that they are doing all they can to prepare for the future. New projects, sometimes mega-projects like desalination, are a way to do that, and smaller-scale desalination efforts are explored when "mega"-sized plants are not feasible. So, from the perspective of a public provider of water, "why desal?"

The discussion of desalination reveals several examples of positions in the space of water institutions and the polarities governing them. On one side, we have water supply agencies focused on securing a water supply and on the other, regulators aiming to secure the water supply but also especially focused on protecting water resource quality and the environment. Such regulators often find themselves competing for better rules to protect existing water resources, whereas the supply-side group looks for new ways of financing and building infrastructure to bring new sources of water to bear. Environmentalists generally see the supply-side, infrastructural model as unsustainable, and align instead with the regulators. For them, this is the only real way to combat the needs of the economy to produce more water for growth. The supply-side group is so strong, however, that the environmentalists' logic has become one of concession in the form of regulation, not to halt supply-side projects, but rather to make them better and more environmentally friendly. Along with the changes that can be demonstrated in environmentalism, changes in water management have also taken place. Today, water policy has overtaken technical capacity in many ways. A capacity to handle legal norms is more vital to the future of infrastructure than any technical ability to manage water agencies and boards. The director of one of the largest water providers in California illustrates this transformation. His career in water began after being a lawyer on land and property rights issues. When he was recruited to his new agency, he felt that the way the law was done in the water sector was largely backward and that there was a great deal of work needed. He also believed

136   *Sharing flows*

that new solutions to problems of water supply in an often water-scarce area did not need to be accomplished through the building of new projects or increasing construction like in the past:

> The challenge is less about building, but about finance or to the political will to build things. So I think the challenges are more political and financial than they are engineering. If you can get the permits and the public and the vote to go build something and get through the lawsuits and the challenges then the engineers can go do their jobs but that's not what holds us up anymore, it's the political institutions these days more than the actual engineering.
>
> (Interview, 2016)

It seems that days of the "water wars" between states like the ones of the early 20th century may have come to a close and been replaced by a more collaborative and consensual atmosphere (Fleck 2016), however a close empirical examination of the current situation in the Western United States reveals the effects of ongoing social transformations. Federal regulation protects people and the environment from blatantly irresponsible practices. Water managers receive years of education, and they study not only engineering, becoming technically competent, but they also become fluent in public relations, basic legal matters, policies, and planning techniques. A heavy layer of regulation, of public comments, of meetings in boardrooms in small water districts all the way to the boardrooms of the most powerful organizations mediates the issues of 21st-century management and we can begin to see how this so-called "hydraulic bureaucracy" really looks and operates.

An analysis of the tendencies, the capacities, the competencies, and the trajectories of the players struggling over the future of the water supply shows that projects like Carlsbad are involved in even considering a major project like ocean water desalination are fertile ground for a comprehensive analysis that accounts for the legal, the political, the institutional and the symbolic nature and importance of water management.

The California case reveals that the sector of water management in the American West cannot be summed up easily by accounting for the technical competence of a cohort of engineers, but must be understood in relation to other agents with new characteristics, new skills, and new expertise, who are trying to find new solutions to the very old problem of water scarcity. The effect of this is the introduction of newer skills and competencies, often political and legal in the case of desalination, as evidenced by some of the biographical details and narratives of the project that have been described. The hydrological crisis in California is configured on the basis of a variety of institutional positions, academic backgrounds, and competencies. On one side environmental bureaucrats and state federal agencies having academic backgrounds linked to environmental issues; this group has also people with academic careers and highly skilled activists working on NGOs. On the other side, water managers work essentially on urban or agricultural water

Sharing flows 137

supply agencies and, more marginally, civil engineers work on smaller urban water agencies. Joining these two sectors shows how professional skills can be linked to public administration, law, and hydro-engineering.

Concerning the solutions promoted to face the drought, the demand-side policies are more likely to appear on the environmental pole whereas supply-side policies appear on the pole linked to management. Supply-side policies are based on hydro-engineering solutions and management tools that correspond to the water manager's expertise. Such solutions are more likely to fit into environmental regulations of the state, in opposition to desalination plants, for example, and are more plausible – at least from short- and mid-term perspectives – than any "mega-project," which will need the support of state and federal agencies. Indeed, the representatives of state and federal agencies are not unanimously in favor of mega-projects, as some administrators wish to promote conservation policies and involve the state. Concerning the managerial pole, there are two other kinds of solutions to the hydraulic crisis: conservation policies of irrigation districts and traditional supply-side solutions. A hypothesis can be formulated from the California case: the emergence of these two solutions on the managerial pole is based on the different resources of these agents in the field. Irrigation districts promoting conservation policies have senior rights, which give them a priority in the use of water in case of cuts in the amount of water reaching California from the Colorado River. This advantaged position, combined with an environmental pole pushing toward conservation policies, makes these advantaged agents embrace regulators' positions in order to protect these senior rights. Small water agencies are the weakest water suppliers as they are dependent on bigger supplier decisions that they do not control in a period of uncertainty. Moreover, these agencies have limited financial resources compared to big city agencies. Finally, they are more likely to employ civil engineers. All these elements bring them to focus on the development of local resources using traditional solutions (e.g. drilling wells) in order to ensure the water supply of their areas.

In summary, if in California the adaptation of water policy to scarcity takes different forms and is not limited to a single position, it is due not only to a fragmented institutional architecture but to the historical process in which market forces and municipal powers have achieved a certain autonomy over the state powers that allows them to be a key factor in the necessary hydrological transition. Furthermore, the developed policies do not merely deal with technical issues, but also with a conflict between these two positions – water suppliers and state and federal agencies. The implementation of water policy results from the equilibrium that each protagonist of the water sector finds to increase or maintain their relative autonomy, their areas of power, combining the resources they have (legal and financial) with the types of solutions that are possible, depending on the socio-professional career of the incumbents (management or technical) and the relations of power between institutions of water management.

138 *Sharing flows*

The California case is different from the Arizona situation. The analysis requires a next step involving these two states in the same framework: they are the most linked historically in terms of competition for the Colorado River water and the biggest users of that water in the lower Colorado Basin. They also share some similar processes in the implementation of water policy. Adaptation to scarcity leads to the confrontation of two strategies in the face of water scarcity:

> First, cities and regional water management units can attempt to gain additional water sources. They can increase the water supply by building pipelines for new surface water, by drilling new production wells, by acquiring new surface water and storage rights, by recharging aquifers for future withdrawal or for the improvement of aquifer water quality, by increasing the storage capacity of surface-water reservoirs, and by building desalination plants. Second, cities can also focus on demand reduction by implementing conservation measures and by recycling waste water.
>
> (Hess et al. 2016: 808)

The problem is thus to understand why some cities or some institutions, in each state, adopt demand-reduction policies even in areas where hydrological institutions are similar. Furthermore, it's not possible to automatically assign a strategy to an institutional property of the water protagonists: in Arizona as well as in California, the uses of policy instruments seem to depend on the social configurations in which they are implemented, breaking with some common schemes according to which public institutions would automatically support conservation policy, while private entities would naturally go for general economic growth (Lorrain & Poupeau 2016). As soon as the focus is brought to the (more detailed) level of the instruments of policy, it appears that conservation measures are sometimes promoted by unexpected operators, in order to guarantee the sustainability of local development; and the introduction of market-oriented instruments can be made by public institutions when their priority would be to regulate water management in a stronger way. For these reasons, it is necessary to study the social logics underlining the adoption of water policy instruments: the notion of field will be used to model the space constituted by the organizations in the Colorado Basin. The structural dynamic of a field allows us to understand how social agents might not be in direct interaction but at the same time they may influence others' decisions; it also brings back the differential resources and the social characteristics of the water protagonists. In that sense, it is necessary to go beyond qualitative analysis to model the space structuring water protagonists' decisions on water policy issues.

5 Implementing water policy
Instruments and their social uses

The research perspective developed in the former chapters can now be articulated into a field analysis that might systematize the different results obtained. First, the social history of water policy in the Western United States has revealed, through the rearrangement of advocacy coalitions, the emergence of a relatively autonomous system of institutions dedicated to the water management of the Colorado River Basin. Beyond each state's specificity, and the territorial struggles for the appropriation of the hydric resources, it showed how common issues have generated environmental norms that all the water protagonists are obliged to follow. This regulation had to face the imperatives of an economic development that prioritizes agro-business, extractivism, and urban growth. Second, the constitution of a world of water professionals helps to explain the progressive implementation of water conservation instruments that remain part of the "water-supply policy as a contested political process" (Hess et al. 2016: 809), and also generates a large and undetermined consensus between the different levels of government and administration. These hydro-policies break with the traditional logics of offer (large projects and infrastructures, etc.) that have driven the development of the Western United States: they provide the impulse for new instruments (water reuse, water storage, etc.) whose uses might vary in terms of the socio-institutional configurations in which they are implemented; and they also benefit from the arrival of a new type of water professional, who is more aware of ecological problems, due to their academic backgrounds and skills, not to mention the history of American water management itself.

Third, we have charted the progressive conversion of a significant fraction of the water protagonists to a form of institutional conservation. In this way, we have also handled the question of social change within the field. This may be understood as a "field effect," and, more precisely, as a product of the struggles in the field and of the relations of power they establish, as "fields are marked by struggles that constantly modify their internal power balances. The question of change within fields is therefore crucial" (Hilgers & Mangez 2015). It is in this sense that it is possible to fully realize the potential for sociological understanding based upon the logic of social fields as elaborated by Bourdieu, wherein one can see the processes of transformation within a coherent system. Indeed, this is one of the advantages of field theory as a general analytical framework, that, contrary to its

140   *Implementing water policy*

detractors' claims, it provides a unique lens through which to view and understand social reproduction, social change, and struggles for autonomy. However, the conversion to a water policy based around principles of conservation does not cover uniform logics: the rapprochement of Arizona's local institutions with regulatory authorities is very different from the implementation of water conservation policies by California's largest operators, who use market instruments such as water transfers, or even building a new supply infrastructure in the form of desalination plants, for example, or pipelines, to support these policies. It is by going back to the principles structuring the field of water policy that it becomes possible to grasp the differential logics at work in the struggles and in the development of a consensus on water conservation that can at the same time see the field of water policy as a coherent system across time and space (e.g. American states), while in the same moment its differentiation is based on policy preferences, historical legacy, and social and institutional characteristics.

Delimiting the field: a selection of specific institutions

The definition of the limits of the field of water policy consists of drawing up an initial list of the agents concerned. But this "mapping" of relevant institutions (Bourdieu & Wacquant 1992) presupposes a certain number of methodological choices concerning the principle of selection applied to those agents, all of them struggling to define their policies. The varying degrees of political and economic influence exerted by specific types of institutions, as well as the particular configurations of each state, made it necessary to identify categories of protagonists attempting to define responses to the drought, and, more broadly, various models of water management. It was less a question of constructing a sample and more a question of identifying the functions of these various organizations.

The first approach consisted of identifying those institutions that had a direct link with the Colorado River Basin at various existing levels of government. Their members meet and debate shared problems, discussing approaches to the drought. For example, the annual meeting of the Colorado River Water Users Association (CRWUA) is held every December in Las Vegas, Nevada, thereby providing an opportunity to observe all the public and private organizations concerned and understand who the key players are. The first step was to list the official institutions for each of the states of the Colorado River Basin responsible for negotiations on distributing water from the river. In Arizona, the most important institution is the Arizona Department of Water Resources, while its Californian counterpart is the Colorado River Board of California, which, independent of political control, is made up of institutions that have contracts with the Bureau of Reclamation (BOR), the federal agency responsible for the Colorado River. The Nevada equivalent is the Southern Nevada Water Authority, which is essentially a metropolitan water agency. Such information can be found on the websites of the agencies of each state. The sample used in this survey also includes institutions responsible for regulating water in each state (including the organizations mentioned above), and that exert influence via two mechanisms. On the one hand, they have the

Implementing water policy 141

capacity to apply existing laws, for example the Groundwater Management Act (1980) in Arizona, most of which focus on the management of groundwater supplies. On the other, these agencies have the power to grant water use permits for specific territories and to draw up guidelines for water management plans. Taking into account the multiplicity of institutions and situations, the overall picture of water policies at the time of the study encouraged the limitation of the detailed analysis to the states of Arizona and California, the main protagonists of the struggle for water distribution, which in many regards employ diametrically opposed approaches, as seen in the previous chapters. Nevertheless, the CRWUA meeting provides an excellent lens allowing one to begin to understand all the players and stakes involved in this diverse field.

Las Vegas: a materialization of the field
The Annual Conference of the Colorado River Water Users Association is held in Caesars Palace, one of Las Vegas's best-known hotels. Attendees include the most important men and women in the management of Colorado River water: the SOI, the commissioner of the Bureau of Reclamation, and the heads of agencies with a contract with the BOR to receive and redistribute water from the Colorado River. Directors of small- and medium-sized agencies are also present. Up to a thousand people attend the conference, an event that serves as an opportunity for the region's managers to meet one another and to hear what leaders in the field of water have to say about risks of shortages and how to deal with them. In terms of the organization of the conference, the tables in the dining room seat nine, giving conference-goers the chance to swop business cards and compare their experiences in the field of water management. This open plan presents a contrast with the closed-door sessions in which heads of the most important Colorado water agencies meet, not only with each other, but also with representatives of the federal government. There is a genuine division of space and the heads of the largest agencies are rarely to be seen in the conference rooms, because they are mostly busy laying the groundwork for future plans with the other important state-level negotiators.

Thus, the conference also provides an opportunity for the "managerial community" to make its presence felt. An important moment of the event happens on the morning of the second day. In one of the hotel's most elegant rooms, the heads of the biggest agencies in the Colorado River Basin report on the water situation and debate policy positions to be taken in regard to federal regulators, drought, etc. In a sense, this morning session is about ensuring that your central message receives a hearing. The day is organized meticulously. The flags of the states located in the Colorado River Basin and of the region's Native American Nations are displayed proudly behind the platform. Representatives of the system's five largest agencies – those located in the Lower Basin that have signed a contract with the federal government granting them the right to receive water from the Colorado River – sit at the same table. Indeed, they even offer commentary on the new presidential situation.

142   *Implementing water policy*

The message to be delivered to the new administration, set to take up its responsibilities, is clear. The agencies have, up until now, dealt reasonably well with the Colorado River Basin crisis. But, if the worst is to be avoided, the states will need help from the federal government. The slogan repeated by these managers is displayed on the screen: "Forge the Future: Collaboration, Innovation and Communication."

In spite of their differences, they have to keep on working together in order to deal with the crisis successfully. During the morning session, the five agency heads announce a new agreement with the director of the federal agency responsible for the Colorado River. The announcement is designed to send out a message of unity and cooperation, which, it has to be said, contrasts fairly sharply with the ongoing tensions characterizing the relationship between them. Nevertheless, the general idea is to present a united front and preserve their prerogatives in terms of managing water from the Colorado River. A secret to no one, this division within the field of water dictates the way in which the conference is organized. The themes presented and debated are hermetic, articulated around the field's dividing lines. For example, there is a session dedicated to agriculture, another on the problems encountered by the Native American Nations, and a third focusing on wastewater recycling, with presentations by urban water agencies.

This division is also visible in the hall hosting the exhibition stands where the agencies present their policies on "good water management." They are arranged in a line, one next to the other. The posters by which they are surrounded let us know that the object of the exercise is to highlight their "successes" and convince us of their value. The stands are full of panels, posters, DVDs, videos, and gifts displaying the logos of the various agencies. Being a good manager today means being able to manage and conserve water efficiently. Recycling is the watchword. Managing water efficiently enables the economy to prosper, a notion that has become a legitimating principle within the field. The skills required to be a good manager stand in contrast to the kind of expertise highlighted during the construction of the major dams and reservoirs of the American West of the past, namely the skills associated with civil engineering underpinning the region's infrastructure.

The identification of organizations allocating water from the Colorado River is made in terms of various types of users. These include municipal companies – operating either independently or in groups, under the aegis of water districts – and irrigation companies, or "irrigation districts," delivering water to the agricultural sector. This list is based on the directory of users of Colorado River water for the year 2015, which is to be found in the annual report of the Colorado River Water User's Association, alongside the water agencies of individual states, cities, and irrigation districts. Conflicts about potential risks of restrictions on the use of Colorado River water also reveal the importance of environmentalist organizations, which, since the 1970s (Gottlieb 1988), have influenced water policy in the American West. There have been a number of agreements, laws, and regulations

Implementing water policy   143

associated with the drought; meetings and symposia on possible responses to the crisis have been held and water projects have been challenged in the courts (for example, the desalination facility near San Diego). Groups of urban and rural water agencies that act as political lobbies vis-à-vis issues related to the drought are also taken into account. One such group is the Association of California Water Agencies (ACWA), which encompasses hundreds of operators in California and about which we learned, through our interviews, that its director had been a very important figure in the elaboration of the Water Plan introduced by the governor of California in 2013.

Water agencies and irrigation districts not allocating water from the Colorado River are not included among the institutions of the sample that we constructed. It should be noted that another group, namely the Native American Nations, was left out of the study for theoretical and practical reasons (Chavarochette 2016). While they do exert a high degree of influence on water policy – they function as operators selling water to local, essentially urban distributors, and receive subsidies from hydroelectric facilities based on their territories, for example – few of them are involved in the decision-making process regarding potential restrictions on the use of water from the Colorado River in the same way that state agencies are. This is at least partly due to their status as priority users, which protects them from restrictions. We observed that Indian Nations were absent in two ways from debates and conflicts associated with the drought. On the one hand, they are rarely represented at public meetings or, especially, in decision-making centers, and, on the other, they are rarely mentioned by other agents in debates and negotiations, except when the issues at hand specifically involve allocations of their water or other interests (e.g. cultural heritage). Consequently, representatives of the Nations monitor approaches to the drought without necessarily playing an active role or taking explicit positions. Compared to other actors on the list of selected organizations, the Nations also account for only a small percentage of total water consumption. With all these considerations in mind, our exploratory survey generated a list of institutions, thereby delimiting, in a provisional manner, the frontiers of the field of water policy in the Colorado River Basin.

The objective of this initial list, which encompasses hundreds of institutions, is to define the principles underpinning the selection of organizations that, in spite of the diversity of institutional situations in the Colorado River Basin, could be meaningfully compared with one another. A series of information-gathering interviews was conducted in Arizona and California in order to verify the pertinence of the choices made. This involved a transition from the preliminary selection phase, based on the institutions involved in the distribution of water from the Colorado River, to a process that took into account information derived directly from water policy professionals. Initially, this adjustment phase in the process of defining the field studied focused not only on the largest water agencies (in terms of demographic and political influence) involved in a de facto way in managing the distribution of water from the basin, but also on the irrigation districts allocated the largest volumes and/or granted priority use of water from the Colorado River (Imperial Irrigation District, Yuma, Palo Verde Irrigation District, Coachella

144   *Implementing water policy*

Valley Irrigation District, etc.). These information-gathering interviews enabled us to gain an understanding of the influence wielded by the secretary of the interior (SOI) as well, and, therefore, by the federal government, in the elaboration of measures taken to counter the effects of the drought. In effect, the secretary of the interior is the only agent with the power to introduce restrictions on water use in the American West. Via the federal agency, the Bureau of Reclamation, the SOI is the political authority responsible for the nation's natural resources and, consequently, for the Colorado River.

Urban operators, which are all, to some degree, dependent on the Colorado River in terms of their access to alternative water sources, and of their position in regard to priority appropriation rights and demographic dynamics, were also studied more closely; indeed, it is vital to take into consideration their influence over approaches to the drought. Only the largest cities in terms of demographics were retained (Phoenix, Las Vegas, Tucson, Los Angeles, San Diego), along with a small number of expanding cities particularly active in regard to water policy due to their dependence on water from the Colorado River. Small, expanding cities attempt to circumvent current environmental rules in order to procure the new water supplies required for their development, while stable cities (like Phoenix and Tucson) tend to apply conservationist measures in order to guarantee water supply (Benites et al. 2016). The end result of these various approaches was a new list of 67 institutions in the states of the Colorado River Basin that are suffering the effects of the drought. This final list constitutes a basis for establishing the ensemble of variables that our documentary research and interviews enabled us to define as pertinent to an understanding of approaches applied to the drought.

Based on the construction of this list of institutions exercising a *field effect*, the delimitation of the field enables the development of a database in which the rows represent the water agents included in the analysis, and the columns represent the variables indispensable to an understanding of water policy. However, it should be pointed out that drawing up a list of pertinent variables is far more difficult than establishing lists of easily identifiable populations of individuals, such as, for example, intellectuals, writers, artists, and economists, for whom variables such as social origin and academic qualifications appear to be self-evident. Indeed, this is the normal approach for those sociologists following Bourdieu's method. For example, compared to the field of publishing (Bourdieu 1997), it is indeed hard to isolate unique economic indicators in the water sector. This may seem surprising, but institutions active in the field of water policy can be regulatory agencies, service providers, or irrigation districts, purchasing, selling, or regulating highly variable volumes of water. Furthermore, the field of water policy does not necessarily offer a homology of social properties between a company and its directors, of the kind observed in a study of the employer class (Bourdieu 1997) or the publishing sector (Bourdieu 1997). In the states considered for this survey, there are water professionals who occupy management positions in the institutions concerned whose career paths have involved directorships in various institutions of which they were not owners (except, perhaps, in the case of irrigation districts). While these positions are not occupied by chance, in the sense that they require certified, recognized skills, the homology applied to other field studies could not be mapped cleanly onto our study of water policies.

In order to define an ensemble of effective variables, the first task is to identify existing conflicts over water shortages and the situation of the Colorado River in each of the regions. For this, press articles on each of the states concerned (particularly California and Arizona in the Lower Basin) are helpful. These conflicts reveal the positions taken by the main policy protagonists – in respect to their priority objectives and instruments of public action – to countering the effects of the drought. This initial phase makes it possible to define various issues faced by individual states concerning access to water and the types of rights and uses they enjoy. For example, the majority of the challenges faced by Nevada are urban, as the bulk of the state's population is residing in Las Vegas, where most of the tax revenue is generated. Meanwhile, in California, most water issues stem from the rural/urban divide; in spite of urban growth, agriculture still accounts for almost 80% of water use. Other states, like Colorado and Arizona, present more contrasted situations in terms of rural/urban water distribution, but while the first enjoys upstream access to water from the river, the second is characterized by a relative shortage due to the fact that it is located downstream, which means that it does not enjoy priority rights. It should also be noted that Arizona's other surface water and groundwater supplies have been affected by decades of intensive use remedied, at least partially, by the Groundwater Management Act in 1980.

Positions taken are defined using documents from various institutions. Although there is a certain consensus about approaches to be taken to the drought, the problem was to find out what actions, beyond injunctions to conservation expressed in decrees issued by the governor or in plans elaborated by state administrations, is actually implemented on an institutional level. Priority public actions are thus analyzed on a case-by-case basis, in order to discern which, out of all those described, are priority actions for the institutions. Differences in positions taken are then defined using a wide variety of sources, such as newspaper articles, in which various managers active in the institutions studied talked about the drought and the desired approaches to countering it. The water plans of the institutions, which include guidelines for their water policy, are also analyzed. All these sources are then subjected to a content analysis carried out with QDAMiner software. Lengthy interviews with each of the institutional managers concerned complete the search for information in addition to our interviews with non-governmental organizations (NGOs) and the other relevant agents (n = 74).

Water policy instruments as position takings

Water policy instruments are generally divided into a number of different categories (Glachand 2004): regulatory instruments (technical norms, administrative authorizations, etc.) destined to constrain behaviors ("command and control approach"); economic instruments used as incentives (subsidies, taxes, permits, procurement contracts, etc.); informational instruments (ecological damage and ways of avoiding or repairing it); and voluntary and negotiated agreements

146 *Implementing water policy*

(industrial commitments to objectives). It is not possible to apply this classificatory system to water policies implemented in the American West, mostly because the organizations selected for the study are involved in very different contexts and levels of action. For example, operators distribute water in a given territory, while state administrations regulate distribution at a broader level by producing norms, delivering permits, and so on. Consequently, the implementation of water policies does not correspond to the criteria elaborated by Christopher Hood (1986). In this area, there is no discernable governance system capable of defining homogeneous modalities, equivalent forms of authority, financial resources operating in a comparable way, and a capacity for direct actions (organization) with similar impacts. Water policies are applied by a variety of organizations in ways that are too different from each other to be able to draw up a coherent list of instruments. Some operators play on their pricing strategies, some authorities apply rating packages, but the fact that they do not directly intervene in the market means that the price of water cannot be considered as a shared instrument.

Consequently, this diversity of functions has been incorporated into the research in order to compare the respective modes of action of the institutions and their contributions to the development and implementation of water policies designed to counter the risk of water shortages. The approach is based on the observation that "a socio-technical system making it possible to intervene in a field of action consists in a large number of instruments that fall into different categories (policy-related, legal, technical)" (Lorrain 2004: 191). In view of the diversity of potential instruments and the various contexts in which they can be applied in the Colorado River Basin as a whole, the focus is placed on the practices of the agents concerned, and on what approaches they take to water shortages in terms of, for example, building new infrastructure to access new sources of supply (canals, dams, desalination facilities, more restrictive regulations, etc.), and of implementing measures intended to reduce consumption (limiting flows, taxation, manipulating prices). This was achieved by means of interviews conducted with professionals in the sector and through an analysis of the water plans of each individual institution as already mentioned.

Based on the idea that "in action, instruments do not exist on their own" (Lorrain 2004: 170), this research enables us to identify the effective functions that define objectives capable of orienting the choice of instruments. If instruments fashion public opinion, ways of seeing and conceiving approaches to the drought draw up the framework, or, more precisely, the principles of vision and division of the social world on the basis of which those instruments are established and applied. For example, a rainwater storage instrument can be implemented and shared by institutions whose objectives are diametrically opposed. It could be used to ecological ends, for example by a conservationist institution like Pima County in Arizona (Poupeau et al. 2018), or to protect priority rights by federal authorities like the Imperial Irrigation District in California. The use of the category "priority orientations" is thus a way of taking into account the social meaning of the instruments applied. These orientations were determined during the empirical research process, according to two principles.

Implementing water policy 147

The first concerns the regime of causality that agents establish to deal with the risk of water shortages. This risk is often associated with excessive water use, a notion that covers a variety of situations. Some observers call into question the modes of production and lifestyles in the American West; others focus on technical issues that can, they believe, be solved via the application of more efficient technologies. But the risk of water shortages can be linked to another causality, this one based on the notion of offer. According to this approach, more effective supply is required in order to deal with the climatic conditions of the American West. Some commentators who take this view emphasize the need to diversify sources of water in order to supply new dams, new wells, and new reservoirs, while others provide a critique of water management, arguing that the fragmented nature of the system prevents water transfers from users in surplus zones to users in deficit zones.

The second principle concerns the objectives of water policies, which oscillate between two extremes. On the one hand, water is seen as a service that underpins and boosts economic and urban growth; on the other, it is considered a natural resource essential for balanced ecosystems and, as such, must be protected by environmental policies against excessive human use. These two structuring principles (regimes of causality and water policy objectives), along with their multiple modalities, can be summarized in terms of five "priority orientations."

- The priority accorded to the protection of ecosystems over economic activities (urbanization, industry, agriculture, etc.) defines an environmentalist approach described as "ecological conservation."
- Water measures designed to boost the economic sector was defined as an "economic development" approach, which acknowledges the threat of scarcity only to the degree that it can be solved with technical means; between these two approaches, different types of orientations were distinguished.
- An orientation characterized by explicit environmental objectives (the conservation of rivers and parks, wastewater processing, reduction of water use as part of an approach to the drought, etc.), which, however, reconcile those objectives with the needs of economic development. This orientation is described as "institutional conservation."
- The promotion of measures (norms, legal rules, etc.) consisting in collectively regulating uses in order to underpin future human activities in a context of recognized water scarcity was defined as "sustainable regulation."
- The emphasis placed on guaranteeing future demand from the economic sector, constitutes a "sustainable management" orientation. It is promoted more at the level of individual organizations than at the collective level.

This classification of instruments also takes into account the distinctions between various types of governance technologies (Lascoumes & Le Galès 2004: 361), based on the various types of political relations defined by instruments and the types of legitimacy they presuppose: legislative and regulatory, economic and fiscal, agreement- and incentive-based, norms and standards, and "best practices."

148 *Implementing water policy*

The models elaborated combine these various aspects in terms of their objectives. Furthermore, a distinction was made between instruments primarily used to achieve those objectives and instruments used in a secondary manner, often to reply to external injunctions to adapt to the drought. Instruments were placed in context thanks to a model incorporating three different aspects: priority objectives, principal instruments, and secondary instruments. Distinctions were made between:

- Legislative and regulatory instruments consisting in (i) protecting ecosystems and guaranteeing the universal right of access to water, (ii) guaranteeing the storage of groundwater, or, inversely, (iii) guaranteeing the priority rights of the longest-established users.
- Economic and fiscal instruments used to provide new sources of supply via (iv) the construction of infrastructure for large-scale water supply, and (v) used to develop technical solutions, some of them designed to reduce use resulting in waste.
- Agreements and incentivizing instruments designed to obtain commitment from institutions, via (vi) ensuring water quality, (vii) introducing water reuse measures (recycling facilities, flooding and stormwater prevention infrastructure), (viii) water plans designed to regulate territorial systems over the long term (storage, reserves).
- Informational instruments consisting in promoting (ix) education about the environment, or (x) strengthening a new institutional framework for regulating water.
- Standardizing "best practice" instruments introducing adjustments in "civil society" and competitive mechanisms with (xi) the introduction of water markets designed to create transfers between institutional users (these are also norms and standards).

Based on these analyses, a list of priorities and preferred water policy instruments was established and structured around, on the one hand, attempts by cities and the agricultural sector to meet future demand (generally satisfied by water agencies), and, on the other, around various environmentalist objectives, ranging from a form of ecological radicalism calling into question the use of water as an economic growth factor to a form of "business environmentalism" (Taylor 2016) intended to provide solutions to the water crisis from a sectorial point of view (water quality, various kinds of risk, etc.). A number of different instruments corresponds to these priorities. Alongside traditional supply-and-demand management instruments used by water managers concerned with "good practices," the instruments of a kind of water governance, thanks to, among other things, closer coordination between institutions, make it possible to manage risks associated with drought in a more effective way. In the same perspective, but outside the bureaucratic realm, certain organizations promote extra-institutional spheres of dialog in which the protagonists of the water sector are able to develop collective solutions to the water crisis. Last, environmentalist groups, which are often locally

Implementing water policy 149

based, essentially use protests and legal approaches to fight against water policies that subordinate ecological concern to the needs of economic development.

This systematic and differentiated understanding of the issues characterizing the field enabled us to identify the social bases of the power of the actors involved. On the one hand, the major cities (Los Angeles, San Diego, Phoenix, Tucson, Las Vegas) exert a demographic and economic influence. This means that, thanks to their political clout in terms of the number of electoral representatives, they are likely to have a major impact on water management decision-making processes during periods of shortage. Consequently, their views are highly influential in official organizations that negotiate how water from the Colorado River is distributed. For example, at the annual meeting of the Colorado Water Users Association, the opinions of the director of the Metropolitan Water District of Los Angeles, which supplies nearly 20 million people, as well as the irrigation districts, and some of the largest water institutions in California (Imperial Valley, Palo Verde, Coachella Valley) and Arizona (Yuma, Pinal County) could make their voices heard, and have an important role to play.

With all these institutions involved, there is of course a great amount of water at stake. The sheer volume of water managed has two impacts. The first is associated with consumption capacity. The more water an institution buys, the greater the impact it has on the profits of the agency selling the water and, in consequence, the more the opinions of the institution tend to be taken into account. This explains why major cities like Los Angeles and Phoenix have so much influence not only on the decision-making processes of agencies that sell water, but also, due to their electoral clout, on measures taken by state governors. This kind of urban electoral impact is particularly noteworthy in states like Arizona and Nevada, where over 80% of the population lives in large cities and their metropolitan areas. A second type of impact is the volume of water managed, considered as an efficient variable in the field. This variable is also associated with water rights. For example, water from the Colorado River is allocated by law to a series of agencies that have contracts with the federal government; access to that water is a right for those agencies, and the federal government is under a legal obligation to ensure that their needs are met. In fact, the water agencies with the highest allocated volumes and the most important priority rights wield a good deal of influence in terms of policy decisions. In California, three irrigation districts receive over 80% of the water from the Colorado River allocated to the state. This is linked to the fact that, due to legislation on water rights in the American West, they have, in times of shortage, priority rights vis-à-vis the cities (O'Neill et al. 2016).

An analysis of conflicts and the issues underlying them thus highlights the role of water rights in terms of the positions taken by institutions in the American West. The legal structure regulating the use in the region of water from the Colorado River finds its roots in a doctrine going back to the 15th century known as "prior appropriation" (see Annex 1). According to this doctrine, the first person to arrive on a piece of land and use available water in a "reasonable" and "beneficial" manner has priority in regard to the use of available water in the region over anyone who came to the same basin at a later date. This doctrine led to the

150 *Implementing water policy*

introduction of a system of priorities in terms of water use, which in the event of water restrictions protects the longest-established users. More concretely, farmers generally enjoy priority rights in regard to water use due to having settled in the West before others. Consequently, the system of priority water use is an important factor in that it grants farmers, who are often, apparently, absent from public debate, a preponderant influence in the field. In terms of their demographic presence and even of the profitability associated with their use of water, they punch far above their weight.

This definition of the limits of the field and of relevant variables makes it possible to elaborate an explanatory model for the strategies developed to counter the effects of the drought. This model is developed by means of a Multiple Correspondence Analysis (MCA), a technique used for analyzing categorical data, which can represent data points (e.g. individuals or institutions) in Euclidean space to reveal patterns of correlation and disjuncture, based on various social characteristics. The fieldwork conducted via interviews, the study of practices, and the observation of meetings serves less as an "empirical validation" of various hypotheses and more as a phase in the construction of the object or as a complement to the elaboration of research hypotheses and the consolidation of relevant variables (Duval 2013).

Constructing pertinent characteristics

In the end, 10 variables divided into 3 groups, are retained with a view to defining the field occupied by the protagonists of the water sector in the American West (Table 1).

- *The capacity of action of institutions (active variables).*

    The "Role" variable is divided into 4 modalities: regulatory institutions (no. = 13), operators (no. = 19), contracting institutions for the Colorado River (no. = 20), expert organizations (NGOs, think tanks, academic institutes, no. = 14).

    The "Type of influence" variable includes 5 modalities: member of a board (no. = 15), lobby (no. = 13), expertise (no. = 13), negotiations and contractualization (no. = 13), promulgation of regulatory norms (no. = 12).

    Because, due to the fact that different types of institutions were included in the analysis (e.g. NGOs, governments, operators), it was impossible to define a homogeneous economic indicator, we took "Volume of water managed" as a proxy of the importance (political and financial capacity) of each institution. Based on our knowledge of the terrain we elaborated four classes distinguishing operators in terms of classifications extrapolated from the surveys. Operators classified on the bases of these criteria as "small," "medium," and "large" were then used to define the first three thresholds (v1: less than 0.1 maf; v2: between 0.1 and 1 maf; v3: between 1 and 4 maf). The fourth threshold (v4: more than 4 maf), which corresponds to the total volume of water from the

Implementing water policy 151

Colorado River allocated to California, enabled us to identify state and federal institutions.

Since priority rights only concern a minority of institutions, most of them in California (and in the Yuma Irrigation District in Arizona), they were not included in the quantitative analysis. They were, however, included in the analysis of strategies.

- *Characteristics of directors of institutions (active variables)*

  The highest qualifications include 4 categories: bachelor's (no. = 10), master's (no. = 30), PhDs (no. = 7), and Juris Doctorate degrees (no. = 14).

  "Types of bachelor's degrees obtained by directors of institutions" are divided into 3 categories: Engineering (no. =19), Natural sciences (no. =18), Social sciences (no. = 26), while Master's and PhDs present 4 modalities: Hydro-engineering (no. = 13), MBAs, or Master's in public administration (no. = 22), environmental studies (no. = 12), no Master's (no. = 17), plus not specified (no. = 5).

  The principal area of expertise in professional careers includes 5 modalities: Natural and environmental sciences (no. = 9), Management and planning of environmental resources (no. = 8), Water management (no. = 11), Water planning (no. = 11), Legal and economic management (no. = 17), plus one not specified (no. = 7).

  Last, the sphere in which professional careers occur has 5 modalities: public institutions (no. = 15), water utilities (no. = 25), NGOs (no. = 10), various environmentalist institutions (no. = 6, for example NGOs to public institutions), managerial institutions (no. = 6, for example public institutions to private institutions).

- *Priority objectives and water policy instruments (passive variables)*

  Priority objectives were divided into 5 modalities: ecological conservation, which rejects an emphasis on the economy (no. = 6), institutional conservation (no. = 14), which focuses on the environment while at the same time ensuring compatibility with economic development, whose affirmation as sole objective constitutes a modality of its own (economic development, no. = 17), then sustainable management, which incorporates environmental norms into water management (no. = 12), and sustainable regulation (no. = 17), which is intended to ensure that environmental norms are respected in economic activities, without unduly hindering those activities.

  Action instruments have 10 modalities: protecting ecosystems and rights of access to water (no. = 6), implementing a new management framework more attentive to environmental issues (no. = 8), measures to ensure good water quality (no. = 1), measures for recycling water (no. = 15), developing water management plans (no. = 11), implementing water markets (no. = 7), small-scale technical solutions (no. = 6), new supply sources via major infrastructure (no. = 8).

152 *Implementing water policy*

Complementary instruments applied by institutions are designed to have the most accurate view on institutions' policy actions. They encompass the following modalities: education about the environment (no. = 3), about transforming demand (no. = 1), and conserving groundwater (no. = 8). Instruments in the preceding category are distributed as follows: implementation of a new management framework more attentive to environmental issues (no. = 12), measures designed to guarantee good water quality (no. = 3), water recycling measures (no. = 17), developing water management plans (no. = 2), implementation of water markets (no. = 5), small-scale technical solutions (no. = 2), new sources of supply via major infrastructure (no. = 10).

The structure of the field of water policy

This Multiple Correspondence Analysis is interesting because the first three axes explain 37.61% of the variance, which is high for such qualitative variables. As shown in Diagrams 1 and 2 (Annex 2 p. 198 and 199), the various protagonists of the water sector are distributed along the first axis (15.03% of the variance) in terms of their role in the institutional sphere, with a very clear opposition between, on the one hand, those exercising a regulatory function on behalf of the governors of California and Arizona, and, on the other, local or metropolitan water operators and local irrigation districts (see Diagram 2). Another important point is the intermediate position of organizations such as the Los Angeles Metropolitan Water District, Association of California Water Agencies, Pima County, and the California Farm Water Coalition: public administrations, operators, and trade associations that, without formally being state institutions, influence the policies of their states due to their size, economic power, and demographics. This axis expresses the two faces of the water market, at once a material good (operators) and a symbolic good (regulators and NGOs). Inevitably, water management consists in ensuring an operational distribution of water supply and promoting an ensemble of norms designed to regulate the principles underpinning it.

The power of operators not having a direct right of use of water from the Colorado River is based on the connections they establish with one another, mainly in terms of participation on the boards of user associations or on the board of contractors (Southern Arizona Water Users Association, Association of California Water Agencies, Metropolitan Water District of Southern California (MET), etc.). For example, if a small urban water agency has a seat on the board of a regional organization it is able to exert influence it would not otherwise have, had it continued to operate on its own. The coalitions formed in the boards of regional water agencies responsible for distributing water from the Colorado River (Metropolitan Water District of Southern California, Central Arizona Project, etc.) and, often, in corporatist bodies such as the Association of California Water Agencies, the Farm Bureau in California, and the Southern Arizona Water Users Association, allow small operators to have their voices heard. The right-hand side of axis 1–2 groups together the institutions that, through these boards – on which other types

Implementing water policy 153

of organization do not sit – form an interconnected, but relatively exclusive world (e.g. Irvine Ranch Water District, San Fernando City, West Basin Municipal Water District). Moreover, the recurrence of these co-presences goes hand in hand with the multi-positionality of certain managers whose power does not so much derive from the fact that they occupy central positions as from their role as go-betweens between institutions. Water professionals like W.T. in Arizona and T.Q. in California provide good examples of the model of water professionals as "multi-positional."

Multi-positional professionals

In February 2016, W.T. was appointed executive director of the Arizona Municipal Water Users Association. As a member of the Governor's Water Augmentation Council, he has also been president of the Arizona Water Association's Water Resources Committee since 2010. The career path traveled by this water professional, who has a BA in history from Arizona State University and a Master's in history from Northern Arizona University, is not that of an engineer moving up the hierarchical ladder of a particular organization, per se. In fact, his professional trajectory is characterized by a diversification of responsibilities. His career initially developed at the local level. In 1994, he became the assistant general manager of the Metro Water District in Pima County, before his election as a member representing Pima County on the board of directors of the Central Arizona Project (CAP). He also served as vice president of the board of directors of the CAP and was president of the board's Finance, Audit & Power Committee. Above all, he played an active role in the establishment of the Water Conservation Alliance of Southern Arizona, and the Southern Arizona Water Users Association (SAWUA), whose memberships include most of the key operators in the southern portion of the state (and not only in the cities). As director of two professional associations, he sat on many management committees, notably the Environmental Working Group of the Water Resources Development Commission set up by the State of Arizona. But, as we can see, this trajectory diverges from the more expected engineering careers. Indeed, it is not totally exceptional, as is revealed by the professional itinerary of another professional from California.

In 2014, T.Q. was appointed director of the Association of California Water Agencies. This position provides him with an important role in defending the interests of cities and irrigation districts. At the interface between the private sector and various water administrations, he is also responsible for reconciling economic development with environmental conservation. His professional itinerary doubtless helped him to acquire such skills. Born in Nebraska in 1951 (his father was an accountant and his mother a librarian), he graduated with a Master's in economics from the University of California at Los Angeles (his dissertation focused on the foundation of groundwater regulations). While studying for his PhD, he worked as a water policy consultant in the well-known Californian consultancy firm, the Rand Corporation.

154 *Implementing water policy*

He was later to say that he had been deeply influenced by his time with the firm and he began developing his ideas on collaborative governance in those years. He understands the importance of consensus, stating the need to "create more political consensus so the policy moves forward" (interview, July 2016). In 1976, at the age of 25, he was hired as a junior economist by the prestigious Council of Economic Advisors at the White House. On his return from Washington, DC, in 1977, he once again took up his post at the Rand Corporation. In 1985, convinced that he no longer wanted to pursue an academic career, but, instead, to use his skills as an economist to contribute to the development of public policy, he joined the Metropolitan Water District of Southern California, where he studied the development of water markets in a context in which major projects were being called into question. In 2007, he became a member of the ACWA, an organization whose objective is to promote "sustainable" water policy in the state as a whole. When he joined the Association, he was aware that "if you want to be a successful water manager, you better care about the environment." Now the head of the ACWA, he is attempting to develop a political agenda shared by all the state's water agencies designed to influence the state policy in the water sector. As executive director of the ACWA, he made the following statement on the transformations of water management:

When I look back on my 30 years in the water world, I see tremendous change in how we manage water. The modus operandi of the 20th century was to build huge projects to move vast amounts of water to support a growing economy. (…) Now the story you hear from water managers is very different. They are investing in local resources – recycling, desalination, cleaning up contaminated groundwater and capturing stormwater. We have done a complete 180 degree turn in California water strategy from the generations that preceded us, and this is what is protecting us today during drought. We are relying on new technologies and new strategies. We are a changed industry. (…) If the drought continues into year 5, 6 and 7, then we may cut into the economic uses of both agricultural and urban areas. That should happen through the market, not regulation. (…) At the ACWA, we've carefully and strategically chosen areas when we can make a difference. We've established policy principles on rethinking storage for the 21st century, headwaters protection, and groundwater sustainability. Some of these principles – particularly groundwater – have been adopted into law. We also developed a Statewide Water Action Plan to look at water comprehensively. Important elements of this strategy have been embraced by the Brown administration. As I approach the end of my career, it is good to know that a comprehensive plan is on the table. Now we need to continue to implement it. I came of age as a teenager in the John F. Kennedy era that placed high value on public service. Making a difference is important to me. Water has turned out to be the most fascinating public policy career I ever could have imagined.

(in Schmidt Sudman & Taylor 2016: 184)

Most regulatory functions are exercised by public institutions in the various states of the Colorado River Basin (Arizona Department of Water Resources, Water Resources (Planning Division), State Water Resources Control Board, etc.) that are very close to federal administrations (SOI, BOR, etc.), as well as by NGOs and think tanks involved in drought management. As shown in Diagrams 1 and 2, their directors generally have environmental skills (left side of Diagram 1) of a different kind (environmental sciences and environmental management) to those acquired by engineers and other professionals in the water sector (engineering skills), whose careers play out as municipal operators, irrigation districts, and in water companies (right side of Diagram 1). The effective capacity to develop and apply water management norms and rules characteristic of state and federal institutions can be exercised via decrees and other legal instruments. Examples include the decree issued by the governor of California obliging water agencies to reduce their per capita consumption by 25%, and the obligation to demonstrate to the Arizona Department of Water Resources the existence of 100 years' worth of water supply before being able to initiate development programs in conformity with the GMA of 1980. Such a capacity can also be exercised by means of incentivizing instruments that define guidelines to be followed, but which present no obligation to respect them. In this perspective, the water action plans elaborated by the Water Departments of the various states are the kinds of water policies most frequently applied.

However, water regulation cannot be considered as a mechanism defined once and for all and applied in a homogenous manner. In and of itself, it constitutes a terrain of struggles to determine not only a legitimate management model, but also the defining principle on which water policies should be based. Indeed, just as T.Q. mentioned, without water professionals who learned how to become "multi-positional" the transformations of the water sector that have been outlined here, might look very different. In that perspective, the second axis (13.68% variance) shows a very clear differentiation within the regulatory side between organizations presenting, on the one hand, environmental management expertise (bottom left side of the second axis) and, on the other, organizations with environmental expertise based on scientific competences (e.g. biology, geology, chemistry) (upper left side of the second axis). On the center of axes 1 and 2 (see Diagram 1) this opposition is mirrored by that between MBAs in public administration, law and economy expertise vs. degrees in natural sciences and also between regulation capacities (bottom center of axis 2) vs. indirect influence on water policy through expertise (top left of axis 2). These two principles of expertise represented by directors belonging, respectively, to public sector institutions and contractors (e.g. MET, Imperial Irrigation District, Coachella Valley) and NGOs (as opposed on axis 2, Diagram 2). These range from water distribution between states in the Colorado River Basin, which is the object of legal negotiations, to environmental approaches focusing, in a broader perspective, on protecting resources. In such approaches, which call upon scientific expertise, engineering and the natural sciences play a central role in defining lobbying actions mainly conducted by NGOs operating at the federal or state level. Additionally, a degree of influence is exerted

156 *Implementing water policy*

by a small number of academic research centers whose directors, for example those of the Water Resources Research Center at the University of Arizona and of the Water Resources Institute in California, are invited to provide advice to the boards of state institutions.

Water regulation involves a number of competing principles of legitimacy, depending on whether water is considered as a natural resource or a service to be distributed among distinct organizations in distinct territories, or as a natural resource whose use must be established independently of institutional differences. Due to the capacity for action and environmental management with which the regulatory institutions (state administrations, coalitions of agencies) are equipped, the first principle plays a role as a dominant temporal power (most of these institutions appear in the bottom left section). Consequently, this principle defines a managerial capital directly involved in managing flows, exemplified by heads of institutions like the director of the Arizona Department of Water Resources (Cf. Chapter 3, p. 94) and F.M., an influential member of the State Water Resources Control Board of California (Cf. Chapter 4, p.122), to which environmentalist regulatory organizations dedicated to ensuring good water quality, protecting ecosystems, and planning water use – such as Natural Conservancy, the Audubon Society, and the Pacific Institute (in the upper left section) – can merely reply with a form of scientific capital primarily based on natural sciences, which is recognized only to the degree that it is seen as "applicable" and "useful" to "policy" decisions. In the late 1980s, she was appointed head of a project on environmental issues in the Los Angeles Department of Public Works. When she left the post of director of the NRDC, she was appointed regional head of the Environmental.

The principles of legitimacy are themselves rivaled by the practical legitimacy of professionals working with operators who are able to accumulate recognized technical skills by means of a basic training in engineering (bachelor of science level) and acquire experience on the ground at the local level in cities and irrigation districts. For example, A.F. the head of Tucson Water, trained as a civil engineer, before spending seven years working for the private engineering firm, CH2M Hill. When he was later appointed head of Tucson Water, he promoted water recycling and storage. After leaving the municipal utility, he returned to the same private firm. In California, the career trajectory of K.L. provides another example of a bridge between the private and public sectors. Born into a working-class family in New York in 1949, he studied industrial engineering. After graduating with a Master of science, he was hired by the Los Angeles County Sanitation District, where he worked from 1972 to 1979. In 1990, after a period as a water resources management consultant in the region, he became head of the Irvine Ranch Water District in Southern California. These are just some of the examples of the profiles, which in many cases deviate from what we expected to be a more homogenous field of engineers, that come to make up the structure of the MCA.

To sum up, axes 1 and 2 reveal an opposition between a regulatory function and a commercial function. This is also an opposition between the competencies of institutions with the most expertise capacity (NGOs, think tanks, academic

Implementing water policy 157

institutes, and expert bodies); regulatory expertise is based on managerial and political skills. It is no doubt here that this is the reason for the polarization of the field of water policy between ecological and economic priorities. However, this dichotomy between regulating and operating functions does not explain the extent to which water conservation policies promoted by all the institutions involved – in terms both of their application and, doubtless, their sincerity – are to varying degrees autonomous vis-à-vis the imperatives of economic development.

The third axis (8.9% variance) provides another principle of differentiation by clearly isolating the group of contractors responsible for transporting and distributing water from the Colorado River (bottom right side of axes 1 and 3; Cf. Diagrams 4 and 5, Annex 2, p. 201 and 202). The most important representatives of this group are the Metropolitan Water District, the Colorado River Board, and the Imperial Irrigation District in California, and the CAP in Arizona. These contractors are opposed to cities' water operators whose political influence is based on their participation on the boards of contractor agencies (upper right side of the axes 1 and 3). Based on legal, political, economic, and managerial competence, the expertise of contractors functioning at the state or interstate level is strongly differentiated from the expertise of other organizations, which tends to be linked to engineering at the local level. The influence of the Metropolitan Water District (MET) in Los Angeles is decisive here, and its general manager occupies a central position in regard to meetings and negotiations between water professionals (Cf. J.K's trajectory, ch4 p. 123).

In Arizona, while the most influential protagonists of the water sector tend to belong to the Arizona Department of Water Resources (ADWR), there is an organization that, due to its responsibility for transporting water from the Colorado River, also plays a central role: the Central Arizona Project, which enjoys a genuine autonomy of action. D.M., its general manager in 2015, but now retired, had 40 years of experience in the water sector (operations, planning, client services, etc.). He was director of Tucson Water and of the City of Phoenix Water Services Department for around 10 years, and was a member of American Water Works, Inc., for 25 years. He worked as vice president of operations for both the Pennsylvania-American and Western Region divisions. In 2003, he was appointed to the board of directors of the Central Arizona Water Conservation District (CAWCD), before becoming, in 2009, general manager of the organization and, as such, responsible for overseeing the CAP. This post is crucial in Arizona in that it involves monitoring the actions of the Central Arizona Groundwater Replenishment District (CAGRD) and the Arizona Water Banking Authority, whose tasks are to manage groundwater supplies via the use of six groundwater recharge facilities. His profile is considerably different from that of the head of the MET, since he obtained a Master's in biology (with a minor in chemistry) at Creighton University in Omaha, Nebraska. Rather than a legal background, his early training was in the natural and physical sciences, still somewhat out of the ordinary for water professionals.

Differences between Colorado River contractors translate into highly dispersed positions on the first two axes. However, they are grouped together on the third

158 *Implementing water policy*

axis (bottom side of the third axis). Moreover, their secondary properties display a high degree of discrimination vis-à-vis the categories to which they primarily belong. Compared, on the one hand, to directors of regulatory institutions, who have advanced academic qualifications in the fields of the environment, science, and, in some cases, law, and, on the other, to members of local operators, who mostly have degrees in civil and hydrological engineering, directors of contractor institutions have more markedly managerial skills (MBAs) focusing on legal and economic expertise. In addition, directors of contracting institutions occupy highly political positions. In many ways, they provide a link between the interests of regulatory institutions and those of local operators. By using their experience with management agencies and their technical skills, they are able to negotiate with federal and state regulators, with whom they share top academic qualifications and competences (management and social sciences skills). In spite of this, however, they are not engineers, and with the operators to whom they sell water from the Colorado River – most of whom have a background in civil or hydrological engineering – they often opt to emphasize their legal and economic expertise, and their contacts with the federal and state authorities impose environmental norms. Based on the promotion good managerial practices and a respect for the environment, this intermediary position is essential to the implementation of a *consensus policy* on water distribution and drought management.

The CAP (and the CAGRD, which depends on it), the Yuma Irrigation District in Arizona, the Metropolitan Water District of Southern California, and the Imperial Irrigation District in California all present another specific characteristic, namely that the quantities of water they manage (v3 and v4) are significantly larger than those managed by local operators (v1 and v2). On axes 2 and 3 (see, Diagram 7, Annex 2, p. 204), contractors are on the left side of the diagram together with other institutions influential in the development of water policy due to their position in the hierarchy of temporal powers (the secretary of the interior, the governor of California, the Central Arizona Project), to the volumes of water they manage in terms of their respective populations (San Diego County, City of Scottsdale), or the academic background of their managers (MBA/social sciences). The various levels of action are, generally speaking, to be found in the different quadrants of axes 1 and 3 (see Diagrams 4 and 5, Annex 2, p. 201 and 202), with, top right, the local and metropolitan level, then a state level at bottom right, with an interstate level on the upper left side. In regard to positions taken by institutions, this differentiation encompasses particular areas of expertise that, together, create a system. These areas include technical capacities in engineering, economic management, and environmental management, as well as expertise qualifications applied to ecological concerns.

From positions to positions taken in water policy

In any discussion of positions taken in the field of water policy, or, in other words, of instruments deployed in terms of defined priorities, structural constraints exercised by the field should be taken into account. However, it does not appear to be

Implementing water policy 159

possible to deduce them directly from those positions as they appear in the space describing the characteristics of institutions. The space describing positions (characteristics of institutions and their directors) and the space describing positions taken (water policy goals and instruments) are not entirely homologous, probably due to the sheer number of instruments used, some of them simultaneously, by the institutions as a whole. Therefore, the problem is to seek the key to the principles underlying these policies in the way in which the field of water policy *retranslates* external constraints into logical frameworks underpinning specific approaches, or, in other words, into differentiated institutional strategies (Cf. Diagrams 3, 6, and 8, Annex 2, pp. 200–205).

Generally speaking, as shown in axes 1 and 2, positions taken and rendered public by institutions and their directors tend to be characterized by two main approaches (Hess et al. 2016): the first, an offer-based policy dependent on finding new sources of supply associated with both traditional infrastructure (dams, canals) and new technological solutions (desalination); the second by reorienting policy and emphasizing a reduction in demand through the storage of surface water or groundwater and the reuse of the resource (individual or collective). In a general perspective, this dichotomy divides institutions between, on the one hand, regulators, which adopt water planning measures and highlight water quality and the promotion of a new water policy that focuses less on new sources than on a transformation of uses (new institutional frame) (see left side of axis 1 in Diagram 3); and, on the other hand, operators, which place an emphasis on technological solutions characterized by the search for new, large-scale sources of supply or the application of small-scale technological solutions designed to improve existing uses (see right side of axis 1 in Diagram 3). This spatial division between, on the one hand, institutional conservation – to which should be added, while bearing in mind its more modest institutional influence, the ecological conservation characteristic of NGOs – and the sustainable regulation approach; and, on the other hand, the priorities granted to economic development and management (sustainable management), is to be found on the first two axes. However, this does mean that instruments like water reuse, groundwater storage and, to a lesser degree, water markets continue to be characterized by a certain degree of uncertainty.

In fact, Diagram 3 reveals information, which at first sight may appear counterintuitive: the centrality of instruments implemented to reduce water demand, which means that they are used by protagonists situated in different positions of the field (and of the MCA). These instruments seem to be much less closely associated with environmental objectives than might be expected. In the field as a whole, they seem to be adopted as a kind of nod in the direction of regulators' demands to make more water savings, while, at the same time, ensuring that economic priorities are not unduly upset.

Axes 2 and 3 deliver a more nuanced description of the various strategies used in the fight against drought. In marginalizing, at least to some degree, the prioritization of ecological conservation and the NGOs that defend it, this description reveals that the institutions involved in managing water distribution and developing the norms by which it is governed (operators, contractors, and regulators)

160   *Implementing water policy*

implement combinations of instruments – which are not, at least initially, easy to decipher – designed for specific purposes. The emphasis placed by contractors responsible for distributing water from the Colorado River (MET, CAP, etc.) on the objectives of sustainable regulation – combining norms governing ecology and economic development – translates as the defense of water markets, with the addition of water reuse and, sometimes, water planning measures. On the other hand, smaller operators, like Pima County and certain cities in Arizona and California, combine water quality measures with changes in demand, while at the same taking on board the technological solutions and water reuse approach promoted by those institutions most closely associated with the economic approach. These operators are inscribed in a space at the opposite end of the spectrum from the one occupied by organizations with priority water rights, characteristic of the longest-established priority water districts in Arizona and California. In both cases, water conservation policies appear to be constrained, but for diametrically opposed reasons. Small, recently established operators appear to face purely ecological constraints associated with the current and future scarcity of the resource, while operators with priority rights face a legal obligation to conform to new environmental norms and to maintain the status quo based on the legal framework established by the Laws of the River.

Water markets and water reuse

In this framework, the ambiguity of water markets becomes apparent. The introduction of water markets can be understood both as a liberal measure consisting in commercializing water, and as an instrument designed to change the rules of the game and transform the existing principles of distribution. Indeed, some institutions focusing on environmental objectives have even adopted them. In effect, water markets can be viewed as an alternative to major technological systems:

> Water markets involve the transfer, lease, or sale of water or water rights from one user to another. (...) A major advantage of market transactions is that water supplies can be shifted between users without the added expense of new dams or reservoirs. As a result, transfers have been blessed – but not always fully supported – by environmentalists. Yet (...) transfers also can have real environmental and economic costs, ranging from urban sprawl, to water cost shifting, and agricultural land fallowing. Negative externalities and mitigation burdens invite conflicts over water transfers.
>
> (Erie 2006: 170)

Water markets: as policy instruments
The function of water markets within the context of water policy instruments applied in the American West has to be referred to the 1980s, the period in which they were first implemented, and to the growing demand of the time on the part of Californian cities: "MET in recent decades has been influenced (...) by a global movement to use market mechanisms to meet burgeoning

urban water needs" (Erie 2006: 169). The difficulty of finding new sources of supply has, in effect, encouraged the use of existing sources in the local agriculture sector:

> The Imperial Irrigation District (IID) is the primary utility company and has some of the most senior rights to Colorado River water, wheeled to farmers through the All-American Canal. The 1988 agreement set up a thirty-five-year water transfer from IID to Los Angeles through a water conservation program that included canal lining and reservoir regulation. Los Angeles' Metro Water District paid for the program in exchange for the water saved – approximately 100,000 acre-feet per year. Ten years later the IID signed a similar agreement with the San Diego County Water Authority (SDCWA) for almost double that amount over a 10-year period. In both 1991 and 1992, California's Department of Water Resources set up emergency drought water banks. In both years the majority of the water sold to the water banks came from fallowing agricultural land.
>
> (Summit 2013: 2012)

The prolonged drought in the American West had provided an opportunity to introduce new procedures for selling water, for example those used for sales between the Palo Verde Irrigation District and the MET. By contrast, the Arizona Water Banking Authority (AWBA) was set up in 1996 with the immediate objective of selling water to Nevada. The AWBA has become an institution that makes it possible to stock water in surface reservoirs and subterranean replenishment areas and is now a key player in the conservation of water resources in the state.

What can be described as an "unlikely coalition of free-market ideologues and environmental activists" (Erie 2006: 189) has served as a transformative force in the field of water policy. In particular, the Central Valley Project Improvement Act (CVPIA, https://www.usbr.gov/mp/cvpia/), designed to protect the environment, made it possible to introduce the practice of transferring water between different institutions. Carl Boronkay, the general manager of the Metropolitan Water District of the time (1984–1993), was able to grasp the opportunity to support the legal text guaranteeing water supply to Los Angeles. He explains: "[P]olitically, we knew that no new dams would be built. Reallocation would be the name of the game" (Boronkay, in Erie 2006: 184ff.). Colorado River contractors have found themselves in a position to change the rules of this game, redefining the issues in order to reconcile contradictory needs deriving from environmental norms promoted by the federal state, risks of water shortages, and increasing calls for economic development. Water, previously a "public resource that farmers used" became a "property right that recipients could buy and sell to other users [...]. [T]he result was the privatization of a publicly developed, common property resource" (Pincetl 2003: 260–261).

162   *Implementing water policy*

However, such analyses, based on privatization (see also Scoville 2015), ignore a point that the MCA successfully brings to light, namely that the use of water policy instruments cannot be reduced to a public/private dichotomy and that some instruments are used by all types of organizations. In fact, the leading promotors of water markets are public organizations that, because they are capable of intervening both on the terrain of local operators and on that of state and federal regulators, have the power to change the rules of the game. "Game changers" like the MET-and, to a lesser degree, the AWBA, merit recognition not only for the "modernizing" solutions they propose, but also for their prudent approach, consisting of keeping one foot in the commercial sector and the other in the public domain. The principles underlying the transformation of water policies should thus be sought in the characteristics of water managers. As the former deputy director general of Metropolitan Water District of Southern California T.Q., explains it:

> Boronkay changed the DNA of the planners of southern California, at that time we were talking about the perfect canal [Delta] it was an engineering solution that we still need, but the votes were going down 90 to 10% in northern California (I assume the public opinion in that issue) nothing goes 90–10% except in communist countries and in Berkeley [...]. Chief planner at MWD that time name was Dan Brooks, he was a civil engineer, he has been around forever, he was a complete state water project guy, one of the most bureaucratically powerful folks, Carl shut them out the door and hired Willy Horne, Willy Horne was not a civil engineer, he had a PhD in water resources modeling, he replaced a civil engineer by a guy who was not a civil engineer, that was 1984... He was a water recycling specialist, a completely different mindset on how you think about the future. MWD went from a civil mentality on State Water Project to a completely different focus on how do we come up with an integrative plan. We were not thinking about sustainability, we were thinking on how do you supply water when you are not gonna get new major supplies of surface water imports, observing environmental revolution, we were not environmentalist, we were water supply managers, but we understood that. We were learning to be good water supply managers.
>
> (Interview, 2016)

This same ambiguity in regard to the use of instruments is also to be found in approaches to water reuse, which are the responsibility of institutions such as the City of Tucson and, to a lesser degree, Pima County, as well as, more surprisingly, Californian institutions such as the Palo Verde Irrigation District (ID), the Imperial Irrigation District, and the West Basin Municipal Water District – or, in other words, institutions that, except for operators in Arizona, give priority to economic development and to a sustainable management of resources that does not call such development into question. First, water recycling should be considered in its relation to the general orientations of individual states. For example, since the 1990s, California has promoted large-scale recycling to counter water scarcity. This is also true of small towns and cities in the state where water resources

Implementing water policy 163

are under stress – for example, West Basin, in whose interest it is to advocate such measures in order to benefit from state aid and reduce the cost of buying water from other operators. On the other hand, the priority given to water planning by the governor of Arizona not only corresponds to a need to reconstitute groundwater reserves, in conformity with the Groundwater Management Act (1980), but also mirrors the stronger regulations applied by state authorities (ADWR) to water transfers. However, this does not exclude the possibility of alliances with local authorities in terms of the introduction of water reuse (see above, Chapter 3). But, beyond the differences between water policies applied by individual states, it can be observed that priorities given to the use of water from the Colorado River are decisive. Consequently, the two organizations with the most rights – Palo Verde ID and Imperial ID in California, Yuma ID in Arizona – undertake markets in order to provide political guarantees enabling them to maintain a constant level of use, and, in the end, to maintain the status quo. The same process is implemented at the urban level in Arizona, where the promotion of water conservation measures in the "major cities" of Phoenix and Tucson (with, in particular, the implementation of water reuse instruments by the Salt River Project (SRP), the CAP, and Pima County), can be interpreted as a way of protecting their current uses from the expansion of real estate in peripheral towns.

Consequently, institutional responses to drought occur within a prism located between two major orientations that are far from incompatible in practice. On the one hand, the promotion of a water market governed by transfers and credits regarding stock; and, on the other, the consolidation of collective regulations applied not only to ecosystems, but also to sources of provision and water planning. These orientations have a common basis, namely the need to organize water conservation with a view to guaranteeing present and future economic development. The introduction of water markets and water reuse measures has to be underpinned by the same objective, namely to secure the provision of the resource and protect the environment. Behind the dichotomy between policies based on offer and policies based on demand, we see the emergence of a more refined differentiation between various water conservation instruments: water markets and water reuse, employed by different institutions for the same objectives, namely a conciliation between environmental and economic interests. Therefore, we can, here, observe, at one and the same time, the limits and advantages of an analysis, based on instruments, applied to an exploration of environmental policies. Although they shed light on the range of stances implied by the general objectives of water policies, those instruments are too malleable and too dependent on their institutional and social contexts of implementation to provide an understanding of the modes of implementation of water policies.

While the implementation of certain instruments is dependent on the place occupied by each of these institutions in the field of water policy, there is no perfect homology between the sphere of positions, and the sphere of stances; consequently, the profile of water managers must be taken into consideration in order to elaborate more precise hypotheses concerning the conditions of implementation of water policy instruments. Water markets are, generally speaking, controlled

164 *Implementing water policy*

by professionals with a background in economics and management, while water reuse instruments are controlled by people with more diverse profiles; while some are economists, most have backgrounds in engineering, hydraulics, and the environment. On the other hand, the development of traditional instruments associated with major projects focusing on offer and increased sources of provision is linked to managers with professional experience in the water management sector (often with a background in engineering, but at no higher than the MSc level).

This analysis of the field of water policies introduces new avenues of research on relations between the various institutional contexts of water policy and the characteristics of professionals in the water sector. It draws attention to the capacity of a number of "game changers" – in California, the head of the MET; in Arizona, the head of Pima County, etc. – to mobilize and combine sometimes divergent interests, notably between operators and regulators. This capacity (linked to their distribution on axes 1 and 2) to introduce links between different organizations and institutions should also be understood in reference to their association with issues linked to the Colorado River (particularly evident on axis 3). From this point of view, they share a number of characteristics distinct from other protagonists in the water sector (technical and managerial skills, social capital, professional experience, etc.), which enables them to go beyond ordinary antagonisms between advocates of economic development and defenders of the environment, and encourage paradoxical dynamics in which the ecological cause ends up supporting economic expansion by producing a consensus about shared objectives. According to the director of a local operator in Arizona:

> I think our biggest challenges are not water resources-related. We are in a very resilient position from a water resources perspective, providing customer service and a good partnership with the business community (…). Water has a very important place in community and what it means to have thriving (…) quality of life, economic development, confidence of the public … Tucson is a good place to live, to raise a family and a good place to raise a business. We are often accused to dry up and blow away the desert … but we are the community in the Southwest least likely to do that because of what we have done from a water supply perspective … We need to make sure that everyone that has a stake in that, has a voice in that.
>
> (Interview 2017)

Conclusion
Dealing with scarcity

The social sciences and environmental policy: questions of method

Although the risk of water shortages in the American West will, perhaps, only become urgent toward the year 2050 (Seager et al. 2007; Barbier 2015), it nevertheless remains true that the main factors of vulnerability exist in an active, perhaps even interactive way – economic growth based on an agro-industrial sector consuming vast quantities of water; urban development with growing energy needs; the already perceptible effects of climate change; and water systems that block a substantial number of initiatives (Perramond 2019). All these factors prefigure "a coming crisis in water supply for the western United States" (Barnett et al. 2008)[1].

The survey presented in this book explores the social logics governing the development and adoption of water policies in a context of scarcity. In this perspective, it does not claim to deliver the kinds of "solutions" that are currently demanded by scientists whose research is supposed to be "applicable" and "useful" to various "stakeholders." Based on a model of specific intelligibility, it develops an explanatory approach to the determinants of water policies. In effect, the notion of the "field" makes it possible to explore the operational aspects of various social universes, the complexity of which renders them too difficult to understand using other approaches. In this perspective, the survey does not consist in developing more or less representative samples (Padowski & Jawitz 2012), but, rather, in elaborating explanatory principles applicable to how those social universes are structured. Here, it highlights systems of relations between water protagonists, which would not become visible if we limited ourselves to the type of categorization usually applied to water management. For example, the way in which water is managed in Tucson, Arizona, is affected by what happens in northern California, not only because it is located in the same watershed, but because the institutional and social logics that underpin how water from the Colorado

---

1 For recent research and data on the drought in the American West, see De Buys (2011), Ingram & Oggins (2013), and Fleck (2016), as well as the publications of the Pacific Institute.

166 *Conclusion: dealing with scarcity*

River is distributed are inscribed in a relational space in which the strategies adopted by any given protagonist depend on those applied by all the others in terms of resources and their characteristics.

The contribution of the social sciences to the study of water policies does not, therefore, consist only in revealing their cognitive frameworks and the way they make their way onto the agenda (Lascoumes & Le Galès 2005), but also of proposing a somewhat different approach to the social logics impacting the management of natural resources and urban services. In the wake of recent research conducted on conflicts about water (Poupeau et al. 2018), this survey takes into account not only the beliefs and norms underpinning the formation of water policy coalitions (Sabatier & Jenkins 1993), but also the role of professional positions (and the specific "capitals" they involve) and the social and educational backgrounds of water protagonists. The interest of this approach in terms of the notion of the "field" is that it makes it possible to simultaneously apprehend a number of active variables in struggles over how water policies should be defined. And while the method developed by Bourdieu has had to be adapted to the particularities of the water sector and the policies by which it is structured, its relational aspect has been retained.

A field of forces governed by structures of relations between water management institutions and water policies, also exist within a field of struggles where coalitions are composed and realigned, which, over the course of time, make it possible to identify and define various water policy "hubs." Our analysis demonstrates how the distinction between regulators and operators expresses an opposition between a normative function and a commercial function, which itself expresses an opposition in terms of skills – between institutions that possess greater administrative capacity (state agencies, non-governmental organizations (NGOs), think tanks, academic institutes, consultancy firms), and institutions whose main activity is to sell water to municipalities, industries, and irrigation districts. This is probably where the reasons for the polarization of the field of water policies between ecological and economic priorities are to be sought.

The field of analysis is not limited to a description, however heuristic, of the structure of the positions taken by protagonists in the water sector. It should explain the positions developed in regard to the issues of the field, in our case the decision-making processes relative to the instruments used in water policy. By treating those instruments as positions taken by protagonists, our analysis reveals the highly structured role of a specific category of contractors, namely those (the Metropolitan Water District of Southern California (MET), the Central Arizona Project (CAP), etc.) tasked with routing and distributing water from the Colorado River (see *supra*, Chapter 6). They are themselves divided into institutions operating across an entire watershed and equipped with the legal, economic, and managerial expertise required to deal with state governments as well as institutions acting at the level of metropolitan cities, counties, and water boards on the basis of engineering or environmental skills. And it is these intermediary characteristics of contractors tasked with distributing water from the Colorado River that enables us to understand the elaboration of the consensus concerning water conservation

Conclusion: dealing with scarcity 167

policy. In effect, the field cannot be reduced to a binary opposition (public/private, regulators/operators, etc.), but, instead, presents itself as a network encompassing many different levels of institutions.

Field effects

These analyses of approaches applied in Arizona and California reveal the conditions in which water conservation policies can be developed and applied. Until the 1970s and 1980s, water management in California was dominated by the imperative of economic development, focusing on agro-industry and urban expansion. But this desire to "make the desert bloom" was confronted by water scarcity, which was exacerbated by recurrent droughts and, as is now apparent, climate change. It was not only major water infrastructure (canals, dams, etc.) that was called into question, but also the power of Californian politicians elected to Congress. The roles of the federal government and its agency, the Bureau of Reclamation, were transformed. The Bureau, formerly responsible for major projects, became a water resource manager and an environmental regulator. In this "era of managers," economists and lawyers developed water conservation instruments, including water transfers, notably between the MET and Imperial Valley, and storage measures. And while the objective was not so much to avoid catastrophe as to support growth in the region, it was nevertheless an important turning point, representing the end of the subordination of water management to a hegemonic economic field, and the emergence of a relatively autonomous field of water policies. Californian contractors (MET, Imperial, Palo Verde, Coachella Valley) started to conserve water, thereby defending their privileges in regard to rights of access to the Colorado River. Requirements linked to administrative concerns encouraged managers more sympathetic to environmental issues to acquire new skills. With such competencies at their disposal, these managers started to advocate more conservation-oriented water policies in the state.

While there was this evolution of approaches to management, which forced California to regulate water consumption, Arizona was characterized by other mechanisms. For example, the regulation of the use of groundwater, introduced in the late 1970s and early 1980s, went hand in hand with the emergence of a relatively autonomous professional milieu dealing with water management at the local level. During this period, the relationships of interdependence between different levels of government (municipality, county, state, and federal institutions) made up this specific subfield, whose operational approach was influenced by evolutions in neighboring California, and which was equipped with specific means of action. The objective of sustainability in water policy was later based on other considerations. Local government institutions (counties, major cities like Tucson and Phoenix) became the principal advocates of water conservation policies designed to guarantee water security, without which economic development would have been imperiled, and to counter attempts by realtors to appropriate water in expanding urban areas. Within these administrations, the arrival of engineers and technicians with a background in environmental management made

168   *Conclusion: dealing with scarcity*

it possible to develop instruments that encourage a more efficient use of water (recycling, stormwater, etc.).

The consensus concerning sustainability-oriented objectives generated in these two subspaces of the field – simultaneously separated and connected – is, therefore, an effect caused by various processes. While, in California, thanks to their economic heft, a small number of organizations enjoy the upper hand, power relations in Arizona are almost entirely different. In the Sunshine State, local institutions, thanks to the coalitions they establish with other governmental levels, are able to reverse the logic underpinning the economic field. But in both cases, water professionals are keen to defend their autonomy, notably in regard to regulatory, state, and federal bodies in the political field. Nevertheless, whether in regard to their alliances with local levels of government in Arizona, or to the ineluctable influence retained by the major Californian organizations, a form of balance was found thanks to a vague and indeterminate consensus about water conservation policy – a consensus that made it possible to formally satisfy ecological imperatives without calling into question land use and economic growth. The field of water policies can thus be seen as a relatively autonomous space located astride the economic and political fields.

In light of the above, we are readily able to understand that the distinction made by Fligstein and McAdam (2011) between two visions of the notion of the field, one fairly agonistic, the other consensual, has no real basis in reality. In order to develop a theory enabling them to explain why order reigns in fields, the authors emphasize the value – in terms of the legitimization of those fields – of negotiated agreements, coalitions, and the development of a form of legitimate institutionalization. They compare this vision to that of "some authors" (including, implicitly, Bourdieu), who

> see fields as highly conflictual arenas that are largely structured on the basis of absolute differences in the resources and coercive power of those who occupy the field. In this view, the struggle for the valued ends of the field will cause one actor or set of actors to try and dominate others. To the degree that they are successful, the field will have a hierarchical structure.
>
> (Fligstein and McAdam 2011: 206)

The problem with this dichotomy is that it fails to acknowledge the fact that the formation of coalitions is itself the result of struggles within the field, and that the constitution of alliances or cooperation networks is more of a "field effect" (as in a field of struggles) than a postponement of competition between agents in the field considered (as a field of forces, or force field).

Consequently, when Fligstein and McAdam mention Powell et al. (2005) and their attempt to map the field using a network analysis approach, they do so because, in their view, the structure of relationships corresponds to the structure of the field. However, the authors do not see that the specificity of the field, in comparison with the network, is that it reveals invisible relationships that cannot be reduced to the sum of visible interactions. Far from opposing the analysis of

Conclusion: dealing with scarcity   169

coalitions and their networks, the model of the field incorporates that analysis as an exploratory phase of the approach. In effect, "fields" – defined as "sites of contest" among their inhabitants known for using their symbolically charged capitals to define hierarchical relations among them – create historical conditions for social networks to emerge as the objective form of "relational structure" (Singh 2016). Another consequence is that the range of social skills used in social games is far wider than the "complex mix of cognitive, affective and linguistic facilities" (Fligstein & McAdam 2011: 216) that facilitate individual strategies, for example participation in forms of collective action. They should be understood as systems of schemas of perception and appreciation that structure social practices within a given field.

Skills therefore exist on two levels. First, at the individual level (a corporal history), as the sum of qualities represented by a particular individual (educational background, qualifications, professional career path, etc.); and, second, at the level of the structure of the field (a reified history). For example, a hydrologist is positioned in an institutional legacy that guides, in terms of its resources, their access to particular organizations (Henry 2012). As in the research on conflicts about water mentioned above, it is, therefore, not possible to explain water policy in terms of beliefs. It is necessary to consider both the structures of the positions in which interactions take place and the academic and professional careers of protagonists in the water sector to understand what holds the field together, in spite of the struggles that structure it. It is to this vision of the basis of the cohesion of fields that we should now return by way of the survey presented in this book.

The instruments of water policy and the question of hydrocracies

In the end, the research results are located at several different levels. The methodological approach consisting of treating instruments as position statements and linking them to the systems underpinning the positions of water management institutions, their organizational characteristics, and the characteristics of their managers, turned out to be useful in terms of understanding how water policies are implemented and positioned. More precisely, the use of these instruments seems to be linked to configurations encompassing not only the state of water resources, but also the characteristics of institutions in the sector, and the specific skills of the water professionals who lead them.

This is how water conservation measures can appear to be directly linked not to the urgency of specific ecological situations, but, instead, to institutional and economic imbalances, for example the need to transfer resources, as has been happening in California since the 1970s (Saliba 1987; Erie 2006). In such cases, it is a market system that, paradoxically, generates ecological measures. It would seem that institutional innovation is correlated to the contribution of new skills, focused less on hydraulic engineering and more on business management. The case of Arizona also reveals an evolution in approaches to management taken by water sector institutions, with public administrations

170   *Conclusion: dealing with scarcity*

importing environmental skills combining aspects of ecology and management. The apparently opposed configurations of two case studies reveal a shared element, namely a calling into question of civil and hydraulic engineering expertise applied in the delivery of technological water distribution services (Teish 2011; Lorrain & Poupeau 2016).

In the end, what water policies reveal about drought is that the "powerful state water bureaucracies" (Molle et al. 2009) that oversaw the implementation of major infrastructure projects operated not only in national administrations, but also at a plurality of different levels of action, sometimes in neighborhoods and communities, sometimes at the subregional level of counties or "XXL metropolises" (Lorrain 2011), and sometimes at a federal or international level that seems not to apply traditional approaches to water management, but nevertheless help to define their operational norms (Doern & Johnson 2006).

Even if they were contested on the grounds of their economic and environmental effects, both in the bureaucratic field itself and by members of "civil society," in which academics are active alongside ecological militants, hydrocracies have attempted to rise to those challenges by taking new approaches and encouraging reform (Molle et al. 2009). Thanks to this perspective, we are able to gain an understanding of how, in the Western United States, the technico-institutional capital of the hydraulic engineers of the 19th century was gradually contested throughout the 20th century due to the importation into the institutions tasked with promoting water policy, of new, more managerial skills, both legal and economic. But it should also be noted that what could be described as "managerial capital" has not enjoyed a dominant position in the water sector. In the United States, the realignment of coalitions in the definition and implementation of water policies provides an insight into the importance of their role in struggles about water. And various protagonists in the water sector outside the inner circle of engineers and political decision makers has allowed for the creation of a specific space in which groups confront one another over the development, promotion, and implementation of water policies.

However, the social history of these struggles, as recounted in this book (see *supra*, Chapters 2 and 3) demonstrates that a binary vision – engineers against managers, technicians against bureaucrats – is inadequate to the task of describing the choice of instruments made by actors in the water sector. This is not only because the hubs highlighted in that social history are never clearly separated, at least not to that degree. It is also because in most cases positions of power are occupied by professionals who have, over the course of their careers, acquired the characteristics of each of the hubs (for example, Newell in Arizona at the beginning of the century, and, more recently, the directors of MET in California), and also because

> in the last two decades water has clearly moved from the purview of experts and engineers to a wider forum where stakeholders articulate different claims, values and interests around water management issues. (...) It reflects on the extent to which new practices have been incorporated in water-related

Conclusion: dealing with scarcity   171

decision-making and reviews the implications in terms of skills needed for tomorrow's water management.

(Molle 2009)

If this analysis apparently fails to acknowledge the "managerial turn" in the 20th century in the American West, it nevertheless succeeds in taking into account the recently acquired skills that diverge from forms of management continually applied throughout the last century.

Current water challenges undoubtedly require a break with past engineering-centered approaches. Notable efforts at changing curriculums and instilling environmentally and socially sensitive practices have been made (...) Consequently, while it remains essential to train creative civil engineers, aquatic ecosystem biologists, or irrigation managers, it also seems vital for a growing number of water professionals to engage in decision-making processes, take part in multi-stakeholder dialogues and consultations, and to contribute to transparency in debates and open up "black boxes."

(Molle 2009)

The "degree of transdisciplinarity" of these new skills, encourages us to see "societal problems as primarily political, in the noble sense of the term, but does not downplay the role of science."

However, the case of water conservation policies observed in a subspace of the field, which mainly concerns established institutions in Arizona and, to a lesser degree, a number of market-oriented organizations in California (see *supra* Chapter 5), shows that these new social skills are based less on a demand for democratic transparency, and more on the promotion of new engineering skills focusing on ecology, the preservation of ecosystems, and environmental management. The networks formed by people possessing these new skills, deriving from minor and less prestigious sources than engineering degrees and MBAs, whose graduates had, until now, filled the most important posts in the sphere of water management, are probably at the origin of a form of implicit solidarity, or at least of shared beliefs, enabling them to establish connections between institutions and to support a form of *ecologization of water policy*. The social basis of water policy and the consensus that has gradually developed in the region in the wake of struggles to appropriate the resource is thus to be found in the transformations of hydrocracies, and the professional characteristics and educational backgrounds of their members.

Water landscapes for the future

The journey undertaken in this book encompasses many reflections on ditches, and more often on canals, those "modern infrastructures" that, since Worster, have replaced the old ditch model with concrete waterways to guide the flow of water. In his now classic work, *Rivers of Empire* (1985), Worster charted the

172 Conclusion: dealing with scarcity

history of California's water management as a quest for empire, that is, for power, authority, and legitimacy through the mastery of water systems. He introduced his argument with a "reflection on a ditch" in California's Imperial Valley, realizing that Thoreau's romantic idea of the West, that place where the future most surely would lie, has proven more problematic for contemporary society than we care to admit (Figure C.1).

The image in Figure C.1 was taken from a canal bed in Arizona. On the one hand, the image shows a physical reality – arid land with no water. However, the foreground of cracked earth and dead branches frames another reality – the human imagination. The drawing in the photo was done by kids who had never seen a river flow. When there is surplus, water flows freely in the canal. On the other side of the canal is a free-flowing river, which has been part of a regional government reclamation project for many years. Today school groups come to visit it, take water samples, and learn about water conservation in one of the most water-scarce regions in the world. The drawing is a mix of what these young students saw, and what they hoped it could be – a living river ecosystem.

One can keep coming back to this image. The drawing is, in many ways, reminiscent of petroglyphs, prehistoric rock drawings featuring animal forms, which can be seen throughout the southwest of the United States. Today it seems that new kinds of petroglyphs can be found in human-made landscapes, those of canals, dams, etc., be they in the form of chalk drawings, or even spray-painted "tags" by local gangs and artists. However, this contemporary petroglyph tells a unique story accompanied by the scene that surrounds it and the juxtaposition that it represents to the waterscape in which it is literally embedded. As Molle et al. (2009) remind us, a "waterscape" is defined by the manner in which surface

Figure C.1 A painting on a canal bed in Arizona. Credit: Brian F. O'Neill 2017.

and groundwater resources interrelate with human, physical, and biotic nature: "Waterscapes are an expression of the interaction between humans and their environment and encompass all of the social, economic and political processes through which water in nature is conceived of and manipulated by societies."

The way in which the human is *written* into the landscape can take physical form with the many dams and canals that dot the American West. These landscaped structures recall water scarcity and its effects, visualized in this image by the cracked earth and concrete and in contrast to the romantic ocean scene written into the concrete wall. In one sense then, our research is a reflection on the attitude of classical high-modernist ideology that James Scott (1999) described, which he called an unfailing belief in state-sponsored projects led by technocratic elites, of the kind that would literally "make the desert bloom." But this image, and the research presented here, also presents another side of the story of dealing with scarcity and its contemporary manifestations. As one Arizona water manager explained, "there is no coming back from what we have done, but we'll have a flowing stream here one day." For many protagonists in the water sector, meeting the challenge of scarcity is not only important in the present, but for future generations as well. They are constantly informed by the problematic relationship that water managers have had with water in the past as they seek a sustainable future. Dealing with scarcity, then, not only involves an unbounded optimism in terms of the technical mastery of nature, but also constitutes an essential part of their work from this point on.

Annex 1: Revisiting the Law of the River

> I've graduated to the point where I can now say, "Aah, that would violate the 'Law of the River.'" [...] He goes way back in the history of representing Arizona's water interest, every time I'd ask a question I felt like [B] would pop up in the audience and say "Well that's prohibited by the Law of the River." Now I've been a lawyer for a long time and I've never heard of the "Law of the River." So I go to the Arizona Revised Statute books and I pull it down and I look it up "River comma Law of" and it's not there. So I thought it must be a federal "Law of the River" so I pull out the US Code and I look up "River comma Law of" and it's not there either. It turns out "The Law of the River" is kind of like the British Constitution, it's whatever the people who have really been hanging around it a long time think it is. It's the embodiment of all kinds of different treaties, acts of Congress, and different complex federal regulations and oral traditions. That's all the "Law of the River," and if you've been around long enough you're allowed to say what it is, but if you haven't been led in the gate, the Water Buffalo ceremonial admittance initiation rights, then you don't get to talk about the "Law of the River."
>
> (Archival interview with a former director of the Central Arizona Project (CAP) board, 2007)

This annex is intended to provide the reader with some additional background material and reading that represent mainly a legal understanding of the issues discussed in this book. It is necessary to explain both in general terms and with some specific examples, but it is also interesting to show how this "Law of the River" has taken on a flexible character and is the point of ongoing debate. Furthermore, the legal norms that it sets out must be articulated at various levels of action, coherent with our field approach.

The regulation of the Colorado River

In 1935, the Los Angeles newspapers were "ecstatic" (Reisner 1986: 258). Governor of Arizona, B.B. Moeur, had decided to deploy "the Arizona Navy" to the site of the Parker Dam, just below the Hoover Dam, where one anchoring cable for a barge had been placed in Arizona soil. "'Moeur's Navy," as the *LA Times* called it, consisted of the Arizona National Guard, the 158th Infantry

Annex 1: Revisiting the Law of the River 175

Regiment, a sergeant, three privates, a cook, and Major F.I. Pomeroy, with orders to engage anyone wishing to place any further obstructions in or on the banks of the Colorado River" (Reisner 1986: 258). After seven months, and a rescue operation by Los Angeles Water and Power to free the Arizona Navy after being caught by the anchoring cable, Governor Moeur deployed the Arizona Militia with machine guns to halt any further construction. It was only then that Secretary of the Interior (SOI) Harold Ickes responded by halting construction. In fact, the Parker Dam had not been authorized by Congress. The Bureau of Reclamation (BOR) just went ahead with the project. In the end, California, the arch rival of Arizona from these early days, was able to pass a bill authorizing the dam. If Arizona wanted to continue to protest, its only other option may have been seceding from the Union (Reisner 1986: 259). Looking at this single event, it would be easy to say that the Colorado River has been the scene of a great battle, both literally and figuratively.

It is stories like these that have caused the Colorado River to be an unending source of fascination for generations of students, scholars, and even water managers. Indeed, "the story of the Colorado River is the great epic of water law and politics in America" (Thompson et al. 2013: 975). Everything starts with the Law of the River, which is the aggregate collection of various contracts and court decisions as well as state and federal laws that constitute a complex and at times seemingly incoherent mire of history (Meyers 1966; Megdal et al. 2011). Any major political or legal movement within the Colorado River Basin must deal with the Law of the River. As a system, it reveals a certain amount of coherence, involving all states within the Colorado River Basin. In a broader context, it will become clear how the managing of water "is not merely a technical field that can be addressed through infrastructure provision and scientific expertise, but a political one that involves human values, behavior and organization" (Linton and Budds 2014: 170): "water is not an inert backdrop for social relations, but that it plays a positive role in social formations" (Linton and Budds 2014: 174).

The Colorado River is a highly complex system of intertwined technical and normative matters. The river water is diverted through a system of dams, reservoirs, canals, and other flow management instruments that bring water to millions of people even outside the river watershed. The Hoover Dam (1936) and the Glenn Canyon Dam (1967) are the two most important dams, and they are capable of holding water in two huge reservoirs (Lake Mead and Lake Powell) that serve to store water for the users of the lower part of the Colorado River Basin when a decrease in flow occurs. There are also dozens of smaller dams and other reservoirs, canals, etc. along the course of the river that make up the complex system that supplies large cities like Las Vegas, Phoenix, Tucson, or Denver. This technical system is regulated by the so-called Law of the River established by a compact negotiated by the Colorado River Basin states in 1922. This compact established the beneficial consumptive use of 7,500,000 acre feet of water for the Upper Basin states (Wyoming, Colorado, Utah, and New Mexico) and the same amount for the Lower Basin states (California, Arizona, and Nevada). In 1928 the Boulder Canyon Project Act was signed and the volumes that were to be apportioned to

176   *Annex 1: Revisiting the Law of the River*

each of the Colorado Lower Basin states were established: Arizona (2.8 maf), California (4.4 maf), and Nevada (0.3 maf). This agreement also stated that the secretary of the interior was authorized to enter into contract with urban water agencies and irrigation districts that wished to be served by the Colorado waters. Another agreement signed in 1944 between the US and Mexico set a volume of 1.5 maf for the states of Baja California and Sonora.

The California Seven Party Agreement, signed in 1931, fixed the share of the water that each of the state applicants would be allocated: Palo Verde Irrigation District, Yuma Project, Imperial Irrigation District, Coachella Valley Irrigation District, Metropolitan Water District (MET), and the City and County of San Diego. This agreement allotted to a single user, namely the Imperial Irrigation District in the Imperial Valley, about 70% of the total amount of water of the Colorado that serves California (3.1 maf) while the other applicants in the south of the state were allotted the remaining 1.4 maf with 12% destined to the MET. As a countervailing arrangement, the agreement established that the MET could withdraw an additional amount of water serving California, if the rest of the users of the other states did not use the total share of water allocated to them. This is what the MET had been doing on a recurring basis, and in fact California has received more than 5 maf for many years. This allocation of water emanates from the two great economic actors that have marked the development of California's water policy. One is the agricultural sector and the irrigation districts under its control, and the other refers to the urban areas, which control water suppliers or water districts.

The beneficiaries and users in California agreed upon this water allocation, which in the event of insufficient slow from the Colorado River, is distributed following a system of priority rights ("present perfected rights") signed by the US Supreme Court in 1979. The abovementioned is a decree that assigns priority to the Palo Verde Irrigation District, Imperial Valley, and Yuma over other contractors in the state in the case of insufficient flow from the Colorado River. This agreement puts the major urban agencies in a weak position in the event of a water crisis. Up until 2003, the MET supplemented its allocation on a regular basis from the excess produced by the system. Nevertheless, the increased use of water in many states and the share of water allotted according to the different agreements (16.5 maf), which was exceeding the average flow of the Colorado River (15.5 maf), began to produce an unsustainable situation. The apportionment of the share of waters established for the Upper Basin and the Lower Basin of the Colorado River was based on the river flow in a year of high rainfall, which does not correspond to the average annual flow, and therefore we refer to a "structural deficit."

In the early 1990s, the dry years reduced the Colorado River's water flow, and yet its users continued to withdraw the same amount of water, especially California. The other states of the basin began to protest about California's excessive use of water. The situation peaked in the early 2000s, as the secretary of the interior decided in 2003 that California should live with the 4.4 maf allotted and would not receive any addition to its allocation. The situation of the Colorado River has not improved and in 2015 Lake Mead dropped to an historic low level that predicted potential restrictions on water supply. In addition to this crisis of the Colorado River, there is also the need of the state, empowered by the Water Conservation Act of 2009, to force urban agencies to reduce per capita consumption by 20% by Horizon 2020 and this obligation must be driven by suppliers who sell water to the final consumer or retailers.

The "Law of the River"

Many doctrines play a role in understanding the laws of the Colorado River which collectively come to determine the rights to water. One could find each individual doctrine to be all-consuming; however, the aim here is to provide a concise and comprehensible outline. Western water law gains in complexity, but also coherence, when one considers the strong sense of individuality that runs through the Western states. Over the years, the states have proven to be quite strong-willed in efforts to implement their own laws to govern water (Getches 2009; Thompson et al. 2013).

Indeed, to undertake a comprehensive review of each state's intricacies would seem to be an almost impossible undertaking. However, one of the key doctrines that applies in the Colorado River Basin is the doctrine of prior appropriation. In essence, this means that the first person to use the water has the right to it. The oldest user is legally known as a "senior" rights holder. Arizona was allowed to proceed with the Central Arizona Project Canal, but the catch was that the CAP would hold "junior" priority through the Colorado River Basin Project Act of 1968. Therefore, if and when a shortage is declared, the CAP will see reductions and California will remain unaffected (US Department of the Interior 2007; CAP 2014). It has been argued many times that the prior appropriation doctrine needs to see reform, because it was originally conceived to encourage settlement of the West and was highly conducive to a certain creativity in water management through diversions and dams for beneficial uses. In the end, the prior appropriation doctrine is indicative of the early settlers' views on nature, but also of views on agricultural and industrial progress (Glennon 2012).

In general, under this system of prior appropriation, individuals do not own water rights, but if one has a property right, then it is possible to divert water for a specific use, from a specific source (Davis 2002). However, unlike the riparian doctrine of the Eastern United States, simply owning property does not endow one with a right to use the water that is associated with that land. The important break with riparianism is in the act of diversion, or the making beneficial use of the water source (Thompson et al. 2013: 167–181). Article 17 of the Arizona Constitution sets out most of these rules and clearly establishes that riparianism does not apply. It is a system that is inherently inequitable, and it is made more complicated when dealing with actors who traditionally operate at different "levels" of action.

For example, in the case of the major allocations that have been made for each state in the Colorado River Basin, a large federal project was built so the state could make use of the water. This meant that over time states could pay back

178   *Annex 1: Revisiting the Law of the River*

the government (usually Bureau of Reclamation), but additionally that the states would own the water whereas individual agencies would not. In this way, the Bureau operates projects under state laws and not federal laws (Trelease 1960: 403–404; Thompson et al. 2013: 843–865). Currently, there is a great deal of apprehension when states discuss the future of the Colorado River. Each state owns the rights to certain amounts of water from a specific source; however, the lines become blurred because the federal government represents Native Americans, who are legally seen as sovereign nations and who have senior rights to the Colorado River. Therefore, the states are fear what might happen to their rights if the federal government intervenes, as it operates many of the diversion projects in crucial states like Arizona and California. The federal-level players also realize that this seemingly heavy-handed approach would be highly conducive to outright conflict. The federal government would prefer not to take a side on any shortage negotiation, and to allow the states to continue to work within the parameters initially defined by the Law of the River, which begins with the Colorado River Compact in the early 20th century.

The Compact and the players

The common origin of the Law of the River is the Colorado River Compact of 1922, usually known as the "Compact." This was initially proposed by the states that have come to constitute what is known as the Upper Basin of the Colorado River. These "States of the Upper Division," as described in Article II of the Compact, are Colorado, New Mexico, Utah, and Wyoming, while the "States of the Lower Division" are Arizona, California, and Nevada (70 Cong Rec. 324, 1928). During these early years of Western settlement a great deal of primitive canal building and irrigation was being performed. The settlers of California's Imperial Valley made their opinion known early (and their voices are still the loudest today) when they asked the federal government to create the All-American Canal.

However, the turning point was in 1905 when a massive flood created the Salton Sea in the Imperial Valley (Reisner 1986: 122–125). A dam had to be constructed. Los Angeles, because it saw great electricity potential in a dam project, then began organizing the Metropolitan Water District to lobby in Washington, DC, with help from the Imperial Valley irrigators. It is also important to consider that there was a drought in California at this time, which charged the whole situation with an extra impetus for reform (Thompson et al. 2013: 978). Clearly, California was strategically placing itself in a situation to take advantage of whatever situation was to develop in the coming years. It would therefore seem that the rest of the states were left behind and have been playing catch-up ever since. California did not restrict itself and its aims to simply Los Angeles, or simply to within the state of California. Lobbyists went to Washington DC, thereby allowing California to position itself in the best possible way for the future management of its water supply into the 20th century. This initial political foresight has been a hallmark of California water politics. As stated earlier, even today the future remains uncertain in the Colorado Basin. Arizona has historically been proactive

Annex 1: Revisiting the Law of the River 179

with its conservation and management practices because it was politically late to the game and has been unable to effectively push its agenda against the more powerful California. Therefore, it is easy to see that the concerns of today have simply reproduced themselves from these early times. The Western states are concerned about California, because of its capacity to increase population and because of its relative power. One of the main leaders behind the 1922 Compact was Delphus Emory Carpenter who tried to find innovative ways of securing "win-win" solutions, a logic that still is pervasive in this field.

Trained as a lawyer at the University of Denver and graduating in 1899, Delphus Emory Carpenter had a constant penchant for finding himself in water law disputes as he practiced through 1908 before running for Senate as a Republican, and winning, despite his opposition to the agrarian populist movement. Known as "Give-a-Dam Carpenter" he was truly a gentleman by all accounts and insisted that he get his way, but that the other parties received "a square deal" as well (Tyler 1998: 28). He might even be considered as the father of modern interstate negotiations and of the strategies of working toward "win-win" situations that many current politicians and negotiators utilize (Mostert 1998).

Around 1910, he was made chairman of the Senate Committee on Agriculture and Irrigation and he prepared a report on the Colorado River, its tributaries, and what legal criteria should apply to it. He came to the conclusion that the doctrines of prior appropriation and beneficial use were key components of Western water law and should remain so. Interestingly, he also felt that the states should take responsibility for the Colorado River and prevent the federal government from intervening in the matters of the Basin.

> To Carpenter, the intervention of the Reclamation Service in *Kansas v. Colorado* (206 U.S. 46, 27 S. Ct. 655, 51 L. Ed. 956, 1907) was like a fire-bell in the night. Even though the Supreme Court ultimately decided in 1907 that each state had full jurisdiction over the waters of its streams, the federal government appeared increasingly disposed to build its projects with scant attention to the statutes and judicial decisions of sovereign states.
>
> (Tyler 1998: 29–30)

He was additionally appointed to work on the *Wyoming v. Colorado* (259 U.S. 419, 42 S. Ct. 552, 66 L. Ed. 999, 1922), which further provided a basis upon which interstate rivers might be divided. Eventually, despite initial infighting between them, Herbert Hoover, Warren G. Harding's secretary of commerce, and Carpenter came to work quite closely. Once the final decision in *Wyoming v. Colorado* (1922) was made, Carpenter drew up the 50–50 (7.5 maf–7.5 maf) allocation scheme between basins upon Hoover's request.

The "equitable" division of the Colorado River has proven problematic into the future despite Carpenter's belief that it would decrease future litigation (Tyler 1998). Mainly, Carpenter felt that the "equitable apportionment doctrine" was the best way to proceed, as had been used in *Kansas v. Colorado* (1907). However, it is also necessary to consider that Carpenter, in one stroke, was attempting to

180 *Annex 1: Revisiting the Law of the River*

make a sweeping reform of the West. In doing so he attempted to be sensitive to Arizona's situation and understand that it would take many years for them to ratify the Compact, but he also wished to protect the Upper Basin's supply of water. At the time, everyone was concerned about the rapidity with which major Lower Basin cities were growing.

In the decades following the Compact, almost all involved the fundamental role that Carpenter played. However, it was Sims Ely of Arizona who spoke of the situation with great perception and candor in 1920 and then in 1944 when he wrote

> I shall never forget the prophetic look that came over your face, nor the clarity of your reasoning as you pointed out to me [in 1920] why that allocation [referring to one half of the total flow of the Colorado River to the Upper Basin states] would be demanded by you when the time should come to frame the treaty ... "You and I will not live to see it," you said, "but within the next one hundred years, perhaps within fifty years, water for irrigation will have become so valuable that the easterly side of the Rockies will be pierced by a tunnel or tunnels, and water will thus be conveyed to the Plains below." It was then that you became the prophet of great things to come.
>
> (Tyler 1998: 27)

Arizona would eventually ratify the Compact in 1944 when Mexico was additionally guaranteed 1.5 maf of Colorado River flow. Through Carpenter's savvy legal ability and knowledge of the inner workings of Western water law, he was successfully able to protect the Upper Basin from major future issues with the prior appropriation doctrine. However, one tricky element of the Compact was that it simply divided the Basins and did not provide for intra-Basin allotments. This would be what eventually brought Arizona and California to the courtroom. The states would have to work out the inter-Basin apportionments through prior appropriation themselves.

Interstate conflicts

California continued lobbying for the building of the All-American Canal and Boulder Canyon Dam. In 1928, the Boulder Canyon Project Act (43 U.S.C.§§ 617 sq.) was finalized. This made it possible for the Boulder Canyon Dam, later to be called the Hoover Dam and, along the way, "Hoogivza Dam," to be constructed along with the All-American Canal (Thompson et al. 2013: 980). It was agreed in 1928 that California would be allowed 4.4 maf and 1 maf of unused surplus on the river, a point that is hotly debated between Arizona and California even today. This Act set up a general provision for the entire Lower Basin where Arizona would receive 2.8 maf and Nevada would be allotted 0.3 maf. At this point, the famous *Arizona v. California* (283 US 423, 1931, 373 US 546, 1963, 376 US 340, 1964, 439 US 419, 1979, 531 US 1, 2000) suits begin to take place and it is clear that these decisions created various social norms that take the form

Annex 1: Revisiting the Law of the River 181

of legal and institutional tools despite Carpenter's, as well as the other shapers of the Compact's, initial movement to try to avoid future legal action.

Originally decided in 1931, and most recently adjusted in 2000, this legal Act, if taken as a whole, is one of the longest lasting and most influential Supreme Court rulings regarding the Colorado River. The issue stemmed from California's need to further divert water beyond that which was outlined by the Colorado River Compact of 1922. The 1963 decision is the best known, and the best documented, because the court held that the secretary of the interior is responsible for allocating water according to various formulas outlined in the court's decisions. The initial controversy involved "present perfected rights," rights that have the most senior authority as outlined in the Boulder Canyon Project Act of 1929. The court upheld these allocations, leaving the states to decide how to deal with tributaries. However, in the event of a water shortage, the secretary of the interior determines apportionment after the 1929 rights can be met.

Therefore, *Arizona v. California* is significant because the federal government has the final say in apportionment when water shortages occur. Additionally, in the subsequent 1964 and 1979 decrees, present perfected rights became further defined; therefore, apportionment to Native American Nations and Basin states became clearer. Interestingly, Native American allocations have only recently been significantly considered and will prove an interesting twist to the Law of the River as the drought becomes more severe. MacDonnell et al. (1995) argued early on that if droughts increase in the future, flaws in this aspect of the Law of the River may become glaringly apparent. Major cities such as Los Angeles, Phoenix, and Las Vegas may have to look elsewhere for water because they are not high enough on the totem pole of appropriation rights. Clearly, this is why *Arizona v. California* has been relitigated so many times. Water is a major concern for growing cities, all of which are major stakeholders in terms of citizens, farming, and industry. The federal government has had the largest impact on the policy process as it relates to the Law of the River for more than 100 years, and it will always have the final say in major water appropriation disputes. However, it is not an interest group in the traditional sense. The government's interest lies in the fact that more disputes over the Law of the River, and more drought in the Southwest, necessitate more government intervention. Historically, the Secretary of the Interior has been heavily involved and still holds a great deal of legally endowed power, especially in the way he can control policies and frame debates.

Arizona's groundwater struggle

Despite the fact that there are major issues with which to contend in terms of surface water, Western states face major concerns that have only recently been realized with respect to groundwater. The embedded issues for Arizona here have been that it was pumping groundwater at alarming rates, because it lacked major canal and delivery infrastructure from the Colorado River. By 1972, Lawrence McBride wrote an article for *Ecology Law Quarterly* entitled

182   Annex 1: Revisiting the Law of the River

"Arizona's coming dilemma: water supply and population growth," in which he looked very specifically at demographic data and a variety of hydrologic data collected by the United States Geological Survey (USGS) and other agencies. His article sounded a significant alarm, because it provides a depth of analysis of the basins and population situation. He described the method of governance in Arizona as a "system of diversions because of the lack of surface water to meet demand" (McBride 1972: 359). At that time, the CAP was not yet finished for Tucson or Phoenix, and the challenges of evaporation and the possibility of desalinization plants were seriously considered, along with diversions from Canada and Alaska; meanwhile, groundwater recharge, which was eventually used to solve many problems in Arizona, was only mentioned in the context of Orange County, California. McBride concluded that there was an "impossibility of setting up a recharge program without changes to the law." In order to eventually reach the more holistic system in place in Arizona today, the laws had to allow for the necessary hydrological considerations to be made. In the end, it would take powerful leadership in Washington, DC, and in Arizona, by Cecil Andrus, Bruce Babbitt, and others, to begin to mitigate the years of groundwater overdraft (Connall Jr. 1982). They were able to rise above some lawmakers who referred to hydrology as voodoo (Ambrose and Lynn 1986). Clearly, many strides have been made since this time, although some disconnect still exists between water law and the science of hydrology. In fact, some scholars (Linton and Budds 2014) would go as far as to say that the constant obsession with the hydrologic cycle in areas such as law, which has profound social components, actually serves to obscure the human interaction with water and abstract water beyond comprehension. However, adaptations for the better have been made, even if legal doctrines still hamper the Western United States (Glennon 2007). But finally, despite Delphus Carpenter's efforts, a highly constructed, contentious, and unequitable system has been created, whose effects can be seen in today's methods of water management.

By 1977, President Jimmy Carter was looking for economically unreasonable dam and canal projects, and the Central Arizona Project was one of them. However, after many years of hard-fought battles with California and the federal government for its allotment of 2.8 maf of water, Arizona was not going to allow the CAP to fall by the wayside. It is commonly thought that Governor Babbitt was behind the federal government's threats toward the CAP in order to bring Arizona irrigation districts and developers together on how to solve Arizona's looming groundwater overdraft issue (Connall Jr. 1982; Colby and Jacobs 2007). In hindsight, this seems not to have been much different than the 2007 Shortage Agreement where federal players had to nudge the states along to produce a consensus. Today, it is preferred that collaborative or negotiated efforts are used to resolve conflict because court cases have become so expensive and time consuming, in addition to the fact that they can contain overall undesirable outcomes. However, one example of the way a state was summoned to action was with the Groundwater Management Act, which would not have been possible without the strong and determined leadership of Bruce Babbitt.

Shortage Sharing Agreement (2007)

Considering that many states are quite apprehensive about federal involvement and especially apprehensive about the secretary of the interior mandating an unfavorable model to manage a shortage in the Colorado River Basin, it may be surprising to learn that in 2005 Secretary of the Interior Gale Norton (Colorado) provided the initial impetus by requesting the Bureau of Reclamation to provide "guidelines" under which Lakes Mead and Powell could operate in times of official shortage (Grant 2008: 964). However, this is not at all implausible considering that part of the Colorado River Basin Project Act of 1968 indicates that the Basin states are to be consulted by the secretary to establish long-range plans for reservoirs. Once again, it is clear how the legal structure of the Basin gives rise to the contemporary model of management. The seven states then provided their own proposals and the BOR received public comment. Finally, on December 13, 2007, the secretary issued a final set of guidelines, including operational elements based on the proposal made by the Basin states in April 2007 (Grant 2008: 965). However, as if the case of *Arizona v. California* was not enough to antagonize the two states, the additional barrier for these guidelines was that California had failed to reduce surplus water use according to the 2001 guidelines and so that agreement had been effectively set aside long ago (Grant 2008: 974).

The 2007 Shortage Sharing Agreement is but another example of the complexity and richness of studying the relations that water and society have with one another. It is a fascinating case study, because the clear values, sedimented institutional and conflictual history, instruments, and agencies of each state across the Colorado River Basin, in addition to Mexico, were on full display. It was truly a monumental achievement to be able to produce consensus with so many varying interests attempting to work together.

Legal references

Arizona v. California, 283 U.S. 423, 51 S. Ct. 522, 75 L. Ed. 1154 (1931).
Arizona v. California, 373 U.S. 546, 83 S. Ct. 1468, 10 L. Ed. 2d 542 (1963).
Arizona v. California, 460 U.S. 605, 103 S. Ct. 1382, 75 L. Ed. 2d 318 (1983).
Boulder Canyon Project Act, 43 U.S.C. §§ 617 et seq. (1928).
Kansas v. Colorado, 206 U.S. 46, 27 S. Ct. 655, 51 L. Ed. 956, (1907).
Winters v. United States, 207 U.S. 564, 28 S. Ct. 207, 52 L. Ed. 340 (1908).
Wyoming v. Colorado, 259 U.S. 419, 42 S. Ct. 552, 66 L. Ed. 999, (1922).
ROD, Record of Decision (2007). Colorado River Interim Guidelines for Lower Basin Shortages and the Coordinated Operations for Lake Powell and Lake Mead. December 2007. Retrieved from http://www.usbr.gov/lc/region/programs/strategies/RecordofDecision.pdf
CAP, Central Arizona Project (2014). Issue Brief, Strategic Initiatives and Public Policy: Colorado River Shortage. Retrieved from http://www.cap-az.com/documents/planning/Shortage_Issue_Brief.pdf on March 1, 2015.

Annex 2: Statistical analysis

Table 1 Variables used in the MCA

Role	Regulator
	Water Agency – Irrigation District
	Representative (RP) and contractors
	Think tank and intermediary actors
Type of influence	Board member of a water agency
	Negotiation/contractor
	Regulations
	Expertise
	Lobby
Volume of water managed	0
	1 = < 0.1 maf
	2 = 0.1–0.6 maf
	3 = 0.6–4 maf
	4 ≥ 4 maf
Director's bachelor's	Civil engineer
	Social sciences
	Environmental sciences
	Natural sciences
Director's Master's or PhD	MBA/Administration
	Environmental studies
	Hydro-engineering
	No Master's
Highest qualification of director	Bachelor's
	Master's
	PhD
	Juris doctorate (JD)
Sphere of professional careers	Water agency
	State/federal
	NGO to state/federal
	NGO
Priority objectives of water policies	Ecological conservation
	Economic development
	Institutional conservation
	Sustainable management
	Sustainable regulation
Categories of priority action instruments	Protecting ecosystems and rights of access

	Undefined
	Large-scale water subsidies
	New institutional framework
	Small-scale instruments
	Water markets
	Water planning
	Water quality
	Water reuses
Other instruments used	Education
	Groundwater instruments
	Large-scale water subsidies
	New institutional frameworks
	Small-scale instruments
	Water demand
	Water markets
	Water planning
	Water quality instruments
	Water reuses

Table 2 Water conservation instruments

Institution	Academic BA of the general manager/ director	Academic MA or PhD of the general manager	Highest academic degree of the executive manager	Expertise sustaining his/ her career	Sphere of professional career	Policy goals	Policy instruments
Arizona Blue Ribbon Water panel	Social sciences	No Masters	JD	Law/Econ.	Public institutions	Institutional conservation	Water reuses
Tucson Water/City of Tucson	Engineer	Hydroengineering	MA	Planning	Broker management	Sustainable regulation	Water reuses
Water Now Alliance	Social Sciences	Environmental studies	JD	Env. management	NGO	Institutional conservation	Water reuses
Palo Verde Irrigation District	Engineer	MBA/Public administration	MA	Water manager	Water utility	Economic development	Water reuses
Upper San Gabriel Valley Municipal Water District	Social Sciences	MBA/Public administration	MA	Law/Econ.	Water utility	Sustainable management	Water reuses
West Basin Municipal Water District	Engineer	Hydroengineering	MA	Water manager	Water utility	Sustainable management	Water reuses
Los Angeles Department of Water and Power	Engineer	Hydroengineering	MA	Water manager	Water utility	Sustainable management	Water reuses
Surfrider	Natural sciences	Environmental studies	MA	Env. science	NGO	Ecological conservation	Water reuses
Natural Resources Defense Council	Natural sciences	MBA/Public administration	MA	Env. science	Broker env.	Ecological conservation	Water reuses
California Urban Water Conservation Council		No Masters				Institutional conservation	Water reuses
Imperial Irrigation District	Engineer	No Masters	BA	Law/Econ.	Water utility	Economic development	Water reuses

The International Center For Water Technology	Engineer	Hydroengineering	PhD	Env. science	NGO	Institutional conservation	Water reuses
The Water Resources Institute, California State University	Social sciences	MBA/Public administration	MA	Env. science	NGO	Institutional conservation	Water reuses
Governor CA	Social sciences	MBA/Public administration	JD	Nominated	Public institutions	Sustainable regulation	Water reuses
Arizona Department of Water Resources	Natural sciences	No Masters	BA	Law/Econ.	Public institutions	Sustainable regulation	Water planning
Arizona Municipal Water Users Association	Social sciences	No Masters	JD	Law/Econ	Public institutions	Sustainable management	Water planning
BOR Lower Colorado Office	Natural sciences	Hydroengineering	PhD	planning	Public institutions	Sustainable regulation	Water planning
Central Arizona Project	Natural sciences	MBA/Public administration	MA	Planning	Water utility	Sustainable regulation	Water planning
City of Phoenix	Social sciences	MBA/Public administration	PhD	Planning	Water utility	Sustainable regulation	Water planning
Governor AZ	Social sciences	No Masters	BA	Business ties	Public institutions	Sustainable regulation	Water planning
Metro Water Tucson	Social sciences	MBA/Public administration	MA	Planning	Water utility	Sustainable regulation	Water planning
Morison Institute for Public Policy	Social sciences	No Masters	JD	Law/Econ.	Passeur management	Sustainable regulation	Water planning
Salt River Project	Engineer	Hydroengineering	BA	Planning	Water utility	Sustainable management	Water planning
Southern Arizona Water Users Association	Engineer	No Masters	MA	Planning	Water utility	Sustainable regulation	Water planning
Water Resources Research Center	Social Sciences	MBA/Public administration	PhD	Planning	Broker management	Sustainable regulation	Water planning
Arizona Water Banking Authority	Social sciences	Environmental studies	MA	Planning	Broker env.	Sustainable management	Water markets

(*Continued*)

Table 2 Continued

Institution	Academic BA of the general manager/director	Academic MA or PhD of the general manager	Highest academic degree of the executive manager	Expertise sustaining his/her career	Sphere of professional career	Policy goals	Policy instruments
City of Glendale	Engineer	Hydroengineering	MA	Technical	Water utility	Economic development	Water markets
City of Marana	Social sciences	MBA/Public administration	MA	Business ties	Water utility	Economic development	Water markets
City of Scottsdale	Social sciences	MBA/Public administration	JD	Law/Econ.	Water utility	Economic development	Water markets
Colorado River Negotiating Team	Natural sciences	No Masters	BA	Law/Econ.	Public institutions	Sustainable regulation	Water markets
San Diego County Water Authority	Social sciences	MBA/Public administration	MA	Law/Econ.	Water utility	Sustainable management	Water markets
Association of California Water agencies	Social sciences	MBA/Public administration	PhD	Law/Econ.	Water utility	Sustainable regulation	Water markets

Table 3 Test values (variables)

	F1	F2	F3
Role–Operator (U/ID)	**5,308**	1,009	**2,746**
Role–Regulator	**–3,729**	**–4,728**	**3,333**
Role–Representative and contractor	1,812	–1,862	**–5,716**
Role–Think Tank/IA	**–3,967**	**5,581**	–0,328
Type of influence–Expertise	**–3,398**	**4,373**	–0,602
Type of influence–Lobby	–0,704	1,738	–1,492
Type of influence–Negotiation/Contractor	**2,037**	–1,648	**–4,739**
Type of influence–Regulations	**–3,580**	**–4,913**	**3,359**
Type of influence–board member of a WA	**5,244**	0,670	**3,078**
Volume of water managed/bought/represented from the Colorado river in AF–V0	**–3,801**	**5,674**	–0,177
Volume of water managed/bought/represented from the Colorado river in AF–V1	**3,409**	0,632	**2,710**
Volume of water managed/bought/represented from the Colorado river in AF–V2	**3,601**	–0,141	–0,055
Volume of water managed/bought/represented from the Colorado river in AF–V3	1,859	–0,252	**–3,622**
Volume of water managed/bought/represented from the Colorado river in AF–V4	**–3,602**	**–5,312**	0,635
Academic BA of the General Manager/Director–Engineer	**4,559**	0,408	**2,433**
Academic BA of the General Manager/Director–Natural Sciences	**–3,262**	**2,229**	0,978
Academic BA of the General Manager/Director–Social Sciences	–1,375	**–2,352**	**–3,137**
Academic MA or PhD of the General Manager–Environmental Studies	**–4,277**	–0,406	0.971
Academic MA or PhD of the General Manager–MBA/PAdministration	1,888	–0,584	**–3,159**
Academic MA or PhD of the General Manager–No Masters	0,520	**–2,001**	1,410
Academic MA or PhD of the General Manager–hydroengineering	1,468	**2,955**	1,407
Highest academic degree of the Executive Manager–BA	1,182	–1,902	**3,058**
Highest academic degree of the Executive Manager–JD	**–2,499**	**–3,442**	**–2,330**
Highest academic degree of the Executive Manager–MA	**2,212**	**2,102**	0,138
Highest academic degree of the Executive Manager–PhD	–1,444	**3,195**	–0,467
Expertise sustaining his/her career–Env. Management	**–2,848**	**–2,302**	1,426
Expertise sustaining his/her career–Env. Science	**–2,732**	**4,440**	1,096
Expertise sustaining his/her career–Law/Econ.	0,603	**–2,262**	**–4,200**
Expertise sustaining his/her career–Nominated	–1,556	**–2,329**	0,468
Expertise sustaining his/her career–Water Manager	**3,993**	1,184	**2,007**
Expertise sustaining his/her career–business ties	0,090	–1,843	**2,515**

(*Continued*)

Table 3 Continued

	F1	F2	F3
Expertise sustaining his/her career–ecology	−1,851	0,018	0,810
Expertise sustaining his/her career–planning	1,103	0,882	**−2,075**
Expertise sustaining his/her career–technical	1,607	0,436	1,205
Professional career–Broker Management	−0,490	−0,028	−0,092
Professional career–Envir. Broker	**−2,339**	−0,410	−0,415
Professional career–NGO	**−3,083**	**5,257**	0,391
Professional career–Public Institutions	**−2,978**	**−4,138**	−0,011
Professional career–Water utility	**6,526**	0,064	0,011
Policy goals–Ecological Conservation	**−2,252**	**2,898**	−0,658
Policy goals–Economic Development	**3,679**	0,624	0,304
Policy goals–Institutional Conservation	**−3,935**	−0,605	1,472
Policy goals–Sustainable Management	**3,510**	−0,377	−0,680
Policy goals–Sustainable Regulation	−1,079	−1,598	−0,585
Policy instruments1–Ecosystems & Human Rights	−1,915	0,962	1,894
Policy instruments1–Large-Scale Water Supply	1,458	0,680	−0,041
Policy instruments1–New Inst Frame	**−3,368**	−0,908	1,381
Policy instruments1–Small-Scale Instr.	**2,668**	0,315	**2,954**
Policy instruments1–Water Markets	**2,005**	−1,217	**−2,754**
Policy instruments1–Water Planning	0,061	−0,691	−1,100
Policy instruments1–Water Quality	−1,419	−1,385	0,506
Policy instruments1–Water Reuses	0,151	1,583	−0,922

Les valeurs affichées en gras sont significatives au seuil alpha=0,05

Table 4 Contribution of the variables

	F1	F2	F3
Role–Operator (U/ID)	7,496	0,298	3,390
Role–Regulator	4,062	7,173	5,481
Role–Representative and contractor	0,916	1,063	15,405
Role–Think Tank/IA	4,595	9,997	0,053
Type of influence–Expertise	3,446	6,272	0,183
Type of influence–Lobby	0,161	1,078	1,220
Type of influence–Negotiation/Contractor	1,239	0,891	11,326
Type of influence–Regulations	3,826	7,917	5,691
Type of influence–board member of a WA	7,852	0,141	4,569
Volume of water managed/bought/represented from the Colorado river in AF–V0	4,220	10,330	0,015
Volume of water managed/bought/represented from the Colorado river in AF–V1	3,696	0,139	3,947
Volume of water managed/bought/represented from the Colorado river in AF–V2	3,955	0,007	0,002
Volume of water managed/bought/represented from the Colorado river in AF–V3	1,144	0,023	7,334
Volume of water managed/bought/represented from the Colorado river in AF–V4	3,368	8,048	0,177
Academic BA of the General Manager/Director–Engineer	5,395	0,047	2,596
Academic BA of the General Manager/Director–Natural Sciences	2,969	1,524	0,451
Academic BA of the General Manager/Director–Social Sciences	0,405	1,302	3,561
Academic MA or PhD of the General Manager–Environmental Studies	5,462	0,054	0,476
Academic MA or PhD of the General Manager–MBA/PAdministration	0,833	0,088	3,940
Academic MA or PhD of the General Manager–No Masters	0,083	1,342	1,025
Academic MA or PhD of the General Manager–hydroengineering	0,630	2,802	0,977
Highest academic degree of the Executive Manager–BA	0,453	1,289	5,128
Highest academic degree of the Executive Manager–JD	1,824	3,802	2,679
Highest academic degree of the Executive Manager–MA	0,889	0,882	0,006
Highest academic degree of the Executive Manager–PhD	0,690	3,713	0,122
Expertise sustaining his/her career–Env. Management	2,738	1,965	1,159
Expertise sustaining his/her career–Env. Science	2,373	6,888	0,645
Expertise sustaining his/her career–Law/Econ.	0,106	1,642	8,703
Expertise sustaining his/her career–Nominated	0,880	2,167	0,134
Expertise sustaining his/her career–Water Manager	4,862	0,470	2,076
Expertise sustaining his/her career–business ties	0,003	1,333	3,815
Expertise sustaining his/her career–ecology	1,245	0,000	0,402
Expertise sustaining his/her career–planning	0,371	0,261	2,219
Expertise sustaining his/her career–technical	0,955	0,077	0,907
Professional career–Broker Management	0,083	0,000	0,005
Professional career–Envir. Broker	1,882	0,063	0,100
Professional career–NGO	3,022	9,659	0,082
Professional career–Public Institutions	2,474	5,252	0,000
Professional career–Water utility	9,396	0,001	0,000

Table 5 Coordinates (variables)

	F1	F2	F3
Role–Operator (U/ID)	1,430	0,285	0,962
Role–Regulator	−1,204	−1,600	1,399
Role–Representative and contractor	0,532	−0,574	−2,183
Role–Think Tank/IA	−1,281	1,889	−0,138
Type of influence–Expertise	−1,154	1,557	−0,266
Type of influence–Lobby	−0,305	0,791	−0,841
Type of influence–Negotiation/Contractor	0,692	−0,587	−2,093
Type of influence–Regulations	−1,216	−1,750	1,483
Type of influence–board member of a WA	1,613	0,216	1,231
Volume of water managed/bought/represented from the Colorado river in AF–V0	−1,227	1,920	−0,074
Volume of water managed/bought/represented from the Colorado river in AF–V1	1,380	0,268	1,427
Volume of water managed/bought/represented from the Colorado river in AF–V2	1,292	−0,053	−0,026
Volume of water managed/bought/represented from the Colorado river in AF–V3	0,871	−0,124	−2,205
Volume of water managed/bought/represented from the Colorado river in AF–V4	−0,932	−1,440	0,214
Academic BA of the General Manager/Director–Engineer	1,179	0,111	0,818
Academic BA of the General Manager/Director–Natural Sciences	−0,958	0,687	0,373
Academic BA of the General Manager/Director–Social Sciences	−0,274	−0,492	−0,813
Academic MA or PhD of the General Manager–Environmental Studies	−1,453	−0,145	0,429
Academic MA or PhD of the General Manager–MBA/PAdministration	0,419	−0,136	−0,912
Academic MA or PhD of the General Manager–No Masters	0,187	−0,752	0,657
Academic MA or PhD of the General Manager–hydroengineering	0,474	1,000	0,590
Highest academic degree of the Executive Manager–BA	0,513	−0,865	1,725
Highest academic degree of the Executive Manager–JD	−0,807	−1,165	−0,978
Highest academic degree of the Executive Manager–MA	0,371	0,369	0,030
Highest academic degree of the Executive Manager–PhD	−0,676	1,569	−0,284
Expertise sustaining his/her career–Env. Management	−1,455	−1,233	0,947
Expertise sustaining his/her career–Env. Science	−1,106	1,884	0,577
Expertise sustaining his/her career–Law/Econ.	0,195	−0,765	−1,762
Expertise sustaining his/her career–Nominated	−1,429	−2,242	0,558
Expertise sustaining his/her career–Water Manager	1,432	0,445	0,936
Expertise sustaining his/her career–business ties	0,067	−1,436	2,429
Expertise sustaining his/her career–ecology	−1,700	0,018	0,966
Expertise sustaining his/her career–planning	0,396	0,332	−0,967
Expertise sustaining his/her career–technical	2,105	0,599	2,052
Professional career–Broker Management	−0,277	−0,017	−0,068
Professional career–Envir. Broker	−1,322	−0,243	−0,305
Professional career–NGO	−1,248	2,231	0,206
Professional career–Public Institutions	−0,875	−1,275	−0,004

(*Continued*)

Professional career–Water utility	1,348	0,014	0,003
Policy goals–Ecological Conservation	−1,150	1,552	−0,437
Policy goals–Economic Development	1,320	0,235	0,142
Policy goals–Institutional Conservation	−1,271	−0,205	0,618
Policy goals–Sustainable Management	1,259	−0,142	−0,317
Policy goals–Sustainable Regulation	−0,291	−0,452	−0,205
Policy instruments1–Ecosystems & Human Rights	−0,978	0,515	1,258
Policy instruments1–Large-Scale Water Supply	0,824	0,403	−0,030
Policy instruments1–New Inst Frame	−1,461	−0,413	0,779
Policy instruments1–Small-Scale Instr.	1,701	0,210	2,448
Policy instruments1–Water Markets	0,762	−0,485	−1,361
Policy instruments1–Water Planning	0,022	−0,260	−0,513
Policy instruments1–Water Quality	−1,859	−1,902	0,861
Policy instruments1–Water Reuses	0,049	0,536	−0,387

Table 6 Coordinates (observations)

	F1	F2	F3
Arizona Blue Ribbon Water panel	−0,131	−0,804	−1,066
Arizona Department of Environmental Quality	−0,210	−0,969	1,082
Arizona Department of Water Resources	−0,536	−0,970	0,511
Arizona Municipal Water Users Association	−0,007	−0,536	−0,744
Arizona Water Banking Authority	−0,023	−0,183	−1,013
BOR Lower Colorado office	−0,616	0,104	0,132
CAGRD	0,427	0,165	−0,798
Central Arizona Project	−0,044	−0,328	−0,693
City of Glendale	1,227	0,318	0,708
City of Marana	0,794	−0,114	0,545
City of Phoenix	0,641	0,208	−0,373
City of Scottsdale	0,652	−0,262	−0,287
Colorado River Negotiating Team	−0,081	−0,696	−0,384
Fish and Wildlife Service Southwest Region	−0,996	−0,642	0,611
Governor AZ	−0,467	−1,201	0,886
Governor's Water Augmentation Council AZ	−0,316	−0,456	−0,650
Metro Water Tucson	0,824	0,067	−0,061
Morison Institute for Public Policy	−0,580	0,272	−0,430
Nature Conservancy	−0,984	0,661	0,055
Pima County	0,099	−0,393	0,656
Salt River Project	0,863	0,021	−0,146
Southern Arizona Water Users Association	0,572	0,021	−0,586
Tucson Water/City of Tucson	0,810	0,280	0,321
Watershed Management Group	−0,408	0,751	−0,012
Water Resources Research Center	−0,509	0,828	−0,440
Central Basin Municipal water district	1,147	0,197	0,562
Colorado River Board of California	−0,131	−0,804	−1,066
California Department of Water Resources (Planning division)	−0,655	−0,481	0,618
State Water Resources control board	−1,083	−1,008	0,297
Water now Alliance	−1,112	0,571	−0,086
Irvine Ranch Water District	1,147	0,197	0,562
The Municipal Water District of Orange County	1,142	0,298	0,568
Metropolitan Water District of Southern California	0,372	−0,479	−1,368
Coachella Valley Water District	0,908	−0,051	−0,428
Audubond	−1,007	1,299	0,142
Environmental Defense Fund	−0,897	1,592	0,123
Water foundation	−0,409	0,682	−0,007
Yorba Linda Water district	0,551	0,217	0,869
Palo Verde Irrigation District. Reçoit	0,908	−0,051	−0,428
Upper San Gabriel Valley Municipal Water District	0,810	−0,030	0,021
West Basin Municipal water district	1,142	0,298	0,568
Los Angeles Department of Water and Power	0,926	0,131	−0,059
San Diego County Water Authority	0,572	−0,278	−0,969
Family Farm alliance	−0,004	0,966	0,273
Pacific institute	−0,897	1,592	0,123
Association of California Water Agencies	0,151	−0,022	−0,429
Surfrider	−0,901	1,203	0,070

(Continued)

Natural Resources Defense Council	−0,676	0,895	−0,161
Imperial Irrigation District	0,701	−0,211	−1,038
Santa Monica city	1,135	−0,035	0,970
San Fernando city	1,135	−0,035	0,970
California Department of Fish and Wildlife	−1,083	−1,008	0,297
Natural Resources Agency	−0,880	−0,946	0,461
California Environmental Protection Agency	−1,027	−1,137	0,335
The international Center for Water Technology	−0,630	1,520	0,179
The Water Resources Institute, California State University	−0,688	1,153	−0,174
Governor CA	−0,790	−1,262	0,118
Secretary of the Interior	−0,875	−1,115	0,267

Table 7 Contributions (observations)

	F1	F2	F3
Arizona Blue Ribbon Water Panel	0,051	2,103	5,686
Arizona Department of Environmental Quality	0,131	3,051	5,855
Arizona Department of Water Resources	0,851	3,060	1,303
Arizona Municipal Water Users Association	0,000	0,933	2,765
Arizona Water Banking Authority	0,002	0,109	5,134
BOR Lower Colorado office	1,124	0,035	0,087
CAGRD	0,538	0,088	3,186
Central Arizona Project	0,006	0,350	2,399
City of Glendale	4,452	0,328	2,503
City of Marana	1,867	0,042	1,483
City of Phoenix	1,215	0,141	0,696
City of Scottsdale	1,258	0,223	0,411
Colorado River Negotiating Team	0,019	1,577	0,738
Fish and Wildlife Service Southwest Region	2,935	1,340	1,868
Governor AZ	0,645	4,691	3,927
Governor's Water Augmentation Council AZ	0,296	0,676	2,111
Metro Water Tucson	2,011	0,015	0,019
Morison Institute for Public Policy	0,995	0,240	0,925
Nature Conservancy	2,868	1,420	0,015
Pima County	0,029	0,502	2,149
Salt River Project	2,204	0,001	0,106
Southern Arizona Water Users Association	0,969	0,001	1,717
Tucson Water/City of Tucson	1,941	0,256	0,516
Watershed Management Group	0,493	1,836	0,001
Water Resources Research Center	0,768	2,228	0,969
Central Basin Municipal Water District	3,891	0,126	1,578
Colorado River Board of California	0,051	2,103	5,686
California Department of Water Resources (Planning Division)	1,268	0,751	1,911
State Water Resources Control Board	3,470	3,306	0,441
Water Now Alliance	3,663	1,058	0,037
Irvine Ranch Water District	3,891	0,126	1,578
The Municipal Water District of Orange County	3,862	0,290	1,613
Metropolitan Water District of Southern California	0,410	0,745	9,354
Coachella Valley Water District	2,441	0,009	0,917
Audubond	3,002	5,489	0,101
Environmental Defense Fund	2,382	8,244	0,076
Water Foundation	0,495	1,513	0,000
Yorba Linda Water District	0,898	0,153	3,778
Palo Verde Irrigation District–Reçoit	2,441	0,009	0,917
Upper San Gabriel Valley Municipal Water District	1,943	0,003	0,002
West Basin Municipal Water District	3,862	0,290	1,613
Los Angeles Department of Water and Power	2,538	0,056	0,017
San Diego County Water Authority	0,968	0,251	4,699
Family Farm alliance	0,000	3,035	0,372
Pacific institute	2,382	8,244	0,076
Association of California Water Agencies	0,067	0,002	0,921
Surfrider	2,403	4,709	0,025
Natural Resources Defense Council	1,353	2,606	0,130

(*Continued*)

Imperial Irrigation District	1,454	0,145	5,386
Santa Monica city	3,815	0,004	4,702
San Fernando city	3,815	0,004	4,702
California Department of Fish and Wildlife	3,470	3,306	0,441
Natural Resources Agency	2,291	2,907	1,060
California Environmental Protection Agency	3,122	4,206	0,560
The International Center for Water Technology	1,174	7,515	0,159
The Water Resources Institute, California State University	1,399	4,323	0,151
Governor CA	1,846	5,182	0,070
Secretary of the Interior	2,267	4,044	0,356

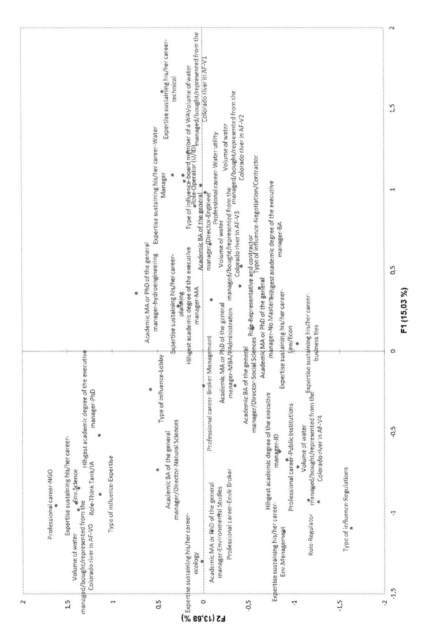

Diagram 1 Active variables axis 1 and 2

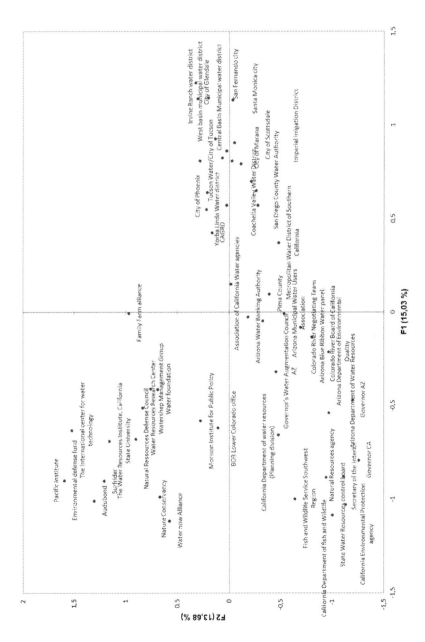

Diagram 2 Observations axis 1 and 2

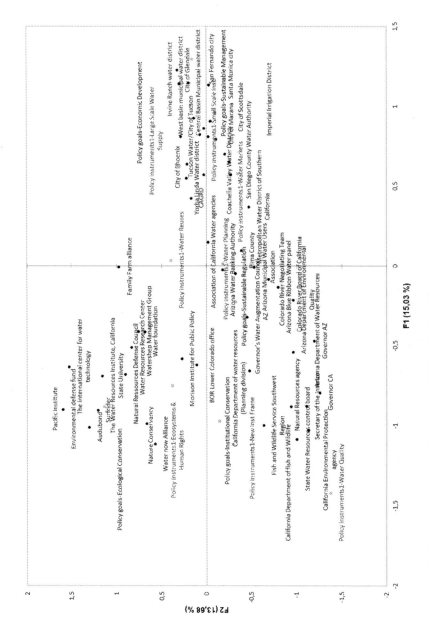

Diagram 3 Observations and supplementary variables axis 1 and 2

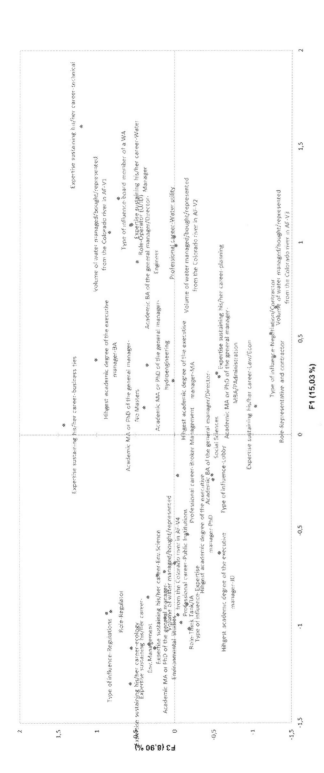

Diagram 4 Active variables axis 1 and 3

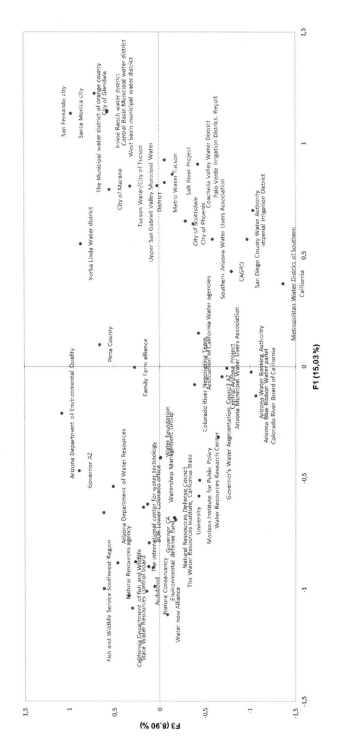

Diagram 5 Observations axis 1 and 3

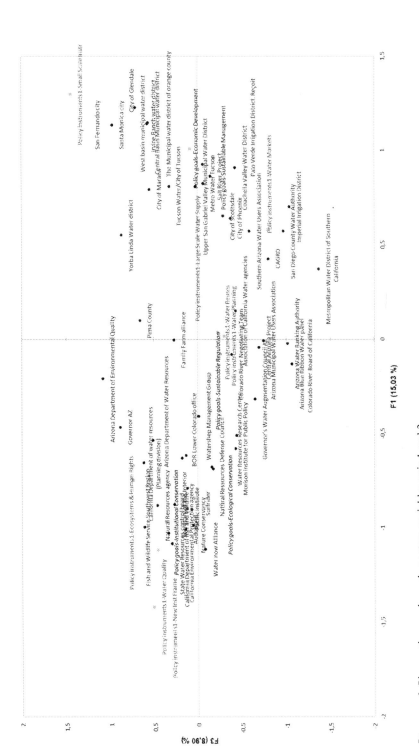

Diagram 6 Observations and supplementary variables axis 1 and 3

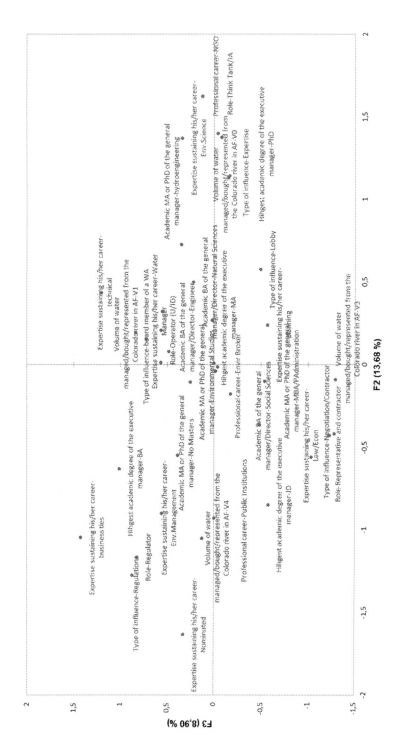

Diagram 7 Active variables axis 2 and 3

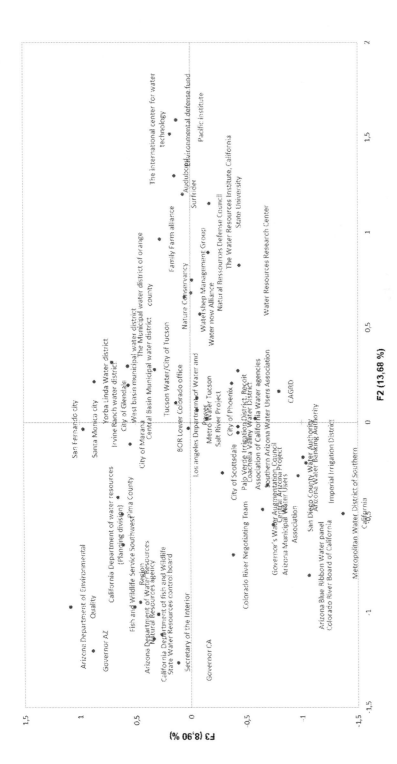

Diagram 8 Observations axis 2 and 3

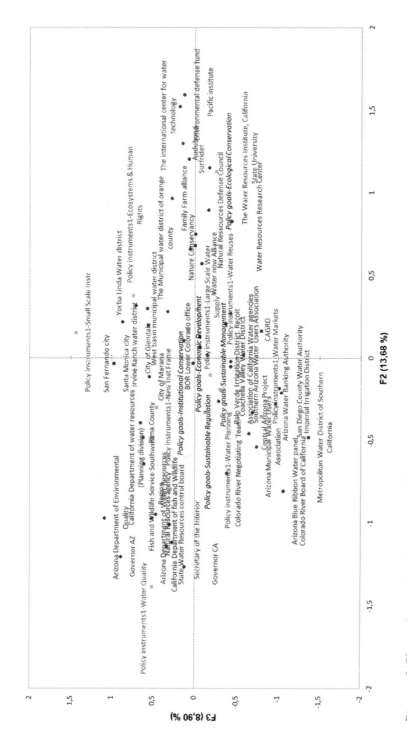

Diagram 9 Observations and supplementary variables axis 2 and 3

Bibliography

Abbey E. (1968). *Desert Solitaire*. Tucson: University of Arizona Press.

Abbott C. (1981). *The New Urban America: Growth and Politics in Sunbelt Cities*. Chapel Hill: Univ. N.C. Press.

Abbott C. (1993). *The Metropolitan Frontier: Cities in the Modern American West*. Tucson: Univ. Ariz. Press.

ADWR (2014). Arizona's Next Century: A Strategic Vision on Water for Water Sustainability. Retrieved from: http://www.azwater.gov/AzDWR/Arizonas_Strateg ic_Vision/documents/ArizonasHistoricalSuccessesinWaterManagement.pdf

Albright James et al. (eds.) (2017). *Bourdieu's Field Theory and the Social Sciences*. Singapore: Palgrave McMillan.

Allan J.T. & Mirumachi N. (2010). Why negotiate? Asymmetric endowments, asymmetric power and the invisible nexus of water, trade and power that brings apparent water security, *Transboundary Water Management: Principles and Practice*. 13–26.

Al-Sabbry M.M., DeVerle H. & Fox R. (2002). An economic assessment of groundwater recharge in the Tucson Basin, *Journal of the American Water Resources Association*, 38(1): 119–131.

Ambrose W.A. & Lynn P. (1986). Groundwater recharge: Enhancing Arizona's aquifers, *Journal of the American Water Works Association*, 78(10): 85–90.

Anand N. (2012). Municipal disconnect: on abject water and its urban infrastructures, *Ethnography*, 13(4): 487–509.

APCLDI (2015). Annual Pima County Local Drought Impact Group Report.

Archer J. (2005). *Architecture and Suburbia: From English Villa to American Dream House*, 1690-2000. Minneapolis: University of Minnesota Press.

Arts B., Leroy P. & van Tatenhove J. (2006). Political modernisation and policy arrangements: A framework for understanding environmental policy change, *Public Organization Review*, 6: 93–106.

August J.L. (1999). *Vision in the Desert. Carl Hayden and Hydropolitics in the American Southwest*. Fort Worth: Texas Christian University Press.

August J.L. (2007). *Dividing Western Waters. Mark Wilmer and Arizona v California*. Fort Worth: TCU Press.

Avery C., Consoli C., Glennon R. & Megdal S. (2007). Good intentions, unintended consequences: The Central Arizona Groundwater Replenishment District, *Arizona Law Review*, (49): 339–359.

Bachelard G. (1999). *Water and Dreams: An Essay on the Imagination of Matter*. Dallas: Institute for Humanities & Culture.

208 *Bibliography*

Bakker D., Eckerberg K. & Zachrisson A. (2014). Political science and ecological restoration, *Environmental Politics*, 23(3): 509–524.

Bakker K. (2010). *Privatizing Water. Governance Failure and the World's Urban Water Crisis*. Ithaca and London: Cornell University Press.

Banister J.M. (2014). Are you Wittfogel or against him? Geophilosophy, hydro-sociality, and the state, *Geoforum*, 57: 205–214.

Barbier D. (2015). Climate change impacts on rural poverty in low-elevation coastal zones, *Estuarine, Coastal and Shelf Science*, 165: A1–13.

Barnet T. et al. (2008). Human-induced changes in the hydrology of the Western United States, *Science*, 319: 1080–1083.

Barraqué B. (2003), The three ages of engineering for the water industry. *Stanford-France STS Conference*, April 7–8, 2003. Retrieved from: https://web.stanford.edu/dept/france-stanford/Conferences/Risk/Barraque.pdf

Barraqué B. (ed.) (2011). *Urban Water Conflicts*. UNESCO IPH, CRC Press.

Barraqué B. (2015). Three engineering paradigms in the historical development of water services: more, better and cheaper water to European cities. In: *Understanding and Managing Urban Water in Transition*, pp. 201–216. Dordrecht: Springer.

Baudot P. Y. (2011). L'incertitude des instruments: L'informatique administrative et le changement dans l'action publique (ann.es 1960–1970). *Revue Française de Science Politique*, 61(1): 79–103.

Beaudry B. (1999, October 18). Yes On Prop 200. *Tucson Weekly*. Retrieved from: http://www.tucsonweekly.com/tucson/yes-on-prop-200/Content?oid=1065474

Beierle T.C. & Cayford J. (2002). *Democracy in Practice: Public Participation in Environmental Decisions*. Washington, DC: Resources for the Future.

Béland D. & Vergniolle de Chantal F. (2014). L'Etat en Amérique. Entre invisibilité politique et fragmentation institutionnelle, *Revue française de science politique*, 64(2): 191–205.

Benites E. (2016). The social logic of urban sprawl: Arizona cities under environmental pressure. In: Poupeau F., Hoshin G., Serrat-Capdevila A., Sans-Fuentes M., Harris S., & Hayde L. (dir.), *Water Bankruptcy in the Land of Plenty*, New York: CRC Press, Taylor & Francis Group, 121–140.

Benites E., Coeurdray M. & Poupeau F. (2016). Une promotion immobilière sous contraintes environnementales. Les logiques sociales du périurbain dans les *Desert Cities* de l'Ouest étasunien, *Revue française de sociologie*, 57(4): 735–765.

Bergeron H., Surel Y. & Valluy J. (1998). *L'Advocacy Coalition Framework*. Une contribution au renouvellement des études de politiques publiques? *Politix*, 11(41): 195–223.

Bezes P. & Le Lidec P. (2016). Politiques de l'organisation. Les nouvelles divisions du travail étatique, *Revue française de science politique*, 66(3): 407–433.

Bezes P. & Le Lidec P. (2016). Politiques de la fusion. Les nouvelles frontières de l'État territorial, *Revue française de science politique*, 66(3): 507–541.

Bichsel C. (2016). Water and the (infra-)structure of political rule: A synthesis. *Water Alternatives*, 9(2): 356–372.

Biggers J. (2012). *State out of the Union. Arizona and the Showdown over the American Dream*. New York: Nations Book.

B.land D. & Vergniolle de Chantal F. (2014). L'Etat en Am.rique. Entre invisibilité politique et fragmentation institutionnelle, *Revue française de science politique*, 64(2): 191–205.

Bibliography 209

Blomquist W., Heikkila T. & Schlager E. (2001). Institutions and conjunctive water management among three western states, *Natural Resources Journal*, 41(3): 653–683.

Bohn S. et al. (2016). *California's Future*. Los Angeles: Public Policy Institute of California. Retrieved from: http://www.ppic.org/main/publication.asp?i=895

Bourdieu P. (1977). La production de la croyance [contribution à une économie des biens symboliques], *Actes de la recherche en sciences sociales*, 13: 3–43. DOI: 10.3406/arss.1977.3493

Bourdieu P. (1991). Le champ littéraire, *Actes de la recherche en sciences sociales*, 89: 3–46. DOI: 10.3406/arss.1991.2986

Bourdieu P. (1996). *The Rules of Art: Genesis and Structure of the Literary Field*. Stanford: Stanford University Press.

Bourdieu P. (1997). Le champ économique, *Actes de la recherche en sciences sociales*, 119: 48–66. DOI: 10.3406/arss.1997.3229

Bourdieu P. (1999). Une révolution conservatrice dans l'édition, *Actes de la recherche en sciences sociales*, 126: 3–28. DOI: 10.3406/arss.1999.3278

Bourdieu P. (2001). *Les Structures sociales de l'économie*. Paris: Seuil.

Bourdieu P. (2005). *The Social Structures of the Economy*. Cambridge: Polity Press.

Bourdieu P. (2008). A conservative revolution in publishing. *Translation Studies*, 1(2): 123–153.

Bourdieu P. (2012). *Sur l'Etat. Cours au Collège de France (1989-1992)*. Paris: Raisons d'agir/Seuil.

Bourdieu P. & Christin R. (1990). La construction du marché. Le champ administratif et la production de la "politique du logement", *Actes de la recherche en sciences sociales*, 88–89: 65–85.

Bourdieu P. & De Saint Martin M. (1978). Le patronat, *Actes de la recherche en sciences sociales*, 20–21: 3–82. DOI: 10.3406/arss.1978.2592

Bourdieu P. & Wacquant L.J. 1992. *An Invitation to Reflexive Sociology*. University of Chicago Press.

Boyer A.-L., Le Gouill C., Poupeau F. & Ramirez-Andreotta M. (2018). Sustainable mining and political participation in semi-arid areas of Western United States: lessons from the Rosemont case study. *Regional Climate Change*, 19(2): 501–513.

Boyer R., Boyer D. & Lafert G. (2007). La connexion des r.seaux comme facteur de changement institutionnel: l'exemple des vins de Bourgogne. PSE Working Papers N. 2007-42. halshs-00587708.

Burt R.S. (1992). *Structural Holes: The Social Structure of Competition*. Cambridge, MA: Harvard University Press.

Burt R.S. (2005). *Brokerage and Closure. An Introduction to Social Capital*. New York: Oxford University Press.

Cadieux K.V. & Taylor L. (eds.). (2013). *Landscape and the Ideology of Nature in Exurbia: Green Sprawl*. Routledge.

Carpenter D.P. (2001). *The Forging of Bureaucratic Autonomy: Reputations, Networks, and Policy Innovation in Executive Agencies, 1862-1928*. Princeton, NJ/Oxford: Princeton University Press.

Carroll P. (2012a). Water and technoscientific state formation in California. *Social Studies of Science*, 31(4): 593–626.

Carroll P. (2012b). Water and technoscientific state formation in California. *Social Studies of Science*, 42(4): 489–516.

Casado-Perez V. (2017). *The Role of Government in Water Markets*. Routledge.

210 Bibliography

Chavarochette C. (2016). Sujet sensible. Enquêter sur l'eau au sud-ouest des États-Unis. *ethnographiques.org*, 32. (http://ethnographiques.org/2016/Chavarochette, 6.10.2016)

Chesnick J. (1999, October 25). Special Report: Prop. 200. *Tucson Citizen*. Retrieved from: http://tucsoncitizen.com/morgue2/1999/10/25/227787-special-report-prop-200/

Coeurdray M., Cortinas J. & Poupeau F. (2014). *Water wars in the Western United States : Crossed Border Disputes and Resolution Conflict*, Bluegrass Project ANR.

Coeurdray M., Cortinas J., O'Neill B. & Poupeau F. (2015). The crossed border disputes over sharing Colorado River between the American Southwestern States – a sociological perspective on environmental policies, *Waterlat Working Papers*, 2(3): 65–78.

Coeurdray M., Poupeau F., Cortinas J. & O'Neill B. (2016a). "Delivering more than water". The salt river project: The invention of an adaptive partnership for water management. In: Lorrain D. & Poupeau F., *Water Regimes. Beyond the Public and Private Sector Debate*. London: Routledge.

Coeurdray M., Cortinas J., O'Neill B. & Poupeau F. (2016b). Sharing the Colorado River: The policy coalitions of the Central Arizona Project (part2). In: Poupeau F., Hoshin G., Serrat-Capdevila A., Sans-Fuentes M., Harris S. & Hayde L. (dir.), *Water Bankruptcy in the Land of Plenty*. New York: CRC Press, Taylor & Francis Group, 79–97.

Colby B. (1987). Do water markets "work"? Market transfers and trade-offs in the southwestern states, *Water Resources Research*, 23(7): 1113–1122.

Colby B.C. & Jacobs K.L. (eds.) (2007). *Arizona Water Policy. Management Innovations in an Urbanizing, Arid Region*. Washington: Resources for the Future Press.

Colby B.G. & Jacobs K.L. (eds.). (2007). *Arizona Water Policy: Management Innovations in an Urbanizing Arid Region*. London: Routledge.

Connall Jr, D.D. (1982). History of the Arizona Groundwater Management Act, *Arizona State Law Journal*, (2) 313–343.

Considine M., Lewis J. & Alexander D. (2009). *Networks, Innovation and Public Policy. Politicians, Bureaucrats and the Pathways to Change inside Government*. New York: Palgrave McMillan.

Cortinas J., Coeurdray M. & Poupeau F. (2015). Du Reclamation act de 1902 aux megaprojets fédéraux – Une perspective socio-historique sur la genèse des politiques hydriques aux USA: le cas de l'Ouest étasunien, *Cuadernos de Desarrollo Rural*, 12(76): 135–153.

Cortinas J., Coeurdray M., O'Neill B. & Poupeau F. (2016a). Les mégaprojets hydriques de l'Ouest étasunien: histoire d'État(s) et gestion des ressources naturelles, *VertigO*, 16(3). Retrieved from: https://vertigo.revues.org/18085, DOI: 10.4000/vertigo.18085

Cortinas J., Coeurdray M. & Poupeau F. (2016b). Coalitions et politiques hydriques dans l'Ouest étasunien. Systèmes techniques, Etat, Environnement, *VertigO*. Retrieved from: https://vertigo.revues.org/18085

Cortinas J., Coeurdray M., O'Neill B. & Poupeau F. (2016c). Water for a New America: The policy coalitions of the Central Arizona Project (part1). In: Poupeau F., Hoshin G., Serrat-Capdevila A., Sans-Fuentes M., Harris S., & Hayde L. (dir.), *Water Bankruptcy in the Land of Plenty*. Delft: CRC Press, Taylor & Francis Group, pp. 77–97.

Cortinas J., O'Neill B. & Poupeau F. (2017). Drought and water policy in the Western United States. Genesis and structure of a multi-level field. In: J. Albright et al. (eds.), *Bourdieu's Field Theory and the Social Sciences*. Sidney: Palgrave, pp. 21–37. Retrieved from: https://doi.org/10.1007/978-981-10-5385-6_2

Bibliography 211

Cortinas J. (2018). La transición hídrica en el Sur de California. Un análisis sociológico de las políticas medioambientales. In Vallejos-Romero et al. (eds.), *Riesgo, Gobernanza y Conflictos Socioambientales*. Santiago de Chile: Ediciones Universidad de la Frontera, pp. 205–245.

Cortinas et al. (2019). Un consensus paradoxal. Conservation des ressources hydriques et croissance économique en Arizona, *Revue française de science politique*, 4(69): 601–630.

Cronon W. (1992). *Nature's Metropolis. Chicago and the Great West*. New York/London: Norton, Co.

Crow-Miller B., Webber M. & Molle F. (2017). The (re)turn to infrastructure for water management? *Water Alternatives*, 10(2): 195–207.

Culp P.W., Glennon R.J. & Libecap G. (2014). *Shopping for Water: How the Market Can Mitigate Water Shortages in the American West*. New York: Island Press.

Dames and Moore Inc. (1995). *CAP Use Study for Water Quality: A Review of CAP-Related Decisions from 1965 to present*. Retrieved on October 3, 2014 from: http://www.savethesantacruzaquifer.info/CAPQualityReport.pdf

Davis S.K. (2001). The politics of water scarcity in the Western States, *The Social Science Journal*, 38: 527–542.

Davis T. (1999, October 25). Water Starts Fires in Tucson Election. High Country News. Retrieved from: https://www.hcn.org/issues/166/5359

deBuys W. (2011). *A Great Aridness. Climate Change and the Future of the American Southwest*. New York: Oxford University Press.

Delli Priscoli J. & Wolf A.T. (2009). *Managing and Transforming Water Conflicts*. Cambridge/New York: Cambridge University Press, International Hydrology Series.

De Nooy W. (2003). Fields and networks: Correspondence analysis and social network analysis in the framework of field theory, *Poetics*, 31(5–6): 305–327. DOI: 10.1016/S0304-422X(03)00035-4

Dezalay Y. (2007). De la défense de l'environnement au développement durable. L'émergence d'un champ d'expertise des politiques européennes, *Actes de la recherche en sciences sociales*, 166–167: 66–79. DOI: 10.3917/arss.166.0067

Doern B. & Johnson R. (eds.) (2006). *Rules, Rules, Rules, Rules. Multi-Level Regulatory Governance*. Toronto: University of Toronto Press.

Douglas Henry A. (2011). Ideology, Power, and the Structure of Policy Networks. *The Policy Studies Journal*, 39(3): 361–383.

Doyle M. (1983). Transportation provisions of Arizona's 1980 groundwater management act: A proposed definition of compensable injury, *The Arizona Law Review*, 25: 655.

Dubois V. (1999). *La Politique culturelle. Genèse d'une catégorie d'intervention publique*. Paris: Belin.

Dubois V. (2014). L'action de l'Etat, produit et enjeu des rapports entre espaces sociaux, *Actes de la recherche en sciences sociales*, 201–202: 13–25.

Durkheim E. (1893/1964). *The Division of Labor in Society*. New York: Free Press of Glencoe.

Duval J. (2006). L'art du réalisme. Le champ du cinéma français au début des années 2000, *Actes de la recherche en sciences sociales*, 161–162: 96–115. DOI: 10.3917/arss.161.0096

Duval J. (2013). L'analyse des correspondances et la construction des champs, *Actes de la recherche en sciences sociales*, 200(5): 110–123. DOI: 10.3917/arss.200.0110

Erie S.P. (2006). *Beyond Chinatown: The Metropolitan Water District, Growth, and the Environment*. Stanford, CA: Stanford University Press.

212   Bibliography

Espeland W. (1998). *The Struggle for Water. Politics, Rationality and Identity in the American Southwest.* Chicago/London: The University of Chicago Press.

Feller J.M. (2007). Adjudication that ate arizona water law. *Arizona Law Review*, 49(2): 405–440.

Fleck J. (2016). *Water is for Fighting Over, and Other Myths about Water in the West.* Washington/Covelo/London: Island Press.

Fligstein N. (1997). Fields, power and social skill: A critical analysis of the new institutionalisms. In: *Recent Work, Center for Culture, Organizations and Politics, Institute for Research on Labor and Employment.* UC Berkeley. Permalink. Retrieved from: http://www.escholarship.org/uc/item/89m770dv

Fligstein N. (2013). Understanding stability and change in fields, *Research in Organizational Behavior*, 33: 39–51.

Fligstein N. & Calder R. (2015). Architecture of markets. In: Scott R. & Kosslyn S. (eds.), *Emerging Trends in the Social and Behavioral Sciences.* John Wiley & Sons.

Fligstein N. & Dauber K. (1989). Structural change in corporate organization, *Annual Review of Sociology*, 15: 73–96.

Fligestein N. & Dauter L. (2007). The sociology of markets, *Annual Review of Sociology*, 33(6): 6–24. DOI: 10.1146/annurev.soc.33.040406.131736

Fligstein N. & Kluttz D. (2016). Varieties in field theory. In: Abrutyn S. (ed.), *Handbook of Contemporary Sociological Theory.* Springer, Handbooks of Sociology and Social Research: ch.10. DOI: 10.1007/978-3-319-32250-6_10

Fligstein N. & McAdam D. (2011). Towards a general theory of strategic action fields, *Sociological Theory*, 29(1): 1–26. Retrieved from: http://www.jstor.org/stable/41057693

Fligstein N. & Shinn T. (2007). Shareholder value and the transformation of the U.S. economy (1984–2000), *Sociological Forum*, 22(4). DOI: 10.1111/j.1573-7861.2007.00044.x

Foster J.B. & Hannah H. (2012). Weber and the environment: Classical foundations for a postexemptionalist sociology. *American Journal of Sociology*, 117(6):1625–1673.

Fowler Don D. (2010). The topographical engineers in the southwest. In: Don D. Fowler (ed.), *A Laboratory for Anthropology. Science and Romanticism in the American Southwest (1846-1930).* Salt Lake City: The University of Utah Press, pp. 38–49.

Fudala J. (2001). *Historic Scottsdale: A Life from the Land.* HPN Books.

Furlong K. & Bakker K. (2008). *Achieving Water Conservation: Strategies for Good Governance, Policy Report – Program on Water Governance*, Municipal Water Supply Project, Canada (www.watergovernance.ca)

Garfin G. (2006). *Arizona Drought Monitoring.* Retrieved from: http://www.researchg ate.net/profile/Gregg_Garfin/publication/267714773_ARIZONA_DROUGHT_MON ITORING/links/548ddd130cf214269f243614.pdf

Garfin G., Jardine A., Merideth R., Black M., & LeRoy S. (eds.) (2013). *Assessment of Climate Change in the Southwest United States: A Report Prepared for the National Climate Assessment.* Washington, DC: Island Press.

Garreau J. (1991). *Edge Cities: Life on the New Frontier.* New York: Doubleday.

Garreau J. (1991). *Edge City: Life on the New Frontier. Random House LLC, New York. Press release (2014, January 23). Andy Tobin Raises More Than $232,000. Sonoran Alliance.* Retrieved on March 6, 2015 from: http://sonoranalliance.com/tag/jim-click/

Garrick D., Jacobs K. & Garffin G. (2008). Models, assumptions, and stakeholders: planning for water supply variability in the Colorado river basin, *Journal of the American Water Resource Association*, 44(2): 381–398.

Genieys W. (2006). Nouveaux regards sur les élites du politique, *Revue française de science Politique*, 56(1): 121–147. DOI: 10.3917/rfsp.561.0121

Bibliography   213

Gensburger S. (2011). Contributions historiennes au renouveau de la sociologie de l'Etat. Regards croisés franco-américains, *Revue française de science politique*, 52(3) : 579–602.

Getches D.H. (2009). *Water Law in a Nutshell* (4th ed.). St. Paul, MN: Thomson/West.

Glachant M. (2004). *Les instruments de la politique environnementale*. Centre d'économie industrielle, Ecole Nationale Supérieure des Mines de Paris.

Glennon R. (2004). *Water Follies. Groundwater Pumping and the Fate of America's Fresh Waters*. New York: Island Press.

Glennon R. & Kavkewitz J. (2013). Smashing Victory: Was Arizona v. California a Victory for the State of Arizona. *Arizona Journal of Environmental Law & Policy*, 4(1): 1–38.

Glennon R.J. (2012). *Water Follies: Groundwater Pumping and the Fate of America's Fresh Waters*. Washington: Island Press.

Glennon R.J. & Culp P.W. (2001). Last green lagoon: How and why the bush administration should save the Colorado river delta. *The Ecology Law Quarterly*, 28(4): 903–992.

Gober P. (2006). *Metropolitan Phoenix: Place Making and Community Building in the Desert*. Philadelphia: University of Pennsylvania Press.

Goldman M. (2007). How "Water for All!" policy became hegemonic: The power of the World Bank and its transnational policy networks, *Geoforum*, 38(5): 786–800.

Gonzales G.A. (2009). *Urban Sprawl, Global Warming and the Empire of Capital*. Albany: State University of New York Press.

Gottlieb R. (1988). *A Life of its Own. The Politics and Power of Water*. San Diego/New York/London: Harcourt Brace Jovanovich Publishers.

Gottlieb R. (2007). *Reinventing Los Angeles. Nature and Community in the Global City*. Cambridge: MIT Press.

Gottlieb R. & FitzSimmons M. (1991). *Thirst for Growth. Water Agencies as Hidden Government in California*. Tucson: University of Arizona Press.

Graham S. & Marvin S. (2001). *Splintering Urbanism: Networked Infrastructures, Technological Mobilities and the Urban Condition*. New York: Taylor & Francis.

Grant D.L. (2008). Collaborative solutions to Colorado River shortages: The Basin States' proposal and beyond, *Nevada Law Journal*, 8(3): 964–993.

Grenfell M. (ed.) (2014). *Pierre Bourdieu. Key Concepts*. London: Routledge.

Gunningham N., Grabosky P. & Sinclair D. (1998). *Smart Regulation: Designing Environmental Policy*. Oxford: Clarendon Press.

Gusfield J.R. (1963). *Symbolic Crusade: Status Politics and the American Temperance Movement*. Urbana and Chicago: University of Illinois Press.

Guttman D. & Willner B. (1976). *The Shadow Government*. New York: Pantheon Books.

Hassenteufel P. (2016). *Sociologie de l'action publique*. Paris: Armand Colin, Kindle Edition.

Hays S.P. (1969). *Conservation and the Gospel of Efficiency*. Pittsburgh: University of Pittsburgh Press.

Henry O. (2012). *Les Guérisseurs de l'économie. Sociogenèse du métier de consultant (1900–1950)*. Paris: CNRS Éditions.

Hess D.J., Wold C.A., Hunter E., Nay J., Worland S., Gilligan J. & Hornberger G.M. (2016). Drought, risk, and institutional politics in the American Southwest, *Sociological Forum*, 31(S1). DOI: 10.1111/socf.12274

Hilgers M. & Mangez E. (eds.) (2015). *Bourdieu's Theory of Social Fields: Concepts and Applications*. London: Routledge.

214   Bibliography

Hirt P., Gustafson A. & Larson K. (2008). The mirage in the Valley of the Sun, *Environmental History*, 13(3): 482–514.

Hofstadter R. (1955). *The Age of Reform*. New York: Vintage Books.

Hood C. (1986). *The Tools of Government*. London: Chatham House Publishers.

Hornberger G.M., Hess D.J. & Gilligan J. (2015). Water conservation and hydrological transitions in cities in the United States. *Water Resources Research*, 51(6): 4635–4649.

Howard C. (1997). *The Hidden Welfare State: Tax Expenditures and Social Policy in the United States*. Princeton, NJ: Princeton University Press

Howitt R., MacEwan D., Medellin-Azuara J., Lund J.R., & Sumner D.A. (2015). *Economic Analysis of the 2015 Draught for California Agriculture*. Davis: Center for Watershed Sciences, University of California.

Huber A., Gorostiza S., Kotsila P., Beltrán M.J. & Armiero M. (2017). Beyond "Socially Constructed" disasters: Re-politicizing the debate on large dams through a political ecology of risk, *Capitalism Nature Socialism*, 28(3): 48–68.

Hundley J.N. (2001). *The Great Thirst: Californians and Water. A History*. Los Angeles: University of California Press.

Hundley N. (1975). *Water and the West. The Colorado River Compact and the Politics of Water in the American West*. Berkeley: University of California Press.

Ingold A. (2008). Les soci.t.s d'irrigation: bien commun et action collective. *Entreprises et histoire*, 50: 19–35.

Ingram H. (1990). *Water Politics: Continuity and Change*. Albuquerque: University of New Mexico Press.

Ingram H. & Oggins C.R. (2013). *Water, the Community and Markets in the West, Western Water Policy Project, Discussion Series Paper n°6*, Natural Resources Law Center, University of Colorado.

Jackson K. (1985). *Crabgrass frontier: The suburbanization of the United States*. New York: Oxford Univ. Press.

Jacobi K. (2003). *Crimes Against Nature: Squatters, Poachers, Thieves, and the Hidden History of American Conservation*. Los Angeles: University of California Press.

Jacobs H. (1998). *Who Owns America? Social Conflicts about Property Rights*. Madison, WI: University of Wisconsin Press.

Jenkins-Smith H. C., St Clair G. K. & Woods B. (1991). Explaining change in policy subsystems: Analysis of coalition stability and defection over time. *American Journal of Political Science*, 35(4): 851–880.

Johnson J.W. (2002). *Arizona Politicians. The Noble and the Notorious*. Tucson: University of Arizona Press.

Johnson R. (1977). *The Central Arizona Project: 1918-1968*. Tucson: The University of Arizona Press.

Kaika M. (2006). Dams as symbols of modernization: The urbanization of nature between geographical imagination and materiality, *Annals of the Association of American Geographers*, 96(2): 276–301.

Kenney D.J. (2009). The Colorado River: What prospect for a 'River No More'? In: Molle F. & Wester P. (eds.), *River Basin Trajectories: Societies, Environments and Development*. CAB International, pp. 12–146.

Kingdon J.W. & Thurber J.A. *Agendas, Alternatives, and Public Policies*. Vol. 45. Boston, MA: Little, Brown and Company, 1984.

Koeble T.A. (1995). The new institutionalism in political science and sociology, *Comparative Politics*, 27(2): 231–243.

Bibliography 215

Kolko G. (1963). *The Triumph of Conservatism: A Reinterpretation of American History, 1900–1916*. New York: The Free Press.

Kraatz M.S. & Zajac E.J. (1996). Exploring the limits of the new institutionalism: The causes and consequences of illegitimate organizational change, *American Sociological Review*, 61(5): 812–836.

Kraft M. E. (2015). *Environmental Policy and Politics*. Madison University of Wisconsin, Pearson Ed. [1996].

Kupel D.E. (2003). *Fuel for Growth: Water and Arizona's Urban Environment*. University of Arizona Press.

Kupel D.E. (2006). *Fuel for Growth: Water and Arizona's Urban Environment*. Tucson, AZ: University of Arizona Press.

Lascoumes P. (2012). *Action Publique et Environnement*. Paris: PUF.

Lascoumes P. & Le Galès P. (2004). De l'innovation instrumentale à la recomposition de l'Etat. In: Pierre Lascoumes P. & Le Galès P. (dir.) *Gouverner par les instruments*. Paris: Presses de Sciences po, pp. 357–369.

Lascoumes P. & Le Galès P. (dir.) (2005). *Gouverner par les instruments*. Paris: Presses de Sciences Po.

Lascoumes P. & Simard L. (2011). L'action publique au prisme de ses instruments. Introduction, *Revue française de science politique*, 61(1): 5–22. DOI 10.3917/rfsp.611.0005

Lash C. (1991). *The True and Only Heaven. Progress and Its Critics*. New York/London: W.W. Norton and Company, Inc.

Lazega E. & Snijders T. (2016). *Multilevel Network Analysis for the Social Sciences. Theory, Methods and Applications*. Heidelberg/New York/Dordrecht/London: Springer International Publishing Switzerland. DOI 10.1007/978-3-319-24520-1

Le Bourhis J.-P. (2003). Complexité et trajectoires d'apprentissage dans l'action publique. Les instruments de gestion durable des ressources en eau en France et au Royaume-Uni, *Revue internationale de politique comparée*, 10(2): 161–175.

LeClair A. (2015, March 18). As California Sets New Water Restrictions, Arizona Resources Dwindle. Arizona Public Media. Retrieved on March 19, 2015 from: https://www.azpm.org/p/crawler-stories/2015/3/18/59276-could-new-california-water-restrictions-become-arizonasfuture/

Le Galès P. & Thatcher M. (1995). *Les Réseaux de politiques publiques. Débats autour des policy networks*. Paris: L'Harmattan.

Le Naour G. (2012). Réseaux et politiques publiques, *Administration et éducation*, 9–13. Retrieved from: halshs-00833770

Lebaron F. (1997). La dénégation du pouvoir. Le champ des économistes français au milieu des années 1990, *Actes de la recherche en sciences sociales*, 119: 3–26. DOI: 10.3406/arss.1997.3226

Lemieux C. (2011). Le crépuscule des champs. Limites d'un concept ou disparition d'une réalité historique? In: Fornel M. de & Oglen A. (dir.), *Bourdieu, théoricien de la pratique*. Paris: Éditions de l'EHESS, pp. 75–99.

Leshy J.D. (2001). The Babbitt Legacy at the Department of the Interior: A preliminary view, *Environmental Law*, 31: 199–228.

Leslie J. (2005). *Deep Water. The Epic Struggle over Dams, Displaced People, and the Environment*. New York: Farrar Strauss & Giroux.

Linton J. & Budds J. (2014). The hydrosocial cycle: Defining and mobilizing a relational-dialectical approach to water. *Geoforum*, 57: 170–180.

216 *Bibliography*

Logan M.F. (2006). *Desert Cities: The Environmental History of Phoenix and Tucson.* Pittsburg: University of Pittsburgh Press.

Lopez-Hoffman, L., McGovern, E., Varady, R.G. & Flessa K.W. (2009). *Conservation of Shared Environments. Learning from the United States and Mexico.* Tucson: The University of Arizona Press.

Lorrain D. (2004). Les pilotes invisibles de l'action publique. Le désarroi du politique ? In: Pierre Lascoumes & Patrick Le Galès (dir.), *Gouverner par les instruments.* Paris: Presses de Sciences po., pp. 163–198.

Lorrain D. (2008). Les institutions de second rang, *Entreprises et histoire*, 50(1): 6–18.

Lorrain D. (2011). Compétitions dans le secteur de l'eau, *Archives ouvertes*, hal-00995122. Retrieved from: https://hal-enpc.archives-ouvertes.fr/hal-00995122

Lorrain D. & Poupeau F. (2016a). What do the protagonists of the water sector do? In: Lorrain D. & Poupeau F. (eds.), *Water Regimes. Beyond the Public and Private Sector Debate.* London: Routledge, pp. 1–13.

Lorrain D. & Poupeau F. (2016b). How socio-technical systems and their operators work. In: Lorrain D. & Poupeau F. (eds.), *Water Regimes: Beyond the Public and Private Sector Debate.* London: Routledge, pp. 187–200.

Lovett L. (2000). Land reclamation as family reclamation: The Family Ideal in George Maxwell's Reclamation and Resettlement Campaigns, 1897–1933. *Social Politics*, 7(1): 80–100.

Lubell M. (2013). Governing institutional complexity: The ecology of games framework. *Policy Studies Journal*, 41(3): 537–559.

Lubell M., Robins G., & Wang P. (2014). Network structure and institutional complexity in an ecology of water management games, *Ecology and Society*, 19(4): 23. Retrieved from: http://www.ecologyandsociety.org/vol19/iss4/art23/

Lynn-Ingram B. & Malamud-Roam F. (2013). *The West Without Water. What Past Floods, Droughts and Other Climatic Clues Tell Us About Tomorrow.* Berkeley/Los Angeles: University of California Press.

MacDonnell L.J., Getches D.H. & Hugenberg W.C. (1995). The law of the Colorado river: Coping with severe sustained drought. *Journal of the American Water Resources Association*, 31(5): 825–836.

Mann D.E. (1963). *The Politics of Water in Arizona.* Tucson: The University of Arizona Press.

Markard J., Raven R. & Truffer B. (2012). Sustainability transitions: An emerging field of research and its prospects, *Research Policy*, 4: 955–967.

Marriott B. (2012). *Legendary Locals of Marana, Oro Valley and Catalina.* Tucson: Arcadia Publisher.

Martin J.L. (2003). What is field theory? *American Journal of Sociology*, 109(1): 1–49.

Massardier G. (1997). P. Le Gales, M. Thatcher (dir.) *Les réseaux de politique publique. Débat autour des policy networks, Politix*, 1997/1(37): 177–183. DOI: 10.3406/polix.1997.1660

Massardier G. et al. (2015). Les coalitions multi-niveaux d'action publique. Un mod.le interpr.tatif des conflits pour l'eau dans les Am.riques, Cahiers des IFRE. Fondation Maison des Sciences de l'Homme, Urbanisme et dérèglement climatique, pp. 63–80.

Mayaux P.-L. (2015). La production de l'acceptabilité sociale, *Revue française de science politique*, 65(2): 237–259.

McBride L. (1972). Arizona's coming dilemma: Water supply and population growth. *Ecology Law Quarterly*, 2(2): 357–384.

Bibliography 217

McClurg S. & Lazer D. (2014). Political networks, *Social Networks*, 36: 1–4. Retrieved from: http://dx.doi.org/10.1016/j.socnet.2013.09.001

McKasson M. & Devine D. (1998, June 25–July 1). Water Log: Think those two votes on direct delivery of CAP water meant something? Think again-CAP water is almost certainly headed back to your tap. *Tucson Weekly*. Retrieved from: http://www.tucsonweekly.com/tw/06-25-98/feat.htm

McKasson (2011). Interview for the Pima County oral history project. https://azmemory.azlibrary.gov/digital/collection/pimacent/id/81/

Megdal S.B. (2007). Arizona's recharge and recovery programs. In: Colby B.G. & Jacobs K.L. (eds.), *Arizona Water Policy: Management Innovations in an Urbanizing, Arid Region*.

Megdal S., Nadeau J. & Tom T. (2011). The forgotten sector: Arizona water law and the environment. *Arizona Journal of Environmental Law & Policy*, 1(2): 243–293.

Meyers C.J. (1966). The Colorado river. *Stanford Law Review*, 19(1): 1–75.

Mizruchi M.S. (2013). *The Fracturing of the American Corporate Elite*. Harvard University Press.

Molle F. (2009). Water and society: New problems, new skills needed, *Irrigation and Drainage*, 58: 1–7.

Molle F., Mollinga P.P. & Wester P. (2009). Hydraulic bureaucracies and the hydraulic mission: Flows of water, flows of power, *Water Alternatives*, 2(3): 328–345.

Molle F. & Wester P. (2009). River basin trajectories: An inquiry into changing waterscapes. In: Molle F. & Wester P. (eds.), *River Basin Trajectories: Societies, Environments and Development*. CAB International, pp. 1–19.

Mollinga P.P (2008). Water, politics and development: Framing a political sociology of water resources management, *Water Alternatives*, 1(1): 7–23.

Mollinga P.P. (2008). Water policy – water politics. Social engineering and strategic action in water sector reform. In: Scheumann W., Neubert S. & Kipping M. (eds.), *Water Politics and Development Cooperation. Local Power Plays and Global Governance*. Berlin/Heidelberg: Springer Verlag, pp. 1–29.

Mostert E. (1998). A framework for conflict resolution. *Water International*, 23(4): 206–215.

Mott Lacroix K. & Megdal S. (2016). Explore, synthesize, and repeat: unraveling complex water management issues through the stakeholder engagement wheel, *Water*, 8(4). Retrieved from: http://www.mdpi.com/2073-4441/8/4/118

Mount J., Hanak H., Lund J., Frank R., Greg Gartrel G., Gray B., Moyle P., and Thompson B.B. (2015). *California's Water: Managing Drought*. Public Policy Institute of California, PPIC Water Policy Center. Retrieved from: http://www.ppic.org/main/publication.asp?i=1132

Mount J. et al. (2016). *Improving the Federal Response to Western Drought Five Areas for Reform*. Los Angeles: Pacific Institute for Public Policy.

Muñoz J., Poupeau F., & Razafimahefa L. (2019). Un consensus paradoxal: Conservation des ressources hydriques et croissance économique en Arizona. *Revue française de science politique*, vol. 69(4), 601–630. doi:10.3917/rfsp.694.0601

Munro J. (1993). California water politics: Explaining policy change in a cognitively polarized subsystem. In: Sabatier P. & Jenkins-Smith H. (eds.), *Policy Change and Learning*. Boulder: Westview Press, pp. 105–128.

Nash R.F. (1967). *Wilderness and the American Mind* (4th ed.). New Haven/London: Yale University Press.

218 Bibliography

Needham A. (2014). *Power Lines: Phoenix and the Making of the Modern Southwest: Phoenix and the Making of the Modern Southwest.* Princeton: Princeton University Press.

Newman H. (1994, June 28). City to settle water suit. *Tucson Citizen.* Retrieved from: http://tucsoncitizen.com/morgue2/1994/06/28/180143-city-to-settle-water-suit/

Nies J. (2013). *Unreal City. Las Vegas, Black Mesa, and the Fate of the West.* New York: Nation Books.

Nies J. (2014). *Unreal City. Las Vegas, Black Mesa, and the Fate of the West.* New York: Nation Books.

O'Leary B. (1998). Bruce Babbitt. Retrieved on April 8, 2015 from: http://www.washingtonpost.com/wp-srv/politics/govt/admin/babbitt.htm

O'Neill B. et al. (2016a). The Making of water policy in the American Southwest: Environmental sociology and its tools. In: Poupeau F., H. Gupta, A. Serrat-Capdevila, M.A. Sans-Fuentes, S. Harris, & L. Hayde (eds.), *Water Bankruptcy in the Land of Plenty,* Delft, CRC Press, pp. 45–64.

O'Neill B., Poupeau F., Coeurdeay M. & Cortinas J. (2016b). Laws of the river: Conflict and cooperation on the Colorado River. In: Poupeau F., H. Gupta, A. Serrat-Capdevila, M.A. Sans-Fuentes, S. Harris, & L. Hayde (eds.), *Water Bankruptcy in the Land of Plenty.* Delft, CRC Press, pp. 101–119.

Orren K. & Skowronek S. (2004). *The Search for American Political Development.* New York: Cambridge University Press.

Ostrom E. (1990). *Governing the Commons: The Evolution of Institutions for Collective Action.* Cambridge University Press.

Ostrom E. (2009). A general framework for analyzing sustainability of social-ecological systems, *Science,* 325(5939): 419–423.

Padowski J.C. & Jawitz J.W. (2012). Water availability and vulnerability of 225 large cities in the United States, *Water Resources Research,* 48. DOI: 10.1029/2012WR012335

Patashnik J. (2014). Arizona v. California and the equitable apportionment of interstate waterways. *Arizona Law Review,* 56(1): 1–51.

Pearce, M.J. (2007). Balancing competing interests: The history of state and federal water laws. In: Colby B.G. & Jacobs K.L. (eds.), *Arizona Water Policy: Management Innovations in an Urbanizing, Arid Region.* Washington: RFF Press.

Perramond E. (2019). *Unsettled Waters: Rights, Law, and Identity in the American West.* Los Angeles: University of California Press.

Pima Association of Governments (2006). Plan 208, Areawide Water Quality Management Plan, Prepared in fulfillment of section 208 of the Clean Water Act.

Pincetl S. (2002). *Transforming California.* Los Angeles: Johns Hopkins University Press.

Pincetl S. (2003). *Transforming California: A Political History of Land Use and Development.* Baltimore: Johns Hopkins University Press.

Pincetl S. (2011). Urban water conflicts in the western US. In: Barraqué B. (ed.), *Urban Water Conflicts.* Paris: UNESCO-IHP, pp. 237–246.

Pincetl S. & Hogue T. (2015). California's new normal? Recurring drought: Addressing winners and losers, *Local Environment,* 20(7): 850–854. DOI: 10.1080/13549839.2015.1042778

Pincetl S., Porse E. & Cheng D. (2016). Fragmented flows: Water supply in Los Angeles County, *Environmental Management,* 58: 208–222. DOI: 10.1007/s00267-016-0707-1

Pisani D.J. (1982). State vs. Nation: Federal Reclamation and Water Rights in the Progressive Era. *Pacific Historical Review,* 51(3): 265–282.

Pisani D.J. (1984). *From the Family Farm to Agribusiness: The Irrigation Crusade in California and the West, 1850-1931.* Berkeley: University of California Press.

Bibliography 219

Pisani D.J. (2000a). Beyond the hundredth meridian: Nationalizing the history of water in the United States. *Environmental History*, 5(4): 466–482.

Pisani D.J. (2000b) Transforming California: A political history of land use and development. *The Journal of American History* 87(3): 1091.

Pisani D.J. (2002). *Water and American Government: The Reclamation Bureau, National Water Policy, and the West, 1902-1935*. Berkeley/London: University of California Press.

Polanyi K. (1983). *La Grande Transformation, Aux origines politiques et économiques de notre temps*. Gallimard [1944].

Poupeau F. et al. (2016a). *Water Bankruptcy in the Land of Plenty. Steps towards a Transatlantic and Transdisciplinary Assessment of Water Scarcity in Southern Arizona, Delpht*. CRC Press.

Poupeau F., Henry O., De Bercegol R., Richard-Ferroudji A., Zérah M.-H. & Dasgupta S. (eds.) (2016b). *Water Regimes Questioned from the "Global South". Agents, practices and knowledge*. Conference Proceedings, Delhi, Center for Policy Research. Retrieved from: https://hal.archivesouvertes.fr/hal01348563/file/Water_Regimes_Conference_P roceedings.pdf

Poupeau F., O'Neill B., Cortinas J. & Coeurdray M. (2016c). The making of water policy in the American southwest: Environmental sociology and its tools. In: Poupeau F., Hoshin G., Serrat-Capdevila A., Sans-Fuentes M., Harris S. & Hayde L. (dir.), *Water Bankruptcy in the Land of Plenty*. New York: CRC Press, Taylor & Francis Group, pp. 45–64.

Poupeau F. et al. (2018). In: Razafimaheva L., Robert J., Jacobi P., Massardier G. & Mercier D. (eds.), *Water Conflicts and Hycrocracy. Coalitions, Networks, Policies*. Sao Paulo: USP Press.

Powell W.W. & Smith-Doerr L. (2005). Networks and economic life. In: *The Handbook of Economic Sociology*, pp. 379–402. Princeton: Princeton University Press.

Press release (2014, January 23). Andy Tobin Raises more than $232,000. Sonoran Alliance. Retrieved on March 6, 2015 from: http://sonoranalliance.com/tag/jim-click/

Rajagopalan B. et al. (2009). Water supply risk on the Colorado River: Can management mitigate? *Water Resources Research*, 45: 1–7. DOI: 10.1029/2008WR007652

Record of Decision [ROD] (2007). Colorado River Interim Guidelines for Lower basin Shortages and the Coordinated Operations for Lake Powell and Lake Mead. Retrieved from: http://www.usbr.gov/lc/region/programs/strategies/RecordofDecision.pdf

Reisner M. (1985). *Cadillac Desert: The American West and its Disappearing Water*. New York: Penguin Books.

Reisner M. (1986). *Cadillac Desert: The American West and Its Disappearing Water*. New York: Penguin Books.

Ross A. (2011). *Bird on Fire – Lessons from the World's Least Sustainable City*. New York: Oxford University Press.

Sabatier P. (1988). An advocacy coalition framework of policy change and the role of policy-oriented learning therein, *Policy Sciences*, 21: 129–168.

Sabatier P. & Jenkins-Smith (1993). The advocacy coalition framework: Assessment, revisions, and implications for scholars and practitioners. In: Sabatier P. & Jenkins-Smith H. (eds.), *Policy Change and Learning*. Boulder: Westview Press, pp. 211–235.

Sabatier P.A. & Jenkins-Smith H.C. (1993). *Policy Change and Learning: An Advocacy Coalition Approach*. Chicago: Westview Press.

Sabatier P., Weible C. & Ficker J. (2005). Eras of water management in the United States: Implications of collaborative watershed approaches. In: Sabatier P., Focht W., Lubell M., Trachtenberg Z., Vedlitz A. & Matlock M. (eds.), *Swimming Upstream.*

220 *Bibliography*

Collaborative Approaches to Watershed Management. Cambridge/London: MIT Press, pp. 23–52.

Saliba B.C. (1987). Do water markets "work"? Market transfers and trade-offs in the southwestern states, *Water Resources Research*, 22(7): 1113–1122.

Sapiro G. (1996). La raison littéraire. Le champ littéraire français sous l'Occupation (1940-1944), *Actes de la recherche en sciences sociales*, 111–112: 3–35.

Schipper J. (2008). *Disappearing Desert. The Growth of Phoenix and the Culture of Sprawl*. Norman: University of Oklahoma Press.

Schmidt Sudman R. & Taylor S. (2016). *Water More or Less. Reflections about the Changing Landscape of California's Water in Stories, Art and Policy Including Diverse Voices of 20 Top Water Leaders*, Pentimo Press.

Scott J. (1999). *Seeing Like a State: How Certain Schemes to Improve the Human Condition Have Failed*. Yale: Yale University Press.

Scott C.A. & Pasqualetti M.J. (2010). Energy and water resources scarcity: Critical infrastructure for growth and economic development in Arizona and Sonora. *Natural Resources Journal*, 50(3): 645–682.

Scoville C. (2015). Reclaiming water politics: California's drought and the eclipse of the public, *Berkeley Journal of Sociology*, 59: 35–43. Retrieved from: http://berkeleyjourn al.org/2015/12/reclaiming-water-politics-californias-drought-and-the-eclipse-of-the-public/

Seager R. et al. (2007). Model projections of an imminent transition to a more arid climate in Southwestern North America, *Science*, 316: 1181–1184.

Serrat-Capdevila A. (2016). The Tucson Basin: A natural and human history. In: Poupeau F., Hoshin G., Serrat-Capdevila A., Sans-Fuentes M., Harris S., Hayde L. (dir.), *Water Bankruptcy in the Land of Plenty*. New York: CRC Press, Taylor & Francis Group, pp. 27–44.

Sheridan T. (2012). *Arizona: A History*. Tucson: The University of Arizona Press.

Sheridan T. (2014). The Sonoran Desert conservation plan and Ranch Conservation in Pima County (Arizona). In: Charnley S., Sheridan T.E. & Nabhan G. (eds.), *Stitching the West Back Together. Conservation of Working Landscapes*. Chicago: University of Chicago Press, pp. 251–266.

Shermer E.T. (2011). *Sunbelt Capitalism: Phoenix and the Transformation of American Politics*. Philadelphia, PA: University of Pennsylvania Press.

Shermer E.T. (2013). *Sunbelt Capitalism: Phoenix and the Transformation of American Politics*. Philadelphia: University of Pennsylvania Press.

Singh S. (2016). What is relational structure? Introducing History to the Debates on the relation between fields and social networks, *Sociological Theory*, 34(2): 128–150. DOI: 10.1177/0735275116648181

Skocpol T. (1992). *Protecting Soldiers and Mothers. The Political Origins of Social Policy in the United States*. Cambridge, MA: Harvard University Press.

Smith C.L. (1972). *The Salt River Project: A Case Study in Cultural Adaptation to an Urbanizing Community*. University of Arizona Press.

Southern Arizona Leadership Council (2014). Internal Report.

Southern Nevada Water Authority (2012). Annual Report. http://epubs.nsla.nv.gov/state pubs/epubs/593031-2012.pdf

Stegner W. (1953). *Beyond the Hundredth Meridian: John Wesley Powell and the Second Opening of the West*. New York: Houghton Mifflin.

Stegner W. (1992(1954)) *Beyond the Hundredth Meridian:* John Wesley Powell *and the Second Opening of the West*. New York: Penguin Books.

Bibliography   221

Sterner T. (2016). *Les instruments de la politique environnementale*. Paris: Collège de France/Fayard.

Strang V. (2016). Infrastructural relations: Water, political power and the rise of a New'Despotic Regime', *Water Alternatives*, 9(2): 292–318.

Strauss A. & Corbin J. (1990). *Basics of Qualitative Research: Grounded Theory, Procedures and Techniques*. Newbury: Sage.

Summit A.R. (2013). *Contested Waters. An Environmental History of the Colorado River*. Boulder: University Press of Colorado.

Swyngedouw E. (2015). *Liquid Power. Contested Hydro-modernities in 20th Century Spain*. Cambridge: MIT Press.

Tarlock A.D. (2001). Future of prior appropriation in the new west. *Natural Resources Journal*, 41: 769–793.

Taylor C., Pollard S., Rocks S. & Angus A. (2012). Selecting policy instruments for better environmental regulation: A critique and future research agenda, *Environmental Policy and Governance*, 22: 268–292. DOI: 10.1002/eet.1584

Taylor D.E. (2016). *The Rise of the American Conservation Movement. Power, Privilege, and Environmental Protection*. Durham and London: Duke University Press.

Terrain.org. (2006, March 22). Interview with Bruce Babbitt. *Terrain.org: A Journal of the Built Natural Environments*. Retrieved on April 7, 2015 from: http://terrain.org/2006/i nterviews/interview-with-bruce-babbitt/

Thatcher M. (1998). The development of policy network analysis: From modest origins to overarching frameworks, *Journal of Theoretical Politics*, 10(4): 389–417.

Teisch J.B. (2011). *Engineering Nature: Water, Development, and the Global Spread of American Environmental Expertise*. University of North Carolina Press.

Teisman G.R. (2000). Models for research into decision-making processes: On phases, streams and decision-making rounds, *Public Administration*, 78(4): 937–956.

Thomas C.S. (ed.) (1991). *Politics and Public Policy in the Contemporary American West*. Albuquerque: University of New Mexico Press.

Thompson B.H., Leshy J.D. & Abrams R.H. (2013). *Legal Control of Water Resources: Cases and Materials* (5th Ed.). Saint-Paul, MN: Thomsen Reuters.

Tirole J. (2016). *Economie du bien commun*. Paris: Presses Universitaires de France.

Topalov C. (1988a). *Laboratoires du nouveau siècle: la nébuleuse réformatrice et ses réseaux en France (1880–1914)*. Paris: EHESS.

Topalov C. (1988b). *Naissance de l'urbanisme moderne et réforme de l'habitat populaire aux États-Unis, 1900–1940. Rapport au Plan Urbain*. Paris: CSU.

Topalov C. (1999). *Laboratoires du nouveau siècle: la nébuleuse réformatrice et ses réseaux en France (1880–1914)*. Paris: EHESS.

Traduction française. (2002). *Le seul et vrai paradis. Une histoire de l'idéologie du progrès et de ses critiques*. Paris: Climats.

Trelease F.J. (1960). Federal limitations on state water law. *Buffalo Law Review*, 10(3): 399–426.

Tyler D. (1997). Delphus Emory Carpenter and the Colorado River Compact of 1922. *University of Denver Water Law Review*, 1(2): 228–274.

Tyler D. (1998). The Silver Fox of the Rockies: Delphus Emory Carpenter and the Colorado River Compact. *New Mexico Historical Review*, 73(1): 25–43.

Udall S.L. (1963). *The Quiet Crisis*. New York: Rinehart and Winston.

Valdez Diaz C. (1996, April 22). City studies water supply options. *Tucson Citizen*. Retrieved on October 15, 2014 from: http://tucsoncitizen.com/morgue2/1996/04/22/3 9002-city-studies-water-supply-options/

222   Bibliography

Van Tatenhove J. & Leroy P. (2003). Environment and participation in a context of political modernisation, *Environmental Values*, 12(2): 155–174.

Varady R. et al. (2016). Adaptive management and water security in a global context: Definitions, concepts, and examples, *Current Opinion in Environmental Sustainability*, 21: 70–77. DOI: 10.1016/j.cosust.2016.11.001

Varady R.G., van Weert F., Megdal S.B., Gerlak A., Iskandar C.A. & House-Peters L. (2013). *Thematic Paper No. 5: Groundwater Policy and Governance*. Rome, Italy: GEFFAO Groundwater Governance Project A Global Framework for Country Action. Retrieved from: http://www.groundwatergovernance.org/resources/thematic-papers/en/

Vincent J.A. (2006). What lies beneath: The inherent dangers of the central Arizona groundwater replenishment district, *Arizona State Law Journal*, 38: 857–880.

Walton J. (1993). *Western Times and Water Wars. State, Culture and Rebellion in California*. Berkeley/Los Angeles/Oxford: University of California Press.

Wang A. (2012, January 30). Arizona's been good to billboard entrepreneur Karl Eller. *AZcentral.com*. Retrieved from: http://www.azcentral.com/business/news/articles/20 11/11/28/20111128arizona-been-good-billboard-entrepreneur-karl-eller.html

Weatherford G.D. & Brown F.L. (1986). *New Courses for the Colorado River*. Albuquerque, NM: University of New Mexico Press.

Weber M. 1978. In: Roth G. & Wittich C. (eds.), *Economy and Society: An Outline of Interpretive Sociology*. Berkeley, CA: University of California Press.

Weible C.M. (2005). Beliefs and perceived influence in a natural resource conflict: An advocacy coalition approach to policy networks, *Political Research Quarterly*, 58(3): 461–475.

Weible C.M. & Sabatier P.A. (2005). Comparing policy networks: Marine protected areas in California, *Policy Studies Journal*, 33(2): 181–201.

White E. (2006, July 23) "Marana's Kais", *Arizona Daily Star*.

Wiersma R. (1995, November 2–8). Vote yes on Prop 200. *Tucson Citizen*. Retrieved from: http://www.tucsonweekly.com/tw/11-02-95/cover.htm

Wiewel W. & Persky J.J. (eds.) (2002). *Suburban Sprawl*. Armonk: M.E. Sharpe.

Wilhite D.A. (ed.) (2014). *Drought and Water Crises: Science, Technology, and Management Issues*. London: CRC Press.

Willey P. & Gottlieb R. (1982). *Empires in the Sun: The Rise of the New American West*. Tucson, AZ: University of Arizona Press.

Wittfogel K. (1957). *Oriental Despotism. A Comparative Study of Total Power*. New Haven: Yale University Press.

WMG (Water Management Group) (2015). We Are Water People. Information online, July 13.

Worster D. (1985). *Rivers of Empire: Water, Aridity, and the Growth of the American West*. New York: Pantheon Books.

Worster D. (1986). *Rivers of Empire: Water, Aridity and the Growth of the American West*. New York: Oxford University Press.

Worster D. (1991). *Under Western Skies: Nature and History in the American West*. Oxford: Oxford University Press.

Worster D. (1992). *Under Western Skies: Nature and History in the American West*. Oxford: Oxford University Press.

Worster D. (2001). *A River Running West: The Life of John Wesley Powell*. New York: Oxford University Press.

Bibliography 223

Zarbin E.A. & McCabe M. (1986). *Salt River Project: Four Steps Forward, 1902-1910.* Salt River Project.

Zarbin E.A. (1997). *Two Sides of the River: Salt River Valley Canals, 1867–1902.* SRP (Salt River Project).

Zeitoun M. & Mirumachi N. (2008). Transboundary water interaction I: Reconsidering conflict and cooperation. *International Environmental Agreements: Politics, Law and Economics,* 8(4): 297–316.

Zetland D. (2009). The end of abundance: How water bureaucrats created and destroyed the southern California oasis, *Water Alternatives,* 2(3): 350–369.

Legal Sources and Official Reports

Arizona v. California, 283 U.S. 423, 51 S. Ct. 522, 75 L. Ed. 1154 (1931).

Arizona v. California, 373 U.S. 546, 83 S. Ct. 1468, 10 L. Ed. 2d 542 (1963).

Arizona v. California, 460 U.S. 605, 103 S. Ct. 1382, 75 L. Ed. 2d 318 (1983).

Arizona Department of Water Resources (ADWR). (2014). *Arizona's Next Century: A Strategic Vision on Water for Water Sustainability.* Retrieved from: http://www.azwa ter.gov/AzDWR/Arizonas_Strategic_Vision/documents/ArizonasHistoricalSuccess esinWaterManagement.pdf

Arizona Department of Water Resources (ADWR). (2015). *Drought Program.* Retrieved from: http://www.azwater.gov/AzDWR/StatewidePlanning/Drought/ADPPlan.htm on March 11, 2015.

Arizona Drought Preparedness Plan (2004). Retrieved from: http://www.azwater.gov/Az DWR/StatewidePlanning/Drought/documents/operational_drought_plan.pdf

Boulder Canyon Project Act, 43 U.S.C. §§ 617 et seq. (1928).

CAP. *Oral History Project. Oral History Transcripts.* Retrieved from: http://www.cap-az.com/about-us/oral-history-transcripts

CAPa. (2014). *Central Arizona Project - Issue Brief: Strategic Initiatives and Public Policy: Colorado River Shortage.* Retrieved March 1, 2015, from: http://www.cap-az.com/documents/planning/Shortage_Issue_Brief.pdf

CAPb. *Central Arizona Project - Issue Brief: Colorado River Shortage, Central Arizona Project,* October 2014. Retrieved from: http://www.cap-az.com/documents/planning/ Shortage_Issue_Brief.pdf on March 1, 2015.

CAPc. (2015). *Central Arizona Project - Property Tax Q&A.* Retrieved July 26, 2015, from: http://www.cap-az.com/departments/finance/property-taxes

CAP. (2014). *Central Arizona Project - Issue Brief: Colorado River Shortage. Central Arizona Project,* October 2014. Retrieved from: http://www.cap-az.com/documents/pla nning/Shortage_Issue_Brief.pdf

CAP. (2014). *Central Arizona Project - Colorado River Supply Report, Agenda Number 9.* April 16, 2014. Retrieved from: http://www.tucsonaz.gov/files/water/docs/The_State _of_the_Colorado_River_April_2014_CAP.pdf

City of Tucson Water Department Drought Preparedness and Response Plan (2012). Retrieved from: http://www.tucsonaz.gov/files/water/docs/drought_plan_update_spri ng_2012.pdf

CVPIA. (1992). *Central Valley Project Improvement Act.* Retrieved from: https://www. usbr.gov/mp/cvpia/

Farmers Investment Company v. Bettwy, 113 Ariz. 520, 558 P.2d 14 (1976).

224   *Bibliography*

Farmers Investment Company v. Bettwy, 558 P.2d 14 Ariz. (1976).

Governor of Arizona. (2014). *Executive Order 2014-10: The Governor's Council on Water Supply Sustainability.*

Hurley v. Abbott, 259 F. Supp. 669 D. Ariz. (1966).

Kansas v. Colorado, 206 U.S. 46, 27 S. Ct. 655, 51 L. Ed. 956 (1907).

Pima County. (2014). *Drought Plan*. Retrieved from: http://webcms.pima.gov/UserFiles/Servers/Server_6/File/Government/Drought%20Management/LDIG/DroughtVulner abilityMemo.pdf

ROD, Record of Decision. (2007). *Colorado River Interim Guidelines for Lower Basin Shortages and the Coordinated Operations for Lake Powell and Lake Mead*. Retrieved from: http://www.usbr.gov/lc/region/programs/strategies/RecordofDecision.pdf

Sims Ely to Carpenter, box 37, Carpenter Papers, NCWCD (1944, 18 April).

SRP (2014). *Making Connections*, SRP 2014 Annual Report.

USBOR (2010). Field Hearing: Collaboration on the Colorado River. Retrieved on March 19, 2015 from: http://www.usbr.gov/newsroom/testimony/detail.cfm?RecordID=1622

U.S. Bureau of Reclamation (BOR). (2012). *Colorado River Basin Water Supply and Demand Study*. Retrieved from: http://www.usbr.gov/lc/region/programs/crbstudy/fi nalreport/studyrpt.html

U.S. Department of the Interior (2007). *Final Environmental Impact Statement: Colorado River Interim Guidelines for Lower Basin Shortages and Coordinated Operations for Lakes Powell and Mead*. Boulder City, NV: Bureau of Reclamation.

Winters v. United States, 207 U.S. 564, 28 S. Ct. 207, 52 L. Ed. 340 (1908).

Wyoming v. Colorado, 259 U.S. 419, 42 S. Ct. 552, 66 L. Ed. 999 (1922).

Other Sources

Arizona House of Representatives, Committee of Natural Resources, Agriculture and Environment, February and March 1993.

Arizona Water Resources, *News Bulletin*, January–March 1980.

CAP, Central Arizona Project. (2014). Issue brief, strategic initiatives and public policy, *Colorado River Shortage*. Retrieved from: http://www.cap-az.com/documents/pla nning/Shortage_Issue_Brief.pdf on March 1, 2015.

CAP, Oral History Transcripts. (2007). Retrieved from: http://www.cap-az.com/about-us/oral-history-transcripts

Brandon L. & Mark H. (2015). As the River Runs Dry: The Southwest's Water Crisis, Arizona and the Southwest seek a balance of growth and conservation as supply continues to decline, *Arizona Republic*, February 27, 2015. Retrieved from: http://www .azcentral.com/story/news/arizona/investigations/2015/02/27/southwest-water-cris is-part-one/24011053/ on March 8, 2015.

Byrd D. (2016). Lake Mead reaches a record low, *Earthsky*, June 2nd. Retrieved from: http://earthsky.org/earth/lake-mead-reaches-a-record-low-2016

Davis T. (2014). Tucson, other cities could be hit by CAP shortage much sooner than expected, *Arizona Daily Star*, June 15th. Retrieved from: http://tucson.com/news/sc ience/environment/tucson-other-cities-could-be-hit-by-cap-shortage-much/article_ 795728a5-2884-5d2f-b64d-d60b504ec8fc.html

LeClair A. (2015). As California Sets New Water Restrictions, Arizona Resources Dwindle, *Arizona Public Media*, March 18, 2015. Retrieved from: https://www.azpm.org/p/cr

awler-stories/2015/3/18/59276-could-new-california-water-restrictions-become-ari
zonas-future/ on March 19, 2015.

Terrain.org (March 22, 2006). *Interview with Bruce Babbitt*. Retrieved from: http://terrain.
org/2006/interviews/interview-with-bruce-babbitt/ on April 7, 2015.

Unsigned article in *The Explorer*. (2002). "Kai brothers embroiled in lawsuit", *The
Explorer*, 22/11. Retrieved from: http://www.tucsonlocalmedia.com/import/article_9cd
b2bc4-5572-591f-8c47-19ea466f68a8.html

Index

Abbey, Edward 2
Abbott, C. 38, 70
Active Management Areas (AMA) 59, 65, 91, 93, 107
adaptive capacity 6
Advocacy Coalition Framework (ACF) viii, 16–20, 87, 95, 110, 116
advocacy coalitions 14, 15, 16–25, 27, 28, 29, 31, 33, 42, 48, 49–53, 57–58, 62, 63–64, 65–69, 71, 73, 74, 78, 85–88, 94, 95–97, 107, 108–116, 117, 139, 152, 156, 161, 166, 168–170
agreements 6, 16, 19, 21, 23, 24, 25, 31, 55, 77, 95, 102, 104, 107, 114, 115, 119, 126, 128, 131, 142–143, 145–148, 161, 168, 176, 182, 183
agriculture: and economic growth 71; economic growth/market 28, 31, 36, 52, 62, 71, 72, 76–78, 160; farmer-entrepreneurs 76–78; federal support 2, 33–35, 38, 52, 56; historical context 28; impact of mining companies 64; impact of urbanization 73–78, 145, 148; irrigation needs 4, 5, 11, 20, 39–41, 44, 48, 50, 62, 81, 124–125, 137, 142, 147, 154; organic products 77; Reclamation Act and 33; water shortage and economic crisis 2, 15, 49, 59, 76–78, 127, 142
Akin, Wayne 49
All-American Canal 21, 161, 178, 180
allocation 15, 21, 23–24, 48, 54, 56, 62, 89, 121, 125, 142, 143, 149, 151, 162, 176–181
alternative energy sources 55, 56
Alter Valley 63
Ambrose, W.A. 182
American Dream 4, 5
American Forestry Association 34

American Geographical Society 34
American Homecraft Society 30
American Planning Association 111, 115
American West, historical background 3–6
Anamax Mining Company 61, 63–64
Anderson, Clinton 54
anti-drought action plans 96
Archer, J. 70
Arizona Constitution 177
Arizona Department of Environmental Quality (ADEQ) 66–67, 194, 196
Arizona Department of Water Resources (ADWR) 21, 23, 60, 72, 88, 91, 94, 96, 97, 103, 108, 111, 157, 163
Arizona Game Protective Association 60
Arizona Highline Reclamation Association 53
Arizona Homebuilders Association 79, 80
Arizona Interstate Commission 49
Arizona Interstate Stream Commission 49, 52
Arizona Monitoring Technical Committee (AMTC) 91
Arizona National Guard 45, 174–175
Arizona Public Service 54
Arizona Salt River Project 36
Arizona Superior Court 41
Arizona Task Force 54
Arizona v. California 21, 44–48, 118, 180–183
Arizona Water Banking Authority (AWBA) 93, 157, 161–162, 187, 194, 196
Arizona Water Commission 60
Arizona Water Company 38, 39, 40
Arizona Wildlife Federation 60
Army Corps of Engineers 2, 14, 34–35, 111
Aspinall, Wayne 54

Index 227

Association of California Water Agencies (ACWA) 143, 152, 153, 154, 194, 196
Assured Water Supply (AWS) 72
August, J.L. 45, 48, 51, 53, 54
Avery, C. 59, 61
Avra Valley 63

Babbitt, Bruce 59–62, 65, 76, 182
Bakker, K. 8, 17
Banister, J.M. 11
Barnet, T. 2, 165
Barraqué, B. 6, 8
Basefsky, Mitch 69
Baudot, P. Y. 97, 111
Beaudry, Bob 66, 68
Béland, D. 115
Benites, E. 23, 87, 144
Bichsel, C. 11
biodiversity 86, 95, 108
Blomquist, W. 59
Boronkay, Carl 161
Boulder Canyon Act 48
Boulder Canyon Dam 180
Boulder Canyon Project Act 21, 48, 175, 180–181
Boulder City 96
Boulder Dam 42–43, 180
Boulder Dam Act 42–43
Bourdieu, Pierre viii, 7, 9, 10, 19, 24, 106, 117, 139, 140, 144, 166, 168
Bowyer, David 56
Boyer, R. 116
Bridge Canyon 53
broker 17, 32, 33, 94, 186, 187
Brown, Jerry 120
Budds, J. 175, 182
Bureau of Reclamation (BOR) 2, 13, 15, 31, 35, 41, 44, 52, 55–57, 60, 64, 96, 99, 101, 123, 125, 129, 140, 141, 144, 155, 167, 175, 178, 183, 187, 194, 196
Bush, James 64

Cadbury brothers 30, 37
Cadieux, K.V. 83
Cadillac Desert (Reisner) 5
Calder, R. 9
California: drought 1–2, 4, 21, 118; fragmented water institutions/regulations 118–120; hydrological crisis 136–138; land-use policy 127; water management 117–138; water recycling 162; "Yellow Peril" 36
California Code of Regulations 123
Californian Constitution 23

California Seven Party Agreement 176
California Water Code 133
California Water Plan 143
Cape Town, South Africa 114
capital 3, 11, 12, 13, 14, 15, 31, 37, 41, 58, 98, 101, 129, 156–158, 164, 166, 169, 170
Carlsbad Desalination Plant 127–136
Carpenter, Delphus 179–181, 182
Carpenter, D.P. 33, 35, 39
Carr, James 54
Carroll, Patrick 5, 8, 15, 16
Carson, Charles 49
Carter, Jimmy 57, 64, 182
Central Arizona Groundwater Replenishment Districts (CAGRD) 59–61, 72–73, 77, 78, 157, 194, 196
Central Arizona Project (CAP): coalitions 58–69, 152; construction 21–23, 28, 59, 70; funding 52, 62, 65, 72; groundwater issues 182; implementation 23, 62–73; management 86, 88, 93, 94, 96, 100, 109, 111, 135, 153, 157–158, 166, 174, 177, 182; support/struggles 44–57, 62–65, 182; urban expansion, environmental constraints 71–73, 77, 80–81; water law 23
Central Arizona Project Association (CAPA) 49–50, 52, 54, 59, 65
Central Valley 2, 118, 161
Central Valley Project Improvement Act (CVPIA) 161
Chamber of Commerce 49, 65, 71
Chandler, Thomas 39, 64
Chavarochette, C. 143
Chesnick, J. 67, 68, 69
chloramines 65, 67
Christin, R. 7
Circle K 68
Citizens for Water Protection 66
Citizens Voice to Restore and Replenish Quality Water 65, 66
Citizens' Water Advisory Committee 77
Citizens Water Protection Initiative 67
City of Phoenix Water Services 97, 107, 157
Clearwell Reservoir 65
Click, Jim 66, 68
climate change 1, 2, 6, 23, 27, 85, 111, 117, 118, 124, 131, 165, 167
cloud seeding 97
Coachella Valley 120, 121, 149, 155, 167
Coachella Valley Irrigation District 21, 143–144, 176, 194, 196

228 *Index*

Coalition for Adequate Water Supply 68
Coeurdray, Murielle 14, 15, 23, 61, 70
Colby, B.C. 60, 66, 86, 182
Colorado River: historical/infrastructural
    background 1–24, 174–177; interstate
    water disputes 5, 21, 44–48, 180–182;
    "Law of the River" 21, 44, 46–48,
    177–178; regulation 174–177
Colorado River Aqueduct 21
Colorado River Basin: policy
    implemention 139–164; regional
    map 22; territorial unit 20–24
Colorado River Basin Project Act 51,
    177, 183
Colorado River Board of California
    119, 120, 121, 140, 194, 196
Colorado River Compact 21, 45–46, 48,
    49, 51, 52, 53, 54, 178–180, 181
Colorado River Project Act 21
Colorado River Water Users
    Association (CRWUA) 140, 141, 149
Colter, Fred 52, 53
Columbia Valley 42
Congress 28–32, 35, 39, 42–45, 48–57,
    63, 167, 174, 175
Connall, D.D., Jr 61, 64, 65, 182
conservation: coalitions: institutions/
    professionals 85–116, 165–173;
    ecological 2, 17, 86, 89, 97, 98–99,
    111, 113–116, 117, 134, 139, 147–149,
    151, 157, 158–160, 169, 170, 184, 186,
    190; environmental 81, 86, 115, 147,
    153; management strategy 117–138;
    sustainable practices 85–116; techniques
    80, 85, 89; technology solutions 9, 11,
    117–118
conservation ethic 108
Conservation Land System 109
contamination 7, 8, 20, 67, 123–124, 154
contractor 4, 18, 21, 119, 121–125, 152,
    155, 157, 158, 160, 161, 166, 167,
    176, 184, 189, 191, 192
Cortinas, J. viii, 17, 18, 21, 23, 70,
    72, 116, 120
Critical Groundwater Code 61
Critical Management Area 61
Cronon, W. 12, 21

Dames and Moore Inc. 65, 66, 67
Dauter, L. 9
Davis, Arthur Powell 33
Davis, S.K. 6, 24, 68, 69
Davis, T. 21
DeBolske, Jack 64

decentralization 24, 27, 28, 51, 73
Democrats 31
Department of Agriculture 2, 34
Department of Commerce 2
Department of Fish and Wildlife 119,
    195, 197
Department of the Interior 2, 35, 40, 43,
    45, 51, 54, 56, 60, 62, 119, 177
Department of Transportation and Flood
    Control 110
desalination 9, 25–26, 79, 104, 121,
    126, 127–138
"Desert Cities" 70–71
Desert Solitaire (Abbey) 2
Dezalay, Y. 7
Doyle, M. 64
drought: California 1–2; history/impact
    14, 19–23, 25, 27, 39, 43, 47, 50, 53,
    55, 70, 78, 80, 84, 85, 118; management
    and planning 9–11, 16, 21–26, 27–28,
    86–89, 91, 93–97, 99, 106–115, 129,
    136–148, 150, 154–155, 158, 159–160,
    163, 167, 170, 178, 181; social factors
    1–9
Drought Interagency Coordinating
    Group 93
Drought Task Force 93, 97
Dubois, V. viii, 7, 116
Ducey, Doug 93·
Duval, J. 7, 150

ecology vii, viii, 2–3, 5, 12, 14, 15, 17, 18,
    37, 54, 70, 74, 79, 81, 85–86, 89, 92, 95,
    97–100, 108–109, 113–115, 117–118,
    134, 139, 145–149, 151, 157, 158–160,
    164, 166, 168–171, 181, 184, 186,
    190–193; *see also* environment
economy: Depression 41–44; ecological
    113–115; expansion/overseas market
    32–33; structural reforms, 19th century
    28–31; urban development 68, 69–71
El Dorado 29
electricity 20, 37–39, 41–44, 49, 54,
    55, 62, 178
Eller, Karl 68
Ellis, Brock 64
Ely, Northcutt "Mike" 48
Encina power plant 127, 132
Endangered Species and Antiquities
    Acts 60
energy: alternative sources 55; crises 53,
    165; efficiency 124; production 42,
    113; sources 55, 56
Engel, Claire 54

engineers: "New Engineer" boom 33–37; technical skills 97–103, 115; as water managers 85–138

Environmental Impact Statements (EIS) 96, 129

Environmental Protection Act 86

Environmental Protection Agency 2, 56, 66–67, 120, 122, 156, 195, 197

environment/environmentalism: economic growth and 78–84; ecosystem protection programs 85; experts and activists 129–134

Erie, S.P. 119, 126, 160–161, 169

Espeland, W. 8, 86, 129

extractivism 139

Fannin, Paul 54

farmers: entrepreneurship potential 73–78; failure 33–37; growth of 73–84, 150, 161; Maxwell's support of 30; protest against CAP project 62–65, 73; Reclamation Service and 33, 35–36

Farmers Investment Company (FICO) 63–64

Farmers Investment Company v. Bettwy 61

federal: engineers 24, 85–138; funding 25, 40, 57, 59; and local coalitions 62–71, 91, 94, 108–116, 167; projects/mega-projects 4, 24–30, 33, 39, 41–44, 71–84; water policy/regulation 27–57, 85–138, 158, 161, 165–173

Federal Emergency Management Agency 2

Ferris, Kathy 104

field, notion of vii–viii, 7, 8, 11, 14, 19–24, 26, 29–31, 69, 87–88, 167–169

Fikes, Bradley 132

First World War 36–37

FitzSimmons, M. 86

Fleck, J. 10, 19, 136, 165

Fligstein, N. 7, 9, 168, 169

Flood Control Act 42

Fluid Systems 130

Foster, J.B. 12

Fowler, Benjamin A. 39–40

Fowler, Don, D. 2, 8

Freitas, Chuck 66

Fudala, J. 39

Furlong, K. 17

Garreau, J. 71

General Atomics 130

Getches, D.H. 177

Gila River Adjudication 41

Gila River Indian Community 39

Glen Canyon Dam 4, 21

Glendale 39, 188, 194, 196

Glennon, Robert vii, 1, 177, 182

Gober, P. 21, 71

Golden Age 56

Gonzales, G.A. 58

good governance 108

Gottlieb, Robert 10–11, 86, 119, 142

governance 15, 17, 18, 19, 20, 28, 106, 107, 118, 146, 147, 148, 154, 182

governor 1, 17, 39, 40, 45–49, 52–54, 60–63, 65, 70, 76, 86, 88, 91, 94, 97, 108, 120, 122, 124, 143, 145, 149, 152–156, 158, 163, 174–175, 182, 187, 194, 195, 196, 197

Grand Canyon 2, 55, 56

Grand Canyon National Park 53

Grant, D.L. 1, 9, 183

Great Basin Lunch Mess 34

Great Depression 4, 13, 37, 41–44

Greater Phoenix Leadership Council 80

Green River 2

Grenfell, M. viii, 19

Groundwater Code 61, 62, 63

Groundwater Management Act (GMA) 23, 59–60, 61–62, 64, 65, 71–72, 74, 78, 93, 96, 97, 104, 107, 141, 145, 155, 163, 182

growth 67–68; and environmental concerns 78–84; rural communities 73–75; "smart growth" policy 81; urban/suburban dynamics 69–73, 139

Growth Nation 80, 81

Gulf of California 20

Gulf of Mexico 4

Guttman, D. 71

habitus 19, 25, 98–100, 102, 106, 106, 109

Hannah, H. 12

Hansbrough, Henry 39

Hayden, Carl 46, 49, 50–54

Hayden, Charles Trumbull 50

Hays, S.P. 23, 31, 32, 36

Hess, D.J. 9, 23, 138, 139, 159

Hofstadter, R. 28, 29, 30, 32

homecraft 30

Hood, Christopher 146

Hoover Dam 4, 21, 44

House of Representatives 43, 47, 50, 51, 54, 56

Howell Code 47, 62

Howitt, R. 1

Huckleberry, Chuck 81

230   *Index*

Hundley, J.N. 45, 46, 53
Hunt, George, W.P. 45–46
Huntington Beach 128
Hurley v. Abbott 47
hydraulic society 11–16
hydrocracy 15, 16, 27–57, 169–171

Idaho 32
IDE Technologies 15, 128
Imperial Irrigation District (IDD) 17, 21,
    47, 48, 119, 121, 125, 143, 146, 155,
    157, 158, 161, 162, 176, 186, 195, 197
Imperial Valley 4, 21, 23, 42, 47, 51, 52,
    120, 131, 149, 167, 172, 176, 178
inequality 15, 23, 95
Ingram, H. 9, 165
institutions: categories/diverse field/
    functions 139–164; consensus 107–116;
    fragmented architecture 15, 18, 73, 91,
    115, 118–120, 137, 147; implementation
    strategies 165–183; local/municipal
    25, 92; political 37, 85, 117–138;
    professionals skills/regulators 85–138;
    public/private 107, 131, 161, 167;
    state/federal 2, 16–20, 25, 69, 93–94,
    107–116; sustainable 85–116
instruments (of water policy) 85–138
intermediary 73, 82, 122, 158, 166,
    184; *see also* broker
irrigation: efficient technologies 124–125;
    history 1–17, 21–23, 27, 180; issues/
    challenges 92, 95, 171; large-scale/
    federal 14, 27–33, 38–57, 84, 117–138,
    142–151; primitive methods 39, 62, 70,
    178; small-scale/local 33–37, 76–84,
    152–158, 160–162

Jackson, Henry 54
Jackson, K. 70
Jacobs, K.L. 24, 60, 66, 86, 182
Jawitz, J.W. 165
Jefferson, Thomas 4, 34, 51
Jenkins-Smith, H. C. 16
job creation 78
Johnson, Hiram 42
Johnson, James 64
Johnson, Lyndon 55
Johnson, J.W. 53, 56
Jones, John, S. 67
Juliani, Gerald "Jerry" 66, 68

Kai family 76–77
Kennedy, John F. 53, 56
Kent, Edward 47

Kent Decree 41, 47
Kibbey, H. 47
Kibbey Decision 47
Kingdon, J.W. 88
Klamath 36
Klamath Project 36
Kluttz, D. 7
Kolko, G. 31
Kraft, M. E. 86
Kuchel, Thomas 54
Kupel, D.E. 37, 59, 65, 66, 67
Kyl, Jon 64

Lake Mead 21, 23, 91, 175, 176–177
Lake Powell 21, 23, 91, 175
Lake Tahoe 36
land use 1, 73–74, 81, 86, 109, 127, 168
Land Use Plan 110
Lascoumes, P. 9, 147, 166
Lash, C. 31
Las Vegas 5, 140, 141–145, 149, 175, 181
law/lawyer 10, 23, 28, 29, 31–33, 35, 37,
    39, 42, 46–51, 53–57, 61, 64–65, 67,
    72–73, 75, 81, 87, 93, 103, 105, 118,
    122–125, 129–131, 133–136, 149, 154,
    155, 156, 158, 167; Common Law 3;
    law of the river 21, 44, 46–48, 174–183;
    see also regulation
Lazer, D. 17
lead air quality planning agency 89
League of 14 49
League of Arizona Cities and Towns 64
Lebaron, F. 7
Legal Aid Association 56
Le Galès, P. 147, 166
Lemieux, C. 7
Le Naour, G. 17
Leroy, P. 86
Leshy 61
Leshy, J.D. 60, 61
Linton, J. 175, 182
Logan, M.F. 21, 37, 71
Lopez-Hoffman, L. 85
Lorrain, D. 7, 8, 115, 138, 146, 170
Los Angeles 4–5, 68, 122, 123, 144;
    County Sanitation District 123, 156;
    federal water projects 4, 5; MET
    21, 119, 121, 131, 149, 152, 157,
    160–161, 178; Peripheral Canal 17;
    Water and Power department 126,
    175, 186, 194, 196; water disputes 48;
    Water District 86
Louisiana Reclamation Commission 30
Lovett, L. 30

Index 231

Lower Colorado Basin 23, 48, 138, 187, 194, 196
Lubell, M. 18
Lynn-Ingram, B. 1, 23
Lynn, P. 182

McAdam, D. 168, 169
McBride, Lawrence 181–182
McClurg, S. 17
MacDonnell, L.J. 181
McFarland, Ernest 46, 49, 63
McKasson, Molly 66, 67–69, 69, 109
Malamud-Roam, F. 1, 23
manager/management *see* water managers/management
Mann, D.E. 37, 49, 62, 63
Marana 69, 74–80, 82–83, 188, 194, 196
Marana Development Services 82–83
Marana Irrigation Trust 74, 75
Marble Canyon 53
Maricopa County 38, 41, 46, 47, 72
Markard, J. 6
Marriott, B. 75
Martin, J.L. 7
Massardier, G. 17
Maxwell, George H. 29–31, 32, 33, 39–40
mega-projects 4, 24, 26, 41–44, 70, 86, 117, 121, 128, 134–135, 137
Megdal, S.B. 86, 175
Mesa 39
MET (Metropolitan Water District) 17, 21, 23, 45, 119, 121, 125–126, 131, 134–135, 149, 152–154, 157, 160–162, 164, 166–167, 170, 176, 178, 194, 196
Meyers, C.J. 175
mining companies vii, 29, 39, 61–65, 71–72, 86, 111
Mississippi River, 1927 flood 42
model 6–12, 15–19, 24, 26, 32, 37–41, 62, 78, 81, 83, 98, 99, 101, 108, 127, 135, 138, 140, 148, 150, 153, 162, 165, 169, 171, 183
Moeur, Benjamin Baker 45
Mojave Desert 5
Molle, François 8, 15, 20, 170, 171, 172–173
Mollinga, P.P. 8
Montana 32
Moore, Ed 66
Morrison Institute for Public Policy 87
Mostert, E. 179
Mott Lacroix. K. 86
Mount, J. 1, 80

Multiple Correspondence Analysis (MCA) 150, 152, 156, 159, 162, 168–169, 184
Munro, J. 17

National Association of Manufacturers 29
National Board of Trade 29
National Businessmen's League 29
National Environmental Policy Act 55
National Environmental Protection Agency 56
National Geographic Society 34
National Irrigation Act 40
National Irrigation Association 29, 30
National Irrigation Congress 30
National Oceanographic and Atmospheric Association (NOAA) 88
National Outstanding Plan Award 110
National Reclamation Act 38, 40
Native American Nations 141, 142, 143, 181
natural resource (management) 3, 6–11, 23, 34, 37, 40, 43, 49, 55, 70, 73, 74, 81, 84–87, 107, 113, 115, 122, 127, 144, 147, 156, 166, 186, 195, 196, 197
Needham, A. 40
neoliberalism 63
networks viii, 7, 8, 11, 12, 16–20, 23, 26, 51, 58, 82, 86, 89–91, 106, 115–116, 122, 127, 167, 168–169, 171
Nevada 4, 21, 31, 35, 36, 39, 46, 48, 96, 140, 145, 149, 161, 175, 176, 178, 180
New Deal 4, 44, 45, 49, 104
Newell, FrederickH. 33
New Engineers 33–34, 171
Newlands, Francis G. 29, 31, 33, 36, 39
Newman, H. 67
New Mexico 1, 48, 54, 175, 178
NGO's 8, 87, 88, 99, 108, 121, 122, 123, 126, 127, 133, 136, 145, 150, 151, 152, 155, 155, 156, 159, 166, 184, 186, 187, 190, 191, 192
Nies, J. 5
North Dakota 32, 39–40
Norton, Gale 183

Ohio State Water Conservation Board 30
O'Neill Brian, F. 21, 149
operator viii, 8, 18, 21, 23, 118, 120–121, 138, 140, 143, 144, 146, 150, 152–153, 155, 156–160, 162–164, 166–167, 189, 190, 192
Oregon 36, 133

232 *Index*

Orland Project 36
Oro Valley 78, 83
Osborn, Chase 49, 62
Ostrom, E. 5
ozone 65, 67

Pacific Gas and Electric Company 39
Pacific Institute in California 87
Pacific Southwest Water Plan (PSWP)
 53, 54
Padowski, J.C. 165
Palo Verde Irrigation District 21,
 120–121, 125, 143, 161, 163,
 176, 186, 194, 196
Parker Dam 45, 174, 175
Pasqualetti, M.J. 70
Pearce, M.J. 62
Persky, J.J. 70
Phoenix 4, 5, 21; and CAP 52, 65, 182;
 economic growth 52, 53, 71, 149;
 electricity 37, 38, 39; environmental
 concerns 144; irrigation needs 38–39;
 National Reclamation Association 40;
 urban expansion, effects of 63, 69–84,
 144; water management/managers 23,
 113–114, 149, 162; water supply/policy/
 management 38–39, 52, 58–59, 64–65,
 67, 144, 157, 175, 181
Phoenix Chamber of Commerce 49
Phoenix Suns 68
Pima Association of Governments
 (PAG) 89
Pima County vii, 72; environmental
 projects 90; local/federal conservative
 measures 108–116
Pima County Local Drought Impact
 Group 88
Pima County Oral History Project 67,
 96, 109
Pinal County 65, 72, 149
Pincetl, S. viii, 18, 19, 21, 119, 161
Pisani, D.J. 4, 29, 31, 33, 37, 39, 41, 42, 43
Planning, Programming, and
 Budgeting System (PPBS) 96
Polanyi, K. 7
populism 31–32, 179
Poseidon Water 127, 128–130, 132, 133
Poupeau, F. vii, viii, 8, 14, 15, 70, 72, 138,
 146, 166, 170
Powell, John Wesley 2–3, 28
power 6, 7, 8, 10, 11, 14, 18, 19–20, 23,
 24, 28–41, 42–44, 48, 50, 55, 59, 62, 63,
 69, 71, 73, 96, 115, 119–120, 124–127,

 132, 134, 137–139, 144, 149, 152, 153,
 156, 158, 162, 167, 168, 170, 172,
 179, 181, 182
Power and Reclamation Subcommittee
 of the Interior Committee 54
Present Perfected Rights 23
private/public 8, 12–15, 18, 30–31, 37, 40,
 65, 73, 84, 87, 93, 96, 97, 106, 107, 109,
 111, 122, 123, 129–131, 138, 140, 151,
 153, 156, 161, 167
Pro-Development Coalition 66, 68
pro-growth lobby groups 71, 79–81, 117
Pure Water Coalition 68

Quantification Settlement Agreement
 (QSA) 131
Quiet Crisis, The (Udall, Stewart) 55

real estate vii, 4, 25, 47, 58, 59, 71, 72, 74,
 76, 78, 80, 81, 87, 93, 109, 163
Reclamation Act 28, 30, 31–33, 34, 37,
 38, 40, 70
Reclamation Service 31–36, 41–44,
 86, 179
Recon Environmental Inc. 109
regulation 4, 9, 17, 21, 27, 29, 31, 62,
 64, 67, 71–72, 83, 92, 103, 105, 120,
 122–123, 130, 133–137, 139, 142,
 146, 147, 151, 153–156, 160–163,
 167, 174–177, 184, 186, 187, 188,
 189, 190, 191, 192
Regulatory and Permitting Group 93
Reisner, Marc 4, 5, 36, 41, 44, 58, 65,
 107, 174–175, 178
Republicans 31
reverse osmosis 130
river *seespecific rivers*
river basin trajectories 20
Rivers of Empire (Worster) 11, 171–172
Rocky Mountains 4, 14, 20, 97, 180
Roosevelt, Franklin D. 34, 35, 40, 41, 51
Roosevelt Dam 40, 70
Roosevelt Water Conservation District 46
Rose, Mark 47–48
Ross, A. 5, 21, 23

Sabatier, P. 16, 18, 166
Safe and Sensible Water Committee 66
Safe Drinking Water Act (SDWA) 66, 67
Sahuarita-Continental Critical
 Groundwater Area 61, 64
Salton Sea 178
Salt River 38, 41, 47, 48, 50

Index 233

Salt River Project (SRP) 36–41, 46, 50–53, 54, 58, 59, 64, 70, 135, 163, 187, 194, 196
Salt River Valley 38–41, 47, 50
Salt River Valley Land 47
Salt River Valley Water Users' Association 38–41, 47
San Diego 21, 109, 121, 125, 127–136, 143, 144, 149, 158, 161, 176, 188, 194
San Diego Coastkeeper 131, 133
San Diego County Water Authority (SDCWA) 119, 128–132, 134, 161, 188, 194, 196
San Francisco 5, 18, 29, 123, 133, 134
Santa Cruz River vii
Santa Cruz Valley 63–64
Sapiro, G. 7
Saylor, John 54
scarcity vii, 6–11, 19, 26, 27, 37, 84, 131, 136–138, 147, 160, 162, 165–183
Schmidt Sudman R. 154
Schwarzenegger, Arnold 120
Scott, James 173
Scott, C.A. 70
Scottsdale 39, 58, 81, 158, 188, 194, 196
Scoville, C. 162
Seager, R. 165
Second World War 49, 58, 70
Senate 32, 43, 50; Committee on Agriculture and Irrigation 179; Committee on Energy and Natural Resources 113; Interior Committee 54; Subcommittee on Irrigation and Reclamation 49
Serrat-Capdevila, A. 86
Seven Party Agreement 21, 176
Sheridan, T. 52, 71, 85, 86
Shermer, E.T. 40, 71
shortages vii, 1, 2, 9, 11, 18, 25, 27, 57, 62, 69, 89, 94, 111, 118, 132, 141, 145–149, 161, 165, 177, 178, 181, 183
Shortage Sharing Agreement 183
Shoshone 36
Simard, L. 9
Singh, S. viii, 169
"smart growth" policy 81
Smith, C.L. 38, 40, 50, 70
Smithsonian Institution 3
Snell and Wilmer law firm 46
snowball sampling 87
snowmelt 2, 21
sociology vii, 7–9, 25, 116

Sonora Desert 5
Sonoran Desert Conservation Plan (SDCP) 109, 110
Southern Arizona Leadership Council (SALC) 66, 68–69
Southern Nevada Water Authority 21, 140
state: institutions/coalitions 2, 4, 6, 8, 12–18, 22–24, 27, 35, 36, 43, 49–57; interstate crises 44–48, 58–84; projects 36, 38, 43–44, 139–164; water management 24–25, 30, 85–138, 165–173
State Water Resources Control Board 24, 120, 121, 122, 155, 156, 194, 196
Stegner, Wallace 3
Stevens, Bill 64
stormwater 93, 109, 110–111, 148, 154, 168
Strauss, A. 87
Summit, A.R. 4, 10, 20, 161
Sun Corridor 4, 52, 70, 71, 74, 81, 82, 84, 87
supply 1, 2, 4, 5, 9–10, 16, 18, 23, 24, 39–41, 53, 58–60, 63, 66–68, 72–75, 81–83, 93–94, 96, 107–108, 113, 118, 122–152, 155, 160–164, 165, 177, 178, 180, 182, 190, 193
Supreme Court 23, 44–48, 53, 56, 61–64, 118, 176, 179, 181
Surfrider Foundation 127, 131, 133, 186, 194, 196
sustainability 7, 9, 20, 37–38, 58–59, 69, 78, 81, 84, 85–115, 117, 135, 138, 147, 151, 154, 159, 162, 167–168, 173, 176, 184, 186, 187, 188, 190, 193
Swing, Phil 42
Swyngedouw, E. 127

Taylor, D. 110, 148
Taylor, C. 9
Taylor, L. 83
Taylor, S. 154
Teisch, J.B. 5, 8
Teisman, G.R. 115
Tempe 39
Thatcher, M. 95
think tanks 8, 34, 87, 121, 123, 150, 155, 156, 166, 184, 189, 191, 192
Thomas, C.S. 45, 50
Thompson, B.H. 175, 177, 178, 180
Thurber, J.A. 88
Tonton Basin 40

234 *Index*

Topalov, C. 8, 30
tourism 1, 5, 62, 71
Trelease, F.J. 178
Truckee Irrigation Project 31
Tubbs, Mike 66, 67
Tucson: and CAP 52, 58, 60, 65–66; economic growth 52, 53, 71; post-war expansion 71; urban expansion, effects of 63–64, 69–84; water conservation measures 23; water quality campaigns 66–68; water supply/policy/management 59, 61–62, 65–69, 92, 94, 98, 108, 109–110, 144, 149, 156–157, 162, 164, 165, 167, 175, 182, 186, 187, 194, 196
Tucson City Council 66, 67, 109
Tucson Water 65–69, 82, 89, 156, 157, 186, 194, 196
Tucson Water "Ambassador Program" 68
Turley, Stan 65
Tyler, D. 179, 180

Udall, Morris 53–54, 76
Udall, Stewart 53, 55–56
underground water 79
United States Geological Survey (USGS) 88, 182
University of Arizona Water Resources Research Center 87
Upper Colorado Basin 48
urban sprawl 1, 38, 69–71, 73, 74, 78, 160
US Geological Survey 3, 33, 34
Utah 4, 46, 48, 175, 178

Valdez Diaz, C. 59, 67
Valley of the Sun 113
Van Tatenhove, J. 86
Varady, R.G. 6
Vergniolle, de ChantalF. 115
Vietnam War 67
Vincent, J.A. 72

Wacquant, L.J. 7, 19, 140
Walkup, Bob 69
Walton, J. 5, 8, 86
Wang, A. 68
Washington 32; and Arizona water dispute 45–46; institutional coalitions/networks 14, 28, 32, 38, 40, 44–45, 51, 53, 55–57, 61, 63–64, 71, 96, 154, 178, 182
wastewater reuse 9, 76, 78, 80, 89, 93, 101, 103, 105, 108, 113, 142, 147 *see* water reuse

Water Advisory Group 77, 93
water alternatives viii, 31, 52, 57, 79
water banking 59, 93, 157, 161, 187, 194, 196
Water Coalition 68, 80
water conservation: future prospects 171–173; "green sprawl" approach 79–84; local/federal measures 85–86, 108–116, 169–171
Water Conservation Act 23, 177
Water Consumer Protection Act (WCPA) 67, 68
Water Consumer Protection Coalition 67, 68
water law 23, 47, 50–51, 118, 175, 177, 179, 180, 182
water management: Arizona 109–116; California 117–138
water managers: classes and characteristics 91–95, 150–152; general activities 87–88; interpersonal skills 102–103; legal skills 123–124; management skills 98–106, 117–138; network 89–91, 106; "new guard" 129–133; non-technical skills 103–106; objectives and assessments of issues 95–97; regulatory expertise/power 124–126, 152–160; technical skills 98–103
water markets 8–11, 17, 26, 126–129, 148, 151–152, 154, 160–164, 184, 185, 187, 188, 190, 193
Water Program of the Pacific Institute 123
water quality 9, 23–24, 28, 66–69, 89, 119, 122, 138, 148, 151, 152, 156, 159, 160, 185, 190, 193
Water Resources Development Commission 93, 153
water reuse 9, 76, 78, 80, 89, 93, 102, 104, 107, 113, 142, 147, 160–164
water rights 8, 15, 19, 38–40, 75–76, 78, 89, 93, 120, 125, 126, 149, 160; appropriative rights 120; riparian rights 120
waterscape 172–173
water shortage *see* shortages
water transfers 9, 17, 125, 140, 147, 161, 163, 167
water treatment 65, 101, 105
water use, definition of 20
Weber, Max 7, 12
Weible, C.M. 18
Wellton-Mohawk Irrigation District 96

Index   235

West Basin Municipal Water District 153, 162, 186, 194, 196
Wester, P. 20
White, E. 76
Wiersma, Richard 65, 66
Wiewel, W. 70
Wilmer, Mark Bernard 46–48, 64
Wittfogel, K. 11–12, 14

Worster, Donald 2, 3, 11–15, 29, 32, 33, 171–172
Wyoming 32, 48, 175, 178

Yuma Irrigation District 86, 151, 158
Yuma Project 21, 36, 176

Zarbin, E.A. 38, 40, 41, 70

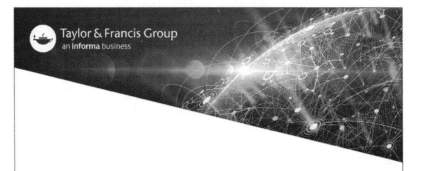

Printed in the United States
by Baker & Taylor Publisher Services